# INNS AND TAVERNS OF OLD LONDON

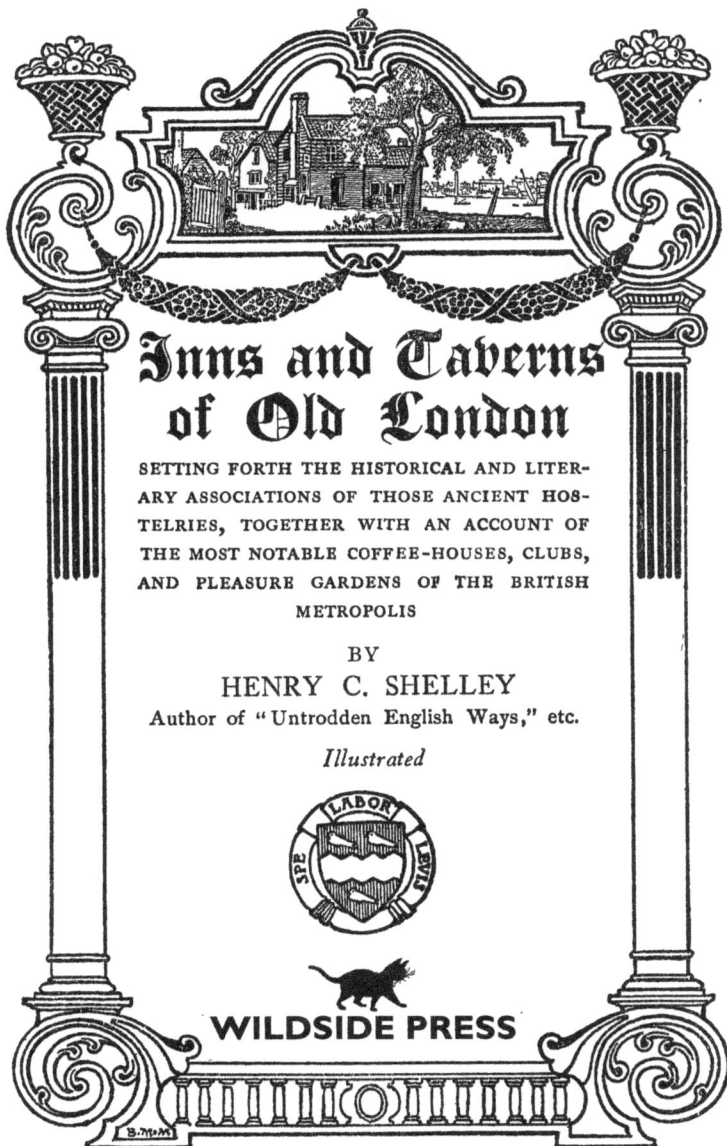

# Inns and Taverns of Old London

SETTING FORTH THE HISTORICAL AND LITER-
ARY ASSOCIATIONS OF THOSE ANCIENT HOS-
TELRIES, TOGETHER WITH AN ACCOUNT OF
THE MOST NOTABLE COFFEE-HOUSES, CLUBS,
AND PLEASURE GARDENS OF THE BRITISH
METROPOLIS

BY

HENRY C. SHELLEY
Author of "Untrodden English Ways," etc.

*Illustrated*

**WILDSIDE PRESS**

Published by
Wildside Press, LLC
P.O. Box 301
Holicong, PA 18928-0301 USA
www.wildsidepress.com


Wildside Press Edition: MMIII

# PREFACE

For all races of Teutonic origin the claim is made that they are essentially home-loving people. Yet the Englishman of the sixteenth and seventeenth and eighteenth centuries, especially of the latter, is seen to have exercised considerable zeal in creating substitutes for that home which, as a Teuton, he ought to have loved above all else. This, at any rate, was emphatically the case with the Londoner, as the following pages will testify. When he had perfected his taverns and inns, perfected them, that is, according to the light of the olden time, he set to work evolving a new species of public resort in the coffee-house. That type of establishment appears to have been responsible for the development of the club, another substitute for the home. And then came the age of the pleasure-garden. Both the latter survive, the one in a form of a more rigid exclusiveness than the eighteenth century Londoner would have deemed possible; the other in so changed a guise that frequenters of the prototype would scarcely recognize the relationship. But the coffee-house and the inn and tavern of old London exist but as a picturesque memory which these pages attempt to revive.

Naturally much delving among records of the past has gone to the making of this book. To enumerate all the sources of information which have been laid under contribution would be a tedious task and need not be attempted, but it would be ungrateful to omit thankful acknowledgment to Henry B. Wheatley's exhaustive edition of Peter Cunningham's "Handbook of London," and to Warwick Wroth's admirable volume on "The London Pleasure Gardens of the Eighteenth Century." Many of the illustrations have been specially photographed from rare engravings in the Print Room of the British Museum.

H. C. S.

# CONTENTS

CHAPTER                                                    PAGE

     PREFACE . . . . . . . . . v

## I.  INNS AND TAVERNS OF OLD LONDON

  I. FAMOUS SOUTHWARK INNS . . . . . 1
 II. INNS AND TAVERNS EAST OF ST. PAUL'S . . 30
III. TAVERNS OF FLEET STREET AND THEREABOUTS 62
 IV. TAVERNS WEST OF TEMPLE BAR . . . 102
  V. INNS AND TAVERNS FURTHER AFIELD . . 136

## II.  COFFEE-HOUSES OF OLD LONDON

  I. COFFEE-HOUSES ON 'CHANGE AND NEAR-BY . 163
 II. ROUND ST. PAUL'S . . . . . . . 185
III. THE STRAND AND COVENT GARDEN . . . 200
 IV. FURTHER WEST . . . . . . . 222

## III.  THE CLUBS OF OLD LONDON

  I. LITERARY . . . . . . . . 243
 II. SOCIAL AND GAMING . . . . . . 267

## IV.  PLEASURE GARDENS OF OLD LONDON

  I. VAUXHALL . . . . . . . . . 291
 II. RANELAGH . . . . . . . . . 312
III. OTHER FAVOURITE RESORTS . . . . . 335
   INDEX . . . . . . . . . 357

# LIST OF ILLUSTRATIONS

|  | PAGE |
|---|---|
| KING'S HEAD TAVERN, FLEET STREET | *Frontispiece* |
| GEOFFREY CHAUCER | 8 |
| TABARD INN, SOUTHWARK, IN 1810 | 12 |
| BRIDGE-FOOT, SOUTHWARK, SHOWING THE BEAR INN IN 1616 | 16 |
| COURTYARD OF BOAR'S HEAD INN, SOUTHWARK | 22 |
| GEORGE INN | 24 |
| WHITE HART INN, SOUTHWARK | 28 |
| OLIVER GOLDSMITH | 34 |
| COCK INN, LEADENHALL STREET | 46 |
| PAUL PINDAR TAVERN | 51 |
| ANCIENT VIEW OF CHEAPSIDE, SHOWING THE NAG'S HEAD INN | 57 |
| A FRENCH ORDINARY IN LONDON | 60 |
| YARD OF BELLE SAUVAGE INN | 76 |
| THE CHESHIRE CHEESE — ENTRANCE FROM FLEET STREET | 79 |
| THE CHESHIRE CHEESE — THE JOHNSON ROOM | 80 |
| DR. SAMUEL JOHNSON | 90 |
| TABLET AND BUST FROM THE DEVIL TAVERN | 95 |
| BEN JONSON | 98 |
| FEATHERS TAVERN | 136 |
| ADAM AND EVE TAVERN | 154 |
| A TRIAL BEFORE THE PIE-POWDER COURT AT THE HAND AND SHEARS TAVERN | 156 |
| FALCON TAVERN, BANKSIDE | 159 |
| GARRAWAY'S COFFEE-HOUSE | 176 |
| MAD DOG IN A COFFEE-HOUSE | 179 |
| TOM'S COFFEE-HOUSE | 180 |
| LLOYD'S COFFEE-HOUSE | 182 |

PAGE

GRECIAN COFFEE-HOUSE . . . . . . . . 202

JOHN DRYDEN . . . . . . . . . . 210

JOSEPH ADDISON . . . . . . . . . 215

SIR RICHARD STEELE . . . . . . . . 217

LION'S HEAD AT BUTTON'S COFFEE-HOUSE . . . 218

BRITISH COFFEE-HOUSE . . . . . . . . 223

SLAUGHTER'S COFFEE-HOUSE . . . . . . . 225

OLD PALACE YARD, WESTMINSTER . . . . . 234

DON SALTERO'S COFFEE-HOUSE . . . . . . 238

ST. JAMES'S STREET, SHOWING WHITE'S ON THE LEFT
    AND BROOKS'S ON THE RIGHT . . . . . 268

THE BRILLIANTS . . . . . . . . . 274

"PROMISED HORRORS OF THE FRENCH INVASION " . . 276

GAMBLING SALOON AT BROOKS'S CLUB . . . . 279

TICKETS FOR VAUXHALL . . . . . . . 296

ENTRANCE TO VAUXHALL . . . . . . . 300

THE CITIZEN AT VAUXHALL . . . . . . . 302

SCENE AT VAUXHALL . . . . . . . . 308

VENETIAN MASQUERADE AT RANELAGH, 1749 . . . 318

THE ASSAULT ON DR. JOHN HILL AT RANELAGH . . 327

MARYLEBONE GARDENS . . . . . . . 340

WHITE CONDUIT HOUSE . . . . . . . 342

BAGNIGGE WELLS . . . . . . . . 348

FINCH'S GROTTO, SOUTHWARK . . . . . . 354

# INNS AND TAVERNS
# OF OLD LONDON

———◆———

I

## CHAPTER I

### FAMOUS SOUTHWARK INNS

UNIQUE among the quaint maps of old London is one which traces the ground-plan of
Southwark as it appeared early in the sixteenth
century. It is not the kind of map which would
ensure examination honours for its author were
he competing among schoolboys of the twentieth century, but it has a quality of archaic
simplicity which makes it a more precious possession than the best examples of modern car-
tography. Drawn on the principle that a min-
imum of lines and a maximum of description
are the best aid to the imagination, this plan of
Southwark indicates the main routes of thoroughfare with a few bold strokes, and then fills

1

in the blanks with queer little drawings of churches and inns, the former depicted in delightfully distorted perspective and the latter by two or three half-circular strokes. That there may be no confusion between church and inn, the possibility of which is suggested by the fact that several of the latter are adorned with spire-like embellishments, the sixteenth-century cartographer told which were which in so many words. It is by close attention to the letterpress, and by observing the frequent appearance of names which have age-long association with houses of entertainment, that the student of this map awakens to the conviction that ancient Southwark rejoiced in a more than generous provision of inns.

Such was the case from the earliest period of which there is any record. The explanation is simple. The name of the borough supplies the clue. Southwark is really the south-work of London, that is, the southern defence or fortification of the city. The Thames is here a moat of spacious breadth and formidable depth, yet the Romans did not trust to that defence alone, but threw up further obstacles for any enemy approaching the city from the south. It was from that direction assault was most likely to come. From the western and southern counties of England, and, above all, from the Continent, this was the high road into the capital.

All this had a natural result in times of peace. As London Bridge was the only causeway over the Thames, and as the High street of Southwark was the southern continuation of that causeway, it followed that diplomatic visitors from the Continent and the countless traders who had business in the capital were obliged to use this route coming and going. The logical result of this constant traffic is seen in the countless inns of the district. In the great majority of cases those visitors who had business in the city itself during the day elected to make their headquarters for the night on the southern shore of the Thames.

Although no definite evidence is available, it is reasonable to conclude that the most ancient inns of Southwark were established at least as early as the most ancient hostelries of the city itself. To which, however, the prize of seniority is to be awarded can never be known. Yet on one matter there can be no dispute. Pride of place among the inns of Southwark belongs unquestionably to the Tabard. Not that it is the most ancient, or has played the most conspicuous part in the social or political life of the borough, but because the hand of the poet has lifted it from the realm of the actual and given it an enduring niche in the world of imagination.

No evidence is available to establish the actual date when the Tabard was built; Stow speaks of it as among the "most ancient" of the locality; but the nearest approach to definite dating assigns the inn to the early fourteenth century. One antiquary indeed fixes the earliest distinct record of the site of the inn in 1304, soon after which the Abbot of Hyde, whose abbey was in the neighbourhood of Winchester, here built himself a town mansion and probably at the same time a hostelry for travellers. Three years later the Abbot secured a license to erect a chapel close by the inn. It seems likely, then, that the Tabard had its origin as an adjunct of the town house of a Hampshire ecclesiastic.

But in the early history of the hostelry no fact stands out so clearly as that it was chosen by Chaucer as the starting-point for his immortal Canterbury pilgrims. More than two centuries had passed since Thomas à Becket had fallen before the altar of St. Benedict in the minster of Canterbury, pierced with many swords as his reward for contesting the supremacy of the Church against Henry II.

"What a parcel of fools and dastards have I nourished in my house," cried the monarch when the struggle had reached an acute stage, "that not one of them will avenge me of this one upstart clerk!"

Four knights took the king at his word, posted with all speed to Canterbury, and charged the prelate to give way to the wishes of the sovereign.

"In vain you threaten me," A Becket rejoined. "If all the swords in England were brandishing over my head, your terrors could not move me. Foot to foot you will find me fighting the battle of the Lord."

And then the swords of the knights flashed in the dim light of the minster and another name was added to the Church's roll of martyrs. The murder sent a thrill of horror through all Christendom; A Becket was speedily canonized, and his tomb became the objective of countless pilgrims from every corner of the Christian world.

In Chaucer's days, some two centuries later, the pilgrimage had become a favourite occupation of the devout. Each awakening of the

year, when the rains of April had laid the dust
of March and aroused the buds of tree and
herb from their winter slumber, the longing to
go on a pilgrimage seized all classes alike.

> " And specially, from every shires ende
> Of Engelond, to Caunterbury they wende,
> The holy blisful martir for to seke,
> That hem hath holpen, whan that they were seke."

Precisionists of the type who are never satisfied unless they can apply chronology in the
realm of imagination will have it that Chaucer's pilgrimage was a veritable event, and
that it took place in April, 1388.  They go
further still and identify Chaucer's host with
the actual Henry Bailley, who certainly was in
possession of the Tabard in years not remote
from that date.  The records show that he
twice represented the borough of Southwark in
Parliament, and another ancient document
bears witness how he and his wife, Christian
by name, were called upon to contribute two
shillings to the subsidy of Richard II.  These
are the dry bones of history; for the living
picture of the man himself recourse must be
had to Chaucer's verse:

> " A semely man our hoste was with-alle
> For to han been a marshal in an halle;

A large man he was with eyen stepe,
A fairer burgeys is ther noon in Chepe:
Bold of his speche, and wys, and well y-taught,
And of manhood him lakkede right naught.
Eke thereto he was right a merry man."

No twentieth century pilgrim to the Tabard inn must expect to find its environment at all in harmony with the picture enshrined in Chaucer's verse. The passing years have wrought a woeful and materializing change. The opening lines of the Prologue are permeated with a sense of the month of April, a " breath of uncontaminate springtide " as Lowell puts it, and in those far-off years when the poet wrote, the beauties of the awakening year were possible of enjoyment in Southwark. Then the buildings of the High street were spaciously placed, with room for field and hedgerow; to-day they are huddled as closely together as the hand of man can set them, and the verdure of grass and tree is unknown. Nor is it otherwise with the inn itself, for its modern representative has no points of likeness to establish a kinship with the structure visualized in Chaucer's lines. It is true the poet describes the inn more by suggestion than set delineation, but such hints that it was " a gentle hostelry," that its rooms and stables were alike spacious, that the food was of the best and the wine of the strongest go further with the imagination than concrete statements.

Giving faith for the moment to that theory which credits the Canterbury Tales with being based on actual experience, and recalling the quaint courtyard of the inn as it appeared on that distant April day of 1388, it is a pleasant exercise of fancy to imagine Chaucer leaning over the rail of one of the upper galleries to watch the assembling of his nine-and-twenty " sondry folk." They are, as J. R. Green has said, representatives of every class of English society from the noble to the ploughman. " We see the ' verray perfight gentil knight ' in cassock and coat of mail, with his curly-headed squire beside him, fresh as the May morning, and behind them the brown-faced yeoman in his coat and hood of green with a mighty bow in his hand. A group of ecclesiastics light up for us the mediæval church — the brawny hunt-loving monk, whose bridle jingles as loud and clear as the chapel bell — the wanton friar, first among the beggars and harpers of the courtly side — the poor parson, threadbare, learned, and devout (' Christ's lore and his apostles twelve he taught, and first

GEOFFREY CHAUCER.

he followed it himself ') — the summoner with his fiery face — the pardoner with his wallet ' full of pardons, come from Rome all hot ' — the lively prioress with her courtly French lisp, her soft little red mouth, and *Amor vincit omnia* graven on her brooch. Learning is there in the portly person of the doctor of physics, rich with the profits of the pestilence — the busy sergeant-of-law, ' that ever seemed busier than he was ' — the hollow-cheeked clerk of Oxford with his love of books and short sharp sentences that disguise a latent tenderness which breaks out at last in the story of Griseldis. Around them crowd types of English industry; the merchant; the franklin in whose house ' it snowed of meat and drink '; the sailor fresh from frays in the Channel; the buxom wife of Bath; the broad-shouldered miller; the haberdasher, carpenter, weaver, dyer, tapestry-maker, each in the livery of his craft; and last the honest ploughman who would dyke and delve for the poor without hire.''

Smilingly as Chaucer may have gazed upon this goodly company, his delight at their arrival paled before the radiant pleasure of mine host, for a poet on the lookout for a subject can hardly have welcomed the advent of the pilgrims with such an interested anticipation of profit as the innkeeper whose rooms they were to occupy and whose food and wines they were to consume.  Henry Bailley was equal to the auspicious occasion.

> " Greet chere made our hoste us everichon,
>     And to the soper sette he us anon;
>     And served us with vitaille at the beste.
>     Strong was the wyn, and wel to drinke us leste."

But the host of the Tabard was more than an efficient caterer; he was something of a diplomatist also.  Taking advantage of that glow of satisfaction which is the psychological effect of physical needs generously satisfied, he appears to have had no difficulty in getting the pilgrims to pay their " rekeninges," and having attained that practical object he rewarded his customers with liberal interest for their hard cash in the form of unstinted praise of their collective merits.  In all that year he had not seen so merry a company gathered under his roof, etc., etc.  But of greater moment for future generations was his suggestion that, as there was no comfort in riding to Canterbury dumb as a stone, the pilgrims should beguile their journey by telling stories.  The suggestion was loudly acclaimed and the scheme unanimously pledged in further copious draughts of wine. And then, to '' reste wente echon,'' until the dawn came again and smiled down upon that brave company whose tale-telling pilgrimage has since been followed with so much delight by countless thousands.

By the time Stow made his famous survey of London, some two centuries later, the Tabard was rejoicing to the full in the glories cast around it by Chaucer's pen. Stow cites the poet's commendation as its chief title to fame, and pauses to explain that the name of the inn was '' so called of the sign, which, as we now term it, is of a jacket, or sleeveless coat, whole before, open on both sides, with a square collar, winged at the shoulders; a stately garment of old time, commonly worn of noblemen and others, both at home and abroad in the war, but then (to wit in the wars) their arms embroidered, or otherwise depict upon them, that every man by his coat of arms might be known from others.'' All this heraldic lore did not prevent the subsequent change — for a time — of the name Tabard to the meaningless name of Talbot, a distortion, however, which survives only in antiquarian history.

At the dissolution of the monasteries this inn, which up till then had retained its connection with the church through belonging to Hyde Abbey, was granted to two brothers named Master, and in 1542 its annual rent is fixed at nine pounds. An authority on social life in England during the middle of Queen Elizabeth's reign ventures on the following description of the arrangements of the inn at that period. '' On the ground-floor, looking on to the street, was a room called ' the darke parlour,' a hall, and a general reception-room called ' the parlour.' This was probably the dining-room of the house, as it opened on to the kitchen on the same level. Below the dark parlour was a cellar. On the first floor, above the parlour and the hall, were three rooms — ' the middle chamber,' ' the corner chamber,' and ' Maister Hussye's chamber,' with garrets or ' cock lofts ' over them. Over the great parlour was another room. There were also rooms called ' the Entry Chamber ' and ' the Newe chamber,' ' the Flower de Luce ' and ' Mr. Russell's chamber,' of which the position is not specified.''

When, in 1875, the old Tabard, the inn, that is, of George Shepherd's water-colour drawing of 1810, was demolished, making way for the present somewhat commonplace representative of the ancient hostelry, many protests were

TABARD INN, SOUTHWARK, IN 1810.

made on the plea that it was sheer vandalism
to destroy a building so intimately associated
with the genius of Chaucer. But the protests
were based upon lack of knowledge. Chaucer's
inn had disappeared long before. It is sometimes stated that that building survived until
the great Southwark fire of 1676, but such assertions overlook the fact that there is in existence a record dated 1634 which speaks of the
Tabard as having been built of brick six years
previously upon the old foundation. Here,
then, is proof that the Tabard of the pilgrims
was wholly reconstructed in 1628, and even that
building — faithful copy as it may have been
of the poet's inn — was burnt to the ground in
1676. From the old foundations, however, a
new Tabard arose, built on the old plan, so
that the structure which was torn down in 1875
may have perpetuated the semblance of Chaucer's inn to modern times.

Compared with its association with the Canterbury pilgrims, the subsequent history of the
Tabard is somewhat prosaic. Here a record
tells how it became the objective of numerous
carriers from Kent and Sussex, there crops up
a law report which enshrines the memory of a
burglary, and elsewhere in reminiscences or
diary may be found a tribute to the excellence

of the inn's rooms and food and the reasonableness of the charges. It should not be forgotten, however, that violent hands have been laid on the famous inn for the lofty purposes of melodrama. More than sixty years ago a play entitled "Mary White, or the Murder at the Old Tabard" thrilled the theatregoer with its tragic situations and the terrible perils of the heroine. But the tribulations of Mary White have left no imprint on English literature. Chaucer's pilgrims have, and so long as the mere name of the Tabard survives, its recollection will bring in its train a moving picture of that merry and motley company which set out for the shrine of A Becket so many generations ago.

Poetic license bestows upon another notable Southwark inn, the Bear at Bridge-foot, an antiquity far eclipsing that of the Tabard. In a poem printed in 1691, descriptive of "The Last Search after Claret in Southwark," the heroes of the verse are depicted as eventually finding their way to

"The Bear, which we soon understood
Was the first house in Southwark built after the flood."

To describe the inn as "the first house in Southwark" might have been accurate for

those callers who approached it over London
Bridge, but in actual chronology the proud distinction of dating from post-deluge days has
really to give place to the much more recent
year of 1319. There is preserved among the
archives of the city of London a tavern lease
of that date which belongs without doubt to the
history of this hostelry, for it refers to the inn
which Thomas Drinkwater had " recently built
at the head of London Bridge." This Thomas
Drinkwater was a taverner of London, and the
document in question sets forth how he had
granted the lease of the Bear to one James
Beauflur, who agrees to purchase all his wines
from the inappropriately named Drinkwater,
who, on his part, was to furnish his tenant with
such necessaries as silver mugs, wooden ha-
naps, curtains, cloths and other articles.

A century and a half later the inn figures in
the accounts of Sir John Howard, that warlike
" Jacke of Norfolk " who became the first
Duke of Norfolk in the Howard family and
fatally attested his loyalty to his king on Bos-
worth Field. From that time onward casual
references to the Bear are numerous. It was
probably the best-known inn of Southwark, for
its enviable position at the foot of London
Bridge made it conspicuous to all entering or

leaving the city.  Its attractions were enhanced by the fact that archery could be practised in its grounds, and that within those same grounds was the Thames-side landing stage from whence the tilt-boats started for Greenwich and Gravesend.  It was the opportunity for shooting at the target which helped to lure Sir John Howard to the Bear, but as he sampled the wine of the inn before testing his skill as a marksman, he found himself the poorer by the twenty-pence with which he had backed his own prowess.  Under date 1633 there is an interesting reference which sets forth that, although orders had been given to have all the back-doors to taverns on the Thames closed up, owing to the fact that wrong-doers found them convenient in evading the officers of the law, an exception was made in the case of the Bear owing to the fact that it was the starting-place for Greenwich.

Evidence in abundance might be cited to show that the inn was a favourite meeting place with the wits and gallants of the court of Charles I and the Restoration.  " The maddest of all the land came to bait the Bear,'' is one testimony; " I stuffed myself with food and tipple till the hoops were ready to burst,''

BRIDGE-FOOT, SOUTHWARK.
(*Showing the Bear Inn in 1616.*)

is another. There is one figure, however, of
the thirties of the seventeenth century which
arrests the attention. This is Sir John Suckling, that gifted and ill-fated poet and man of
fashion of whom it was said that he " had the
peculiar happiness of making everything that
he did become him." His ready wit, his strik-
ingly handsome face and person, his wealth and
generosity, his skill in all fashionable pastimes
made him a favourite with all. The preferences
of the man, his delight in the joys of the town
as compared with the pleasures of secluded
study in the country, are clearly seen in those
sprightly lines in which he invited the learned
John Hales, the " walking library," to leave
Eton and " come to town ":

> " There you shall find the wit and wine
> Flowing alike, and both divine:
> Dishes, with names not known in books,
> And less among the college-cooks;
> With sauce so pregnant, that you need
> Not stay till hunger bids you feed.
> The sweat of learned Jonson's brain,
> And gentle Shakespeare's eas'er strain,
> A hackney coach conveys you to,
> In spite of all that rain can do:
> And for your eighteenpence you sit
> The lord and judge of all fresh wit."

Nor was it in verse alone that Suckling celebrated the praises of wine. Among the scanty
remains of his prose there is that lively sally,
written at the Bear, and entitled: " The Wine-
drinkers to the Water-drinkers." After mock-
ingly commiserating with the teetotalers over
the sad plight into which their habits had
brought them, the address continues: " We
have had divers meetings at the Bear at the
Bridge-foot, and now at length have resolved
to despatch to you one of our cabinet council,
Colonel Young, with some slight forces of
canary, and some few of sherry, which no doubt
will stand you in good stead, if they do not
mutiny and grow too headstrong for their com-
mander. Him Captain Puff of Barton shall
follow with all expedition, with two or three
regiments of claret; Monsieur de Granville,
commonly called Lieutenant Strutt, shall lead
up the rear of Rhenish and white. These suc-
cours, thus timely sent, we are confident will
be sufficient to hold the enemy in play, and, till
we hear from you again, we shall not think of
a fresh supply. . . . Given under our hand at
the Bear, this fourth of July."

Somewhere about the date when this drollery
was penned there happened at the Bear an incident which might have furnished the water-

drinkers with an effective retort on their satirist. The Earl of Buccleugh, just returned from military service abroad, on his way into London, halted at the Bear to quaff a glass of sack with a friend. A few minutes later he put off in a boat for the further shore of the Thames, but ere the craft had gone many yards from land the earl exclaimed, " I am deadly sick, row back; Lord have mercy upon me! " Those were his last words, for he died that night.

Another picturesque figure of the seventeenth century is among the shades that haunt the memory of the Bear, Samuel Pepys, that irrepressible gadabout who was more intimately acquainted with the inns and taverns of London than any man of his time. That Thames-side hostelry was evidently a favourite resort of the diarist. On both occasions of his visits to Southwark Fair he made the inn his base of operations as it were, especially in 1668 when the puppet-show of Whittington seemed " pretty to see," though he could not resist the reflection " how that idle thing do work upon people that see it, and even myself too! "

Pepys had other excitements that day. He was so mightily taken with Jacob Hall's dancing on the ropes that on meeting that worthy at a tavern he presented him with a bottle of wine. Having done justice to all the sights of the fair, he returned to the Bear, where his waterman awaited him with the gold and other things to the value of forty pounds which the prudent diarist had left in his charge at the inn " for fear of my pockets being cut."

Pepys himself incidentally explains why he had so friendly a regard for the Bridge-foot tavern. " Going through bridge by water," he writes, " my waterman told me how the mistress of the Beare tavern, at the bridge-foot, did lately fling herself into the Thames, and drowned herself; which did trouble me the more, when they tell me it was she that did live at the White Horse tavern in Lumbard Street, which was a most beautiful woman, as most I have seen."

Yet another fair woman, Frances Stuart, one of the greatest beauties of the court of Charles II, is linked with the history of the Beare. Sad as was the havoc she wrought in the heart of the susceptible Pepys, who is ever torn between admiration of her loveliness and mock-reprobation of her equivocal position at court, Frances Stuart created still deeper passions in men more highly placed than he. Apart from her royal lover, there were two nobles, the Dukes of York and Richmond who contended

for her hand, with the result of victory finally
resting with the latter. But the match had to
be a runaway one. The king was in no mood to
part with his favourite, and so the lovers arranged a meeting at the Bear, where a coach
was in waiting to spirit them away into Kent.
No wonder Charles was offended, especially
when the lady sent him back his presents.

Nearly a century and a half has passed since
the Bear finally closed its doors. All through
the lively years of the Restoration it maintained its reputation as a house of good cheer
and a wholly desirable rendezvous, and it figures not inconspicuously in the social life of
London down to 1761. By that time the ever-
increasing traffic over the Thames bridge had
made the enlargement of that structure a necessity, and the Bear was among the buildings
which had to be demolished.

Further south in the High street, and opposite the house in which John Harvard, the
founder of America's oldest university, was
born, stood the Boar's Head, an inn which was
once the property of Sir Fastolfe, and was by
him bequeathed through a friend to Magdalen
College, Oxford. This must not be confused
with the Boar's Head of Shakespeare, which
stood in Eastcheap on the other side of the

river, though it is a remarkable coincidence
that it was in the latter inn the dramatist laid
the scene of Prince Hal's merrymaking with
the Sir John Falstaff we all know.   The earliest
reference to the Southwark Boar's Head occurs
in the Paston Letters under date 1459.   This
is an epistle from a servant of Fastolfe to John
Paston, asking him to remind his master that
he had promised him he should be made host
of the Boar's Head, but whether he ever attained to that desired position there is no evidence to show.   The inn makes but little figure
in history; by 1720 it had dwindled to a mere
courtyard, and in 1830 the last remnants were
cleared away.

Inevitably, however, the fact that the Boar's
Head was the property of Sir John Fastolfe
prompts the question, what relation had he to
the Sir John Falstaff of Shakespeare's plays?
This has been a topic of large discussion for
many years.   There are so many touches of
character and definite incidents which apply in
common to the two knights that the poet has
been assumed to have had the historic Fastolfe
ever in view when drawing the portrait of his
Falstaff.   The historian Fuller assumed this
to have been the case, for he complains that the
" stage have been overbold " in dealing with

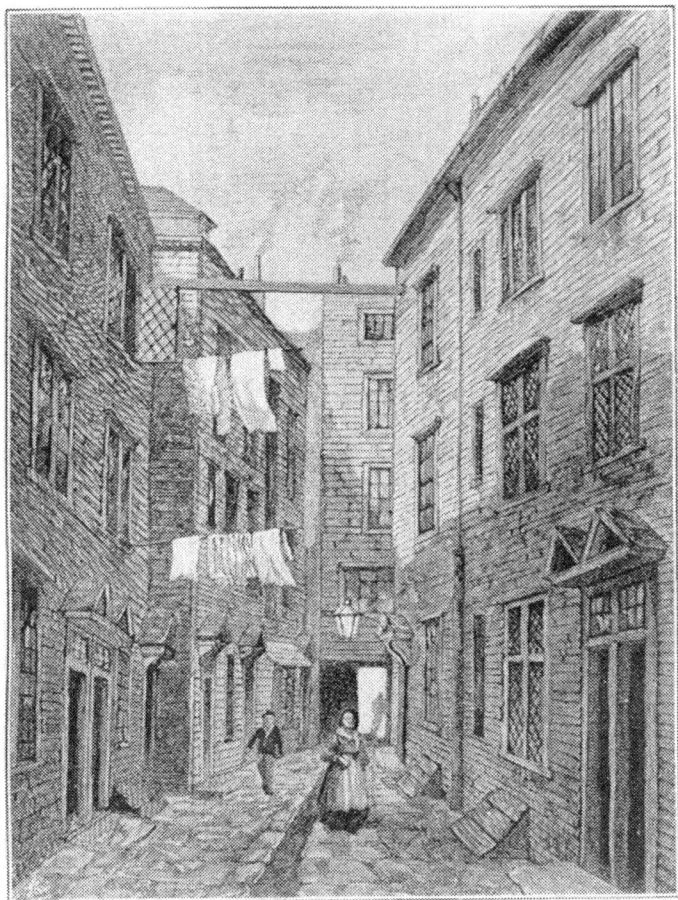

COURTYARD OF BOAR'S HEAD INN, SOUTHWARK.

Fastolfe's memory. Sidney Lee, however, sums up the case thus: " Shakespeare was possibly under the misapprehension, based on the episode of cowardice reported in ' Henry VI,' that the military exploits of the historical Sir John Fastolfe sufficiently resembled those of his own riotous knight to justify the employment of a corrupted version of his name. It is of course untrue that Fastolfe was ever the intimate associate of Henry V when Prince of Wales, who was not his junior by more than ten years, or that he was an impecunious spendthrift and gray-haired debauchee. The historical Fastolfe was in private life an expert man of business, who was indulgent neither to himself nor his friends. He was nothing of a jester, and was, in spite of all imputations to the contrary, a capable and brave soldier.''

Sad as has been the havoc wrought by time and the hand of man among the hostelries of Southwark, a considerable portion of one still survives in its actual seventeenth century guise. This is the George Inn, which is slightly nearer London Bridge than the Tabard. To catch a peep of its old-world aspect, with its quaint gallery and other indubitable tokens of a distant past, gives the pilgrim a pleasant shock. It is such a contrast to the ugly modern structures which impose themselves on the public as " Ye Olde " this and " Ye Olde " that. Here at any rate is a veritable survival. Nor does it matter that the George has made little figure in history; there is a whole world of satisfaction in the thought that it has changed but little since it was built in 1672. Its name is older than its structure. Stow included the George among the " many fair inns " he saw in Southwark in 1598, a fact which deals a cruel blow to that crude theory which declares inns were so named after the royal Georges of Great Britain.

Among the numerous other inns which once lined the High Street of Southwark there is but one which has claims upon the attention on the score of historic and literary interest. This is the White Hart, which was doubtless an old establishment at the date, 1406, of its first mention in historical records. Forty-four years later, that is in 1450, the inn gained its most notable association by being made the headquarters of Jack Cade at the time of his famous insurrection. Modern research has shown that this rebellion was a much more serious matter than the older historians were aware of, but the most careful investigation into Cade's career has failed to elicit any particulars of note

GEORGE INN.

prior to a year before the rising took place.
The year and place of his birth are unknown,
but twelve months before he appears in history
he was obliged to flee the realm and take refuge
in France owing to his having murdered a
woman who was with child. He served for a
time in the French army, then returned under
an assumed name and settled in Kent, which
was the centre of discontent against Henry VI.
As the one hope of reform lay in an appeal to
arms, the discontent broke into open revolt.
" The rising spread from Kent over Surrey
and Sussex. Everywhere it was general and
organized — a military levy of the yeomen of
the three shires." It was not of the people
alone, for more than a hundred esquires and
gentlemen threw in their lot with the rebels;
but how it came about that Jack Cade attained
the leadership is a profound mystery. Leader,
however, he was, and when he, with his twenty
thousand men, took possession of Southwark as
the most desirable base from which to threaten
the city of London, he elected the White Hart
for his own quarters. This was on the first of
July, 1450, and for the next few of those mid-
summer days the inn was the scene of many
stirring and tragic events. Daily, Cade at the
head of his troops crossed the bridge into the

city, and on one of those excursions he caused
the seizure and beheadal of the hated Lord Say.
Daily, too, there was constant coming and going
at the White Hart of Cade's emissaries.  At
length, however, the citizens of London, stung
into action by the robberies and other outrages
of the rebels, occupied the bridge in force.  A
stubborn struggle ensued, but Cade and his men
were finally beaten off.  The amnesty which
followed led to a conference at which terms
were arranged and a general pardon granted.
That for Cade, however, as it was made out
in his assumed name of Mortimer, was invalid,
and on the discovery being made he seized a
large quantity of booty and fled.  Not many
days later he was run to earth, wounded in being captured, and died as he was being brought
back to London.  His naked body was identified
by the hostess of the White Hart, who was
probably relieved to gaze upon so certain an
indication that she would be able to devote herself once more to the entertainment of less
troublesome guests.

For all the speedy ending of his ambitions,
Cade is assured of immortality so long as the
pages of Shakespeare endure.  The rebel is a
stirring figure in the Second Part of King
Henry VI and as an orator of the mob reaches

his greatest flights of eloquence in that speech which perpetuates the name of his headquarters at Southwark. "Hath my sword therefore broke through London gates, that you should leave me at the White Hart in Southwark?"

But English literature was not done with the old inn. Many changes were to pass over its head during the nearly four centuries which elapsed ere it was touched once more by the pen of genius, changes wrought by the havoc of fire and the attritions of the hand of time. When those years had fled a figure was to be seen in its courtyard to become better known to and better beloved by countless thousands than the rebel leader of the fifteenth century. "In the Borough," wrote the creator of that figure, "there still remain some half dozen old inns, which have preserved their external features unchanged, and which have escaped alike the rage for public improvement and the encroachments of private speculation. Great, rambling, queer old places they are, with galleries, and passages, and staircases, wide enough and antiquated enough to furnish materials for a hundred ghost stories. . . . It was in the yard of one of these inns — of no less celebrated a one than the White Hart — that a man was busily employed in brushing the dirt off a pair of boots, early on the morning succeeding the events narrated in the last chapter. He was habited in a coarse-striped waistcoat, with black calico sleeves, and blue glass buttons; drab breeches and leggings. A bright red handkerchief was wound in a very loose and unstudied style round his neck, and an old white hat was carelessly thrown on one side of his head. There were two rows of boots before him, one cleaned and the other dirty, and at every addition he made to the clean row, he paused from his work, and contemplated its results with evident satisfaction.''

Who does not recognize Sam Weller, making his first appearance in '' The Posthumous Papers of the Pickwick Club ''? And who has not revelled in the lively scene in the White Hart when Mr. Pickwick and his friends arrived in the nick of time to prevent the ancient but still sentimental Rachael from becoming Mrs. Jingle? It is not difficult to understand why that particular instalment of '' Pickwick '' was the turning-point of the book's fortunes. Prior to the advent of Sam in the courtyard of the White Hart the public had shown but a moderate interest in the new venture of '' Boz,'' but from that event onward the sales of the succeeding parts were ever on the in-

WHITE HART INN, SOUTHWARK.

crease. Sam and the White Hart, then, had much to do with the career of Dickens, for if " Pickwick " had failed it is more than probable that he would have abandoned literature as a profession.

When Dickens wrote, the White Hart was still in existence. It is so no longer. Till late in the last century this hostelry was spared the fate which had overtaken so many Southwark taverns, even though, in place of the nobles it had sheltered, its customers had become hop-merchants, farmers, and others of lower degree. In 1889, in the month of July, four hundred and thirty-nine years after it had received Jack Cade under its roof, the last timbers of the old inn were levelled to the ground.

# CHAPTER II

BOSWELL relates how, in one of his numerous communicative moods, he informed Dr. Johnson of the existence of a club at "the Boar's Head in Eastcheap, the very tavern where Falstaff and his joyous companions met; the members of which all assume Shakespeare's characters. One is Falstaff, another Prince Henry, another Bardolph, and so on." If the assiduous little Scotsman entertained the idea of joining the club, a matter on which he does not throw any light, Johnson's rejoinder was sufficient to deter him from doing so. "Don't be of it, Sir. Now that you have a name you must be careful to avoid many things not bad in themselves, but which will lessen your character."

Whether Johnson's remark was prompted by an intimate knowledge of the type of person frequenting the Boar's Head in his day cannot be decided, but there are ample grounds for thinking that the patrons of that inn were generally of a somewhat boisterous kind. That, perhaps, is partly Shakespeare's fault. Prior to his making it the scene of the mad revelry of Prince Hal and his none too choice companions, the history of the Boar's Head, so far as we know it, was sedately respectable. One of the earliest references to its existence is in a lease dated 1537, some sixty years before the first part of Henry IV was entered in the Stationers' Register. Some half century later, that is in 1588, the inn was kept by one Thomas Wright, whose son came into a '' good inheritance,'' was made clerk of the King's Stable, and a knight, and was '' a very discreet and honest gentleman.''

But Shakespeare's pen dispelled any atmosphere of respectability which lingered around the Boar's Head. From the time when he made it the meeting-place of the mad-cap Prince of Wales and his roistering followers, down to the day of Goldsmith's reverie under its roof, the inn has dwelt in the imagination at least as the rendezvous of hard drinkers and practical jokers. How could it be otherwise after the limning of such a scene as that described in Henry IV? That was sufficient to dedicate the inn to conviviality for ever.

How sharply the picture shapes itself as the

hurrying dialogue is read! The key-note of merriment is struck by the Prince himself as he implores the aid of Poins to help him laugh at the excellent trick he has just played on the boastful but craven Falstaff, and the bustle and hilarity of the scene never flags for a moment. Even Francis, the drawer, whose vocabulary is limited to " Anon, anon, sir " — the fellow that had " fewer words than a parrot, and yet the son of a woman " — and the host himself, as perplexed as his servant when two customers call at once, contribute to the movement of the episode in its earlier stages. But the pace is increased furiously when the burly Falstaff, scant of breath indeed, bustles hurriedly in proclaiming in one breath his scorn of cowards and his urgent need of a cup of sack. We all know the boastful story he told, how he and his three companions had been set upon and robbed by a hundred men, how he himself — as witness his sword " packed like a hand-saw " — had kept at bay and put to flight now two, anon four, and then seven, and finally eleven of his assailants. We all can see, too, the roguish twinkle in Prince Hal's eyes as the braggart knight embellishes his lying tale with every fresh sentence, and are as nonplussed as he when, the plot discovered, Falstaff finds a way to take credit for his cowardice. Who would not forgive so cajoling a vaunter?

It was later in this scene, be it remembered, that the portly knight was found fast asleep behind the arras, " snorting like a horse," and had his pockets searched to the discovery of that tavern bill — not paid we may be sure — which set forth an expenditure on the staff of life immensely disproportionate to that on drink, and elicited the famous ejaculation — " But one half-pennyworth of bread to this intolerable deal of sack! "

But Shakespeare had not finished with the Boar's Head. More coarse and less merry, but not less vivid, is that other scene wherein the shrill-tongued Doll Tearsheet and the peacemaking Dame Quickly figure. And it is of a special and private room in the Boar's Head we think as we listen to Dame Quickly's tale of how the amorous Falstaff made love to her with his hand upon " a parcel-gilt goblet," and followed up the declaration with a kiss and a request for thirty shillings.

For Shakespeare's sake, then, the Boar's Head is elect into that small circle of inns which are immortal in the annals of literature. But, like Chaucer's Tabard, no stone of it is left. Boswell made a mistake, and so did Goldsmith after him, in thinking that the Boar's Head of the eighteenth century was the Boar's Head of Shakespeare's day. They both forgot the great Fire of London. That disastrous conflagration of 1666 swept away every vestige of the old inn. Upon its foundation, however, another Boar's Head arose, the sign of which, cut in stone and dated 1668, is among the treasures of the Guildhall Museum. This was the building in which Boswell's club met, and it was under its roof Goldsmith penned his famous reverie.

As was to be expected of that social soul, the character of Falstaff gave Goldsmith more consolation than the most studied efforts of wisdom: "I here behold," he continues, "an agreeable old fellow forgetting age, and showing me the way to be young at sixty-five. Sure I am well able to be as merry, though not so comical, as he. Is it not in my power to have, though not so much wit, at least as much vivacity? — Age, care, wisdom, reflection, begone — I give you to the winds! Let's have t'other bottle: Here's to the memory of Shakespeare, Falstaff, and all the merry men of Eastcheap!"

With such zest did Goldsmith enter into his night out at the Boar's Head that when the midnight hour arrived he discovered all his

OLIVER GOLDSMITH.

companions had stolen away, leaving him —
still in high spirits — with the landlord as his
sole companion. Then the mood of reverie began to work. The very room helped to trans-
port him back through the centuries; the oak
floor, the gothic windows, the ponderous chim-
ney-piece, — all were reminders of the past.
But the prosaic landlord was an obstacle to the
complete working of the spell. At last, however, a change came over mine host, or so it
seemed to the dreaming chronicler. '' He in-
sensibly began to alter his appearance; his
cravat seemed quilled into a ruff, and his
breeches swelled out into a farlingale. I now
fancied him changing sexes; and as my eyes
began to close in slumber, I imagined my fat
landlord actually converted into as fat a landlady. However, sleep made but few changes in
my situation: the tavern, the apartment, and
the table, continued as before: nothing suffered mutation but my host, who was fairly
altered into a gentlewoman, whom I knew to be
Dame Quickly, mistress of this tavern in the
days of Sir John; and the liquor we were
drinking seemed converted into sack and
sugar.''

Such an opportunity of interviewing an acquaintance of Falstaff was not to be lost, and

to the credit of Dame Quickly be it said that she was far more communicative than some moderns are under the questioning ordeal. But it was no wonder she was loquacious: had she not been ordered by Pluto to keep a record of every transaction at the Boar's Head, and in the discharge of that duty compiled three hundred tomes? Some may subscribe to the opinion that Dame Quickly was indiscreet as well as loquacious; certainly she did not spare the reputations of some who had dwelt under that ancient roof. The sum of the matter, however, was that since the execution of that hostess who was accused of witchcraft the Boar's Head '' underwent several revolutions, according to the spirit of the times, or the disposition of the reigning monarch. It was this day a brothel, and the next a conventicle for enthusiasts. It was one year noted for harbouring Whigs, and the next infamous for a retreat to Tories. Some years ago it was in high vogue, but at present it seems declining.''

One other son of genius was to add to the fame of the Boar's Head, the American Goldsmith, that is, the gentle Washington Irving. Of course Shakespeare was the moving spirit once more. While turning over the pages of Henry IV Irving was seized with a sudden in-

spiration: " I will make a pilgrimage to Eastcheap, and see if the old Boar's Head tavern
still exists." But it was too late. The only
relic of the ancient abode of Dame Quickly was
the stone boar's head, built into walls reared
where the inn once stood. Nothing daunted,
however, Irving explored the neighbourhood,
and was rewarded, as he thought, by running
to earth Dame Quickly's " parcel-gilt goblet "
in a tavern near by. He had one other " find."
In the old graveyard of St. Michael's, which no
longer exists, he discovered, so he avers, the
tombstone of one Robert Preston who, like the
Francis of " Anon, anon, sir," was a drawer at
the Boar's Head, and quotes from that tombstone the following admonitory epitaph:

> " Bacchus, to give the toping world surprise,
>   Produced one sober son, and here he lies.
>   Though rear'd among full hogsheads, he defied
>   The charms of wine, and every one beside.
>   O reader, if to justice thou'rt inclined,
>   Keep honest Preston daily in thy mind.
>   He drew good wine, took care to fill his pots,
>   Had sundry virtues that excused his faults.
>   You that on Bacchus have the like dependence,
>   Pray copy Bob, in measure and attendance."

Small as was the reward of Irving's quest,
a still more barren result would ensue on a

modern pilgrimage to the Boar's Head. It was
still a tavern in 1785, for a chronicler of that
date described it as having on each side of the
doorway "a vine branch, carved in wood, rising more than three feet from the ground,
loaded with leaves and clusters; and on the top
of each a little Falstaff, eight inches high, in
the dress of his day." But Dame Quickly's
forecast of declining fortune moved on to its
fulfilment. In the last stages of its existence
the building was divided into two, while the
carved boar's head which Irving saw still remained as the one sign of its departed glories.
Finally came the resolve to widen the approach
to London Bridge from the city side, and the
carrying out of that resolve involved the sweep-
ing away of the Boar's Head. This was in
1831, and, as has been said, the only relic of the
ancient tavern is that carved sign in the Guildhall Museum. But the curious in such matters
may be interested to know that the statue of
King William marks approximately the spot of
ground where hover the immortal memories of
Shakespeare, and Goldsmith, and Irving.

Within easy distance of Eastcheap, in Upper
Thames Street, which skirts the river bank,
there stood, in Shakespeare's day and much
later, a tavern bearing the curious name of the

Three Cranes in the Vintry. John Stow, that
zealous topographer to whom the historians of
London owe so large a debt, helps to explain
the mystery. The vintry, he tells us, was that
part of the Thames bank where " the merchants
of Bordeaux craned their wines out of lighters
and other vessels, and there landed and made
sale of them." He also adds that the Three
Cranes' lane was " so called not only of a sign
of three cranes at a tavern door, but rather of
three strong cranes of timber placed on the
Vintry wharf by the Thames side, to crane up
wines there." Earlier than the seventeenth
century, however, it would seem that one crane
had to suffice for the needs of " the merchants
of Bordeaux," and then the tavern was known
simply as the Crane. Two references, dated re-
spectively 1552 and 1554, speak of the sign in
the singular. Twenty years later, however, the
one had become three.

Ben Jonson, whose knowledge of London
inns and taverns was second only to that of
Pepys, evidently numbered the Three Cranes
in the Vintry among his houses of call. Of two
of his allusions to the house one is derogatory
of the wit of its patrons, the other laudatory of
the readiness of its service. " A pox o' these
pretenders to wit! " runs the first passage.

" Your Three Cranes, Mitre, and Mermaid
men! Not a corn of true salt, not a grain of
right mustard amongst them all." And here
is the other side of the shield, credited to Iniquity in " The Devil is an Ass '': —

" Nay, boy, I will bring thee to the bawds and roysters
At Billingsgate, feasting with claret-wine and oysters;
From thence shoot the Bridge, child, to the Cranes in
    the Vintry,
And see there the gimblets how they make their entry."

Of course Pepys was acquainted with the
house. He had, indeed, a savage memory of
one meal under its roof. It was all owing to
the marrying proclivities of his uncle Fenner.
Bereft of his wife on the last day of August,
that easy-going worthy, less than two months
later, was discovered by his nephew in an ale-
house, " very jolly and youthsome, and as one
that I believe will in a little time get him a
wife." Pepys' anticipation was speedily realized. Uncle Fenner had indulged himself with
a new partner by the middle of January, and
must needs give a feast to celebrate the event.
And this is Pepys' frank record of the occasion: " By invitation to my uncle Fenner's,
where I found his new wife, a pitiful, old, ugly,
ill-bred woman, in a hatt, a midwife. Here

were many of his, and as many of her relatives,
sorry, mean people; and after choosing our
gloves, we all went over to the Three Cranes
taverne, and (although the best room of the
house) in such a narrow dogg-hole we were
crammed, (and I believe we were near forty)
that it made me loath my company and victuals;
and a sorry, poor dinner it was."

In justice to the Three Cranes, Pepys must
not be allowed to have the last word. That
particular dinner, no doubt, owed a good deal
of its defects to the atmosphere and the company amid which it was served. At any rate,
the host of the Black Bear at Cumnor — he of
Sir Walter Scott's " Kenilworth " — was
never weary of praising the Three Cranes,
" the most topping tavern in London " as he
emphatically declared.

No one can glance even casually over a list
of tavern signs without observing how frequently the numeral " three " is used. Various explanations have been offered for the pro-
pensity of mankind to use that number, one
deriving the habit from the fact that primitive
man divided the universe into three regions,
heaven, earth, and water. Pythagoras, it will
be remembered, called three the perfect number; Jove is depicted with three-forked light-

ning; Neptune bears a trident; Pluto has his
three-headed dog.  Again, there are three
Fates, three Furies, three Graces and three
Muses.  It is natural, then, to find the numeral
so often employed in the signs of inns and
taverns.  Thus we have the Three Angels, the
Three Crowns, the Three Compasses, the Three
Cups, the Three Horseshoes, the Three Tuns,
the Three Nuns, and many more.  In the city
of London proper the Three Cups was a favourite sign and the Three Tuns was hardly less
popular.  There were also several Three Nuns,
the most famous of which was situated in Ald-
gate High Street, where its modern representative still stands.  In the bygone years it was a
noted coaching inn and enjoyed an enviable
reputation for the rare quality of its punch.
Defoe has a brief reference to the house in
his " A Journal of the Plague Year."

An attempt to enumerate the King's Head
taverns of London would be an endless task.
It must not be overlooked, however, that one of
the most notable houses so named stood in Fenchurch Street, on the site now occupied by the
London Tavern.  This is the tavern for which
a notable historic association is claimed.  The
tradition has it that when the Princess Elizabeth, the " Good Queen Bess " of after days,

was released from the Tower of London on
May 19th, 1554, she went first to a neighbouring church to offer thanks for her deliverance,
and then proceeded to the King's Head to enjoy a somewhat plebeian dinner of boiled pork
and pease-pudding. This legend seems to ignore the fact that the freedom of the Princess
was comparative only; that she was at that
time merely removed from one prison to another; and that the record of her movements
on that day speaks of her taking barge at the
Tower wharf and going direct to Richmond en
route for Woodstock. However, the metal dish
and cover which were used in serving that
homely meal of boiled pork and pease-pudding
are still shown, and what can the stickler for
historical accuracy do in the face of such stubborn evidence?

Two other Fenchurch Street taverns have
wholly disappeared. One of these, the Elephant, was wont to claim a somewhat dubious
association with Hogarth. The artist is credited with once lodging under the Elephant's
roof and with embellishing the walls of the tap-
room with pictures in payment for a long over-
due bill. The subjects were said to have included the first study for the picture which afterwards became famous under the title of

"Modern Midnight Conversation," but treated
in a much broader manner than is shown in the
well-known print.    When the building was
pulled down in 1826 a heated controversy arose
concerning these Hogarth pictures, which were
removed from the walls and exhibited in a
Pall Mall gallery.    The verdict of experts was
given against their being the work of the master for whom they were claimed.    The other
tavern was one of the many mitres to be found
in London during the seventeenth century.
The host, Dan Rawlinson, was so staunch a
royalist that when Charles I was executed he
hung his sign in mourning, an action which
naturally caused him to be regarded with suspicion by the Cromwell party, but "endeared
him so much to the churchmen that he throve
amain and got a good estate."    Something of
that prosperity was due no doubt to the excellent "venison-pasty" of which Pepys was so
fond.    But Dan Rawlinson of the Mitre had his
reverses as well as his successes.    During the
dreaded Plague of London Pepys met an acquaintance in Fenchurch Street who called his
attention to the fact that Mr. Rawlinson's door
was shut up.    "Why," continued his inform-
ant, "after all this sickness, and himself

spending all the last year in the country, one of his men is now dead of the plague, and his wife and one of his maids sick, and himself shut up.'' Mrs. Rawlinson died a day or two later and the maid quickly followed her mistress to the grave. A year later the Mitre was destroyed in the Great Fire of London and Pepys met its much-tried owner shortly after '' looking over his ruins.'' But the tavern was rebuilt on a more spacious scale, and Isaac Fuller was commissioned to adorn its walls with paintings. This was the artist whose fondness of tavern life prevented him from becoming a great painter. The commission at the Mitre was no doubt much to his liking, and Walpole describes in detail the panels with which he adorned a great room in that house. '' The figures were as large as life: a Venus, Satyr, and sleeping Cupid; a boy riding a goat and another fallen down, over the chimney: this was the best part of the performance, says Vertue: Saturn devouring a Child, Mercury, Minerva, Diana, Apollo; and Bacchus, Venus, and Ceres embracing; a young Silenus fallen down, and holding a goblet, into which a boy was pouring wine; the Scarons, between the windows, and on the ceiling two angels supporting a mitre, in a large circle.'' The execution of all this must have kept Fuller for quite a long time amid his favourite environment.

One of the lesser known Cock taverns of London was still in existence in Leadenhall Street during the first quarter of the last century. A drawing of the time shows it to have been a picturesque building, the most notable feature being that the window lights on the first floor extended the entire width of the front, the only specimen of the kind then remaining in London. At the time the drawing was made that particular room was used as the kitchen. From the dress of the boys of the carved brackets, supporting the over-hanging upper story, it has been inferred that the house was originally a charity school. Behind the tavern there stood a brick building dated 1627, formerly used by the bricklayers' company, but in 1795 devoted to the purposes of a Jewish synagogue. As with all the old taverns of this sign, the effigy of the bird from which it took its name was prominently displayed in front. Far more ancient than the Cock is that other Leadenhall Street tavern, the Ship and Turtle, which is still represented in the thoroughfare. The claim is made for this house that it dates back to 1377, and for many generations, down,

COCK INN, LEADENHALL STREET.

indeed, to 1835, it had a succession of widows as hostesses. The modern representative of this ancient house prides itself upon the quality of its turtle soup and upon the fact that it is the meeting-place of numerous masonic lodges, besides being in high favour for corporation and companies' livery dinners.

If the pilgrim now turns his steps toward Bishopsgate Street Within — the " Within " signifying, of course, that that part of the thoroughfare was inside the old city wall — he will find himself in a neighbourhood where many famous inns once stood. Apart from the Wrestlers and the Angel which are mentioned by Stow, there were the Flower Pot, the White Hart, the Four Swans, the Three Nuns, the Green Dragon, the Ball, and several more. The reason for this crowding together of so many hostelries in one street is obvious. It was through Bishop's gate that the farmers of the eastern counties came into the city and they naturally made their headquarters in the district nearest to the end of their journey.

For many years the White Hart maintained its old-time reputation as a " fair inn for the receipt of travellers." That it was an ancient structure is proved by the fact that when it was demolished, the date of 1480 was discovered on

one of its half-timbered bays. The present up-
to-date White Hart stands on the site of the
old inn.

Far greater interest attaches to the Bull inn,
even were it only for the fact of its association
with Thomas Hobson, the Cambridge carrier
whom Milton made famous. In the closing
years of the sixteenth century the house appears to have had a dubious reputation, for
when Anthony Bacon came to live in Bishopsgate Street in 1594 his mother became exceedingly anxious on his account, fearing '' the
neighbourhood of the Bull Inn.'' Perhaps,
however, the distressed mother based her alarm
on the dangers of play-acting, for the house
was notable as the scene of many dramatic performances. That it was the recognized headquarters for Cambridge carriers is shown by
an allusion, in 1637, which reads: '' The Blacke
Bull in Bishopsgate Street, who is still looking
towards Shoreditch to see if he can spy the
carriers coming from Cambridge.'' Hobson, of
course, was the head of that fraternity. He
had flourished amazingly since he succeeded to
his father's business in the university city, and
attained that position of independence which
enabled him to force the rule that each horse
in his stable was to be hired only in its proper

turn, thus originating the proverb, '' Hobson's choice,'' that is, '' this or none.'' Despite his ever growing wealth and advanced years, Hobson continued his regular journeys to London until the outbreak of the plague caused the authorities to suspend the carrier service for a time. This is the fact upon which Milton seized with such humourous effect in his poetical epitaph:

> " Here lies old Hobson. Death hath broke his girt,
> And here, alas! hath laid him in the dirt;
> Or else, the ways being foul, twenty to one
> He's here stuck in a slough, and overthrown.
> 'Twas such a shifter that, if truth were known,
> Death was half glad when he had got him down;
> For he had any time this ten years full
> Dodged with him betwixt Cambridge and The Bull.
> And surely Death could never have prevailed,
> Had not his weekly course of carriage failed;
> But lately, finding him so long at home,
> And thinking now his journey's end was come,
> And that he had ta'en up his latest inn,
> In the kind office of a chamberlain,
> Showed him his room where he must lodge that night,
> Pulled off his boots, and took away the light."

Among the " Familiar Letters " of James Howell is a stately epistle addressed " To Sir Paul Pindar, Knight," who is informed to his face that of all the men of his times he is " one

of the greatest examples of piety and constant
integrity," and is assured that his correspondent could see his namesake among the apostles
saluting and solacing him, and ensuring that his
works of charity would be as a " triumphant
chariot " to carry him one day to heaven. But
Sir Paul Pindar was more than benevolent; he
was a master in business affairs and no mean
diplomatist. His commercial aptitude he put
to profitable use during a fifteen years' residence in Italy; his skill as a negotiator was
tested and proved by nine years' service in
Constantinople as the ambassador of James I
to Turkey. At the date of his final return to
England, 1623, the merchant and diplomat was
an exceedingly wealthy man, well able to meet
the expense of that fine mansion in Bishopsgate
Street Without which perpetuated his name
down to our own day. In its original state Sir
Paul Pindar's house, both within and without,
was equal in splendour and extent to any mansion in London. And, as may be imagined, its
owner was a person of importance in city and
court life. One of his possessions was a great
diamond worth thirty-five thousand pounds,
which James I used to borrow for state occasions. The son of that monarch purchased this
jewel in 1625 for about half its value and suc-

PAUL PINDAR TAVERN.

cessfully deferred payment for even that reduced sum! Sir Paul, indeed, appears to have
been a complacent lender of his wealth to roy-
alty and the nobility, so that it is not surprising many " desperate debts " were owing him
on his death. A century and a quarter after
that event, that is in 1787, the splendid mansion of the wealthy merchant and diplomat had
become a tavern under the names of its builder,
and continued in that capacity until 1890, when
railway extension made its demolition necessary. But the beautifully carved front is still
preserved in the South Kensington Museum.

While there may at times be good reason for
doubting the claims made as to the antiquity
of some London taverns, there can be none for
questioning the ripe old age to which the
Pope's Head in Cornhill attained. This is one
of the few taverns which Stow deals with at
length. He describes it as being " strongly
built of stone," and favours the opinion that it
was at one time the palace of King John. He
tells, too, how in his day wine was sold there at
a penny the pint and bread provided free. It
was destroyed in the Great Fire, but rebuilt
shortly after. Pepys knew both the old and
the new house. In the former he is said to have
drunk his first " dish of tea," and he certainly

enjoyed many a meal under its roof, notably on
that occasion when, with Sir W. Penn and Mrs.
Pepys, he " eat cakes and other fine things."
Another, not so pleasant, memory is associated
with the Pope's Head.  Two actors figured in
the episode, James Quin and William Bowen,
between whom, especially on the side of the
latter, strong professional jealousy existed.
Bowen, a low comedian of " some talent and
more conceit," taunted Quin with being tame
in a certain role, and Quin retorted in kind, declaring that Bowen's impersonation of a character in " The Libertine " was much inferior
to that of another actor.  Bowen seems to have
had an ill-balanced mind; he was so affected
by Jeremy Collier's " Short View " that he
left the stage and opened a cane shop in Holborn, thinking " a shopkeeper's life was the
readiest way to heaven."  But he was on the
stage again in a year, thus resuming the career
which was to be his ruin.  For so thoroughly
was he incensed by Quin's disparagement that
he took the earliest opportunity of forcing the
quarrel to an issue.  Having invited Quin to
meet him, the two appear to have gone from
tavern to tavern until they reached the Pope's
Head.  Quin was averse to a duel, but no sooner
had the two entered an empty room in the Corn-

hill tavern than Bowen fastened the door, and, standing with his back against it and drawing his sword, threatened Quin that he would run him through if he did not draw and defend himself. In vain did Quin remonstrate, and in the end he had to take to his sword to keep the angry Bowen at bay. He, however, pressed so eagerly on his fellow actor that it was not long ere he received a mortal wound. Before he died Bowen confessed he had been in the wrong, and that frank admission was the main cause why Quin was legally freed of blame for the tragic incident in the Pope's Head.

Although there was a Mermaid tavern in Cornhill, it must not be confused with its far more illustrious namesake in the nearby thoroughfare of Cheapside. The Cornhill house was once kept by a man named Dun, and the story goes that one day when he was in the room with some witty gallants, one of them, who had been too familiar with the host's wife, exclaimed, '' I'll lay five pounds there's a cuckold in this company.'' To which another immediately rejoined, '' 'Tis Dun! ''

Around the other Mermaid — that in Cheapside — much controversy has raged. One dispute was concerned with its exact site, but as the building disappeared entirely many generations ago that is not a matter of moment. Another cause of debate is found in that passage of Gifford's life of Ben Jonson which describes his habits in the year 1603. "About this time," Gifford wrote, "Jonson probably began to acquire that turn for conviviality for which he was afterwards noted. Sir Walter Raleigh, previously to his unfortunate engagement with Cobham and others, had instituted a meeting of *beaux esprits* at the Mermaid, a celebrated tavern in Friday Street. Of this club, which combined more talent and genius, perhaps, than ever met together before or since, our author was a member; and here, for many years, he regularly repaired with Shakespeare, Beaumont, Fletcher, Selden, Cotton, Carew, Martin, Donne, and many others, whose names, even at this distant period, call up a mingled feeling of reverence and respect." Many have found this flowing narrative hard of belief. It is doubted whether Gifford had any authority for mixing up Sir Walter Raleigh with the Mermaid, and there are good grounds for believing that Jonson's relations with Shakespeare were not of an intimate character.

All the same, it is beyond dispute that there were rare combats of wit at the Mermaid in Jonson's days and under his rule. For indis-

putable witness we have that epistle which
Francis Beaumont addressed to Jonson from
some country retreat whither he and Fletcher
had repaired to work on two of their comedies.
Beaumont tells how he had dreams of the " full
Mermaid wine," dwells upon the lack of excitement in his rural abode, and then breaks
out:

" Methinks the little wit I had is lost
Since I saw you; for wit is like a rest
Held up at tennis, which men do best
With the best gamesters.   What things have we seen
Done at the Mermaid! heard words that have been
So nimble, and so full of subtle flame,
As if that every one (from whence they came)
Had meant to put his whole wit in a jest,
And had resolved to live a fool the rest
Of his dull life."

That poem inspired another which should
always be included in the anthology of the Mermaid.   More than two centuries after Beaumont penned his rhyming epistle to Jonson,
three brothers had their lodging for a brief
season in Cheapside, and the poetic member of
the trio doubtless mused long and often on
those kindred spirits who, for him far more
than for ordinary mortals, haunted the spot
where the famous tavern once stood.   Thus it

came about that John Keats' residence in
Cheapside was a prime factor in suggesting
his " Lines on the Mermaid Tavern ":

> " Souls of poets dead and gone,
> What Elysium have ye known,
> Happy field or mossy cavern,
> Choicer than the Mermaid Tavern?
> Have ye tippled drink more fine
> Than mine host's Canary wine?
> Or are fruits of Paradise
> Sweeter than those dainty pies
> Of venison?   O generous food!
> Drest as though bold Robin Hood
> Would, with his maid Marian,
> Sup and bowse with horn and can.
>
> " I have heard that on a day
> Mine host's sign-board flew away,
> Nobody knew whither, till
> An Astrologer's old quill
> To a sheepskin gave the story, —
> Said he saw you in your glory,
> Underneath a new-old sign
> Sipping beverage divine,
> And pledging with contented smack
> The Mermaid in the Zodiac.
>
> " Souls of poets dead and gone,
> What Elysium have ye known,
> Happy field or mossy cavern,
> Choicer than the Mermaid Tavern? "

ANCIENT VIEW OF CHEAPSIDE, SHOWING THE NAG'S HEAD INN.

Compared with the Mermaid, the other old taverns of Cheapside make a meagre showing in history. There was a Mitre, however, which dated back to 1475 at the least, and had the reputation of making " noses red "; and the Bull Head, whose host was the " most faithful friend " Bishop Ridley ever had, and was the meeting-place of the Royal Society for several years; and, above all, the Nag's Head, famous as the alleged scene of the fictitious consecration of the Elizabethan bishops in 1559. There is an interesting drawing of 1638 depicting the procession of Mary de Medici in Cheapside on the occasion of her visit to her daughter, the wife of Charles I. This animated scene is historically valuable for the record it gives of several notable structures in the thoroughfare which was at that time the centre of the commercial life of London. In the middle of the picture is an excellent representation of Cheapside Cross, to the right the conduit is seen, and in the extreme corner of the drawing is a portion of the Nag's Head with its projecting sign.

Another of Ben Jonson's haunts was situated within easy distance of the Mermaid. This was the Three Tuns, of the Guildhall Yard, which Herrick includes in his list of taverns favoured by the dramatist.

> " Ah Ben!
> Say how or when
> Shall we thy Guests,
> Meet at those lyric feasts
>     Made at the Sun,
> The Dog, the Triple Tunne;
> Where we such clusters had
> As made us nobly wild, not mad? "

Close at hand, too, in Old Jewry, was that Windmill tavern, of which Stow wrote that it was " sometime the Jews' synagogue, since a house of friars, then a nobleman's house, after that a merchant's house, wherein mayoralties have been kept, and now a wine tavern." It must have been a fairly spacious hostelry, for on the occasion of the visit of the Emperor Charles V in 1522 the house is noted as being able to provide fourteen feather-beds, and stabling for twenty horses. From the fact that one of the characters in " Every Man in His Humour " dates a letter from the Windmill, and that two of the scenes in that comedy take place in a room of the tavern, it is obvious that it also must be numbered among the many houses frequented by Jonson.

One dramatic episode is connected with the history of the Windmill. In the early years of the seventeenth century considerable excitement was aroused in Worcestershire by the doings of John Lambe, who indulged in magical arts and crystal glass enchantments. By 1622 he was in London, and numbered the king's favourite, the Duke of Buckingham, among his clients. That was sufficient to set the populace against him, an enmity which was greatly intensified by strange atmospheric disturbances which visited London in June, 1628. All this was attributed to Lambe's conjuring, and the popular fury came to a climax a day or two later, when Lambe, as he was leaving the Fortune Theatre, was attacked by a mob of apprentices. He fled towards the city and finally took refuge in the Windmill. After affording the hunted man haven for a few hours the host, in view of the tumult outside, at length turned him into the street again, where he was so severely beaten that he died the following morning. A crystal ball and other conjuring implements were found on his person.

Far less exciting was the history of Pontack's, a French ordinary in Abchurch Lane which played a conspicuous part in the social life of London during the eighteenth century. Britons of that period had their own insular contempt for French cookery, as is well illustrated by Rowlandson's caricature which, with

its larder of dead cats and its coarse revelation of other secrets of French cuisine, may be
regarded as typical of the popular opinion.
But Pontack and his eating-house flourished
amazingly for all that. A French refugee in
London in 1697 took pride in the fact that
whereas it was difficult to obtain a good meal
elsewhere '' those who would dine at one or
two guineas per head are handsomely accom-
modated at our famous Pontack's.'' The
owner of this ordinary is sketched in brief by
Evelyn, who frequently dined under his roof.
Under date July 13, 1683, the diarist wrote:
'' I had this day much discourse with Monsieur
Pontaq, son to the famous and wise prime President of Bordeaux. This gentleman was owner
of that excellent vignoble of Pontaq and
Obrien, from whence come the choicest of our
Bordeaux wines; and I think I may truly say
of him, what was not so truly said of St. Paul,
that much learning had made him mad. He
spoke all languages, was very rich, had a handsome person, and was well bred; about forty-
five years of age.''

Hogarth, it will be remembered, paid Pontack a dubious compliment in the third plate
of his Rake's Progress series. The room of
that boisterous scene is adorned with pictures

A FRENCH ORDINARY IN LONDON.
(*From a Rowlandson Caricature*).

of the Roman Emperors, one of which has been removed to give place to the portrait of Pontack, who is described by a Hogarth commentator as " an eminent French cook, whose great talents being turned to heightening sensual, rather than mental enjoyments, has a much better chance of a votive offering from this company, than would either Vespasian or Trajan." These advertisements, however, were all to the good of the house. They were exactly of the kind to attract the most profitable type of customer. Those customers might grumble, as Swift did, at the prices, but they all agreed that they enjoyed very good dinners. The poet, indeed, expressed the unanimous verdict of the town when he asked:

" What wretch would nibble on a hanging shelf,
   When at Pontack's he may regale himself? "

# CHAPTER III

Save for the High Street of Southwark, there was probably no thoroughfare of old London which could boast so many inns and taverns to the square yard as Fleet Street, but ere the pilgrim explores that famous neighbourhood he should visit several other spots where notable hostelries were once to be seen. He should, for example, turn his steps towards St. Paul's Churchyard, which, despite the fact that it was chiefly inhabited by booksellers, had its Queen's Arms tavern and its Goose and Gridiron.

Memories of David Garrick and Dr. Johnson are associated with the Queen's Arms. This tavern was the meeting-place of a select club formed by a few intimate friends of the actor for the express purpose of providing them with opportunities to enjoy his society. Its members included James Clutterback, the city merchant who gave Garrick invaluable financial aid when he started at Drury Lane, and John Paterson, that helpful solicitor whom the

62

actor selected as one of his executors. These
admirers of " little David " were a temperate
set; " they were none of them drinkers, and
in order to make a reckoning called only for
French wine." Johnson's association with the
house is recorded by Boswell as belonging to
the year 1781. " On Friday, April 6," he
writes, " he carried me to dine at a club which,
at his desire, had been lately formed at the
Queen's Arms in St. Paul's Churchyard. He
told Mr. Hoole that he wished to have a *City
Club*, and asked him to collect one; but, said
he, ' Don't let them be *patriots*.' The company
were to-day very sensible, well-behaved men."
Which, taken in conjunction with the abstemi-
ous nature of the Garrick club, would seem to
show that the Queen's Arms was an exceedingly decorous house.

Concerning the Goose and Gridiron only a
few scanty facts have survived. Prior to the
Great Fire it was known as the Mitre, but on
its being rebuilt it was called the Lyre. When
it came into repute through the concerts of a
favourite musical society being given within its
walls, the house was decorated with a sign of
Apollo's lyre, surmounted by a swan. This
provided too good an opportunity for the wits
of the town to miss, and they promptly renamed

the house as the Goose and Gridiron, which recalls the facetious landlord who, on gaining
possession of premises once used as a music-
house, chose for his sign a goose stroking the
bars of a gridiron and inscribed beneath, " The
Swan and Harp." It is an interesting note in
the history of the St. Paul's Churchyard house
that early in the eighteenth century, on the re-
vival of Freemasonry in England, the Grand
Lodge was established here.

Almost adjacent to St. Paul's, that is, in
Queen's Head Passage, which leads from Pa-
ternoster Row into Newgate Street, once stood
the famous Dolly's Chop House, the resort of
Fielding, and Defoe, and Swift, and Dryden,
and Pope and many other sons of genius. It
was built on the site of an ordinary owned by
Richard Tarleton, the Elizabethan actor whose
playing was so humorous that it even won the
praise of Jonson. He was indeed such a merry
soul, and so great a favourite in clown's parts,
that innkeepers frequently had his portrait
painted as a sign. The chief feature of the establishment which succeeded Tarleton's tavern
appears to have been the excellence of its beef-
steaks. It should also be added that they were
served fresh from the grill, a fact which is
accentuated by the allusion which Smollett

places in one of Melford's letters to Sir Walkin Phillips in "Humphry Clinker": "I send you the history of this day, which has been remarkably full of adventures; and you will own I give you them like a beef-steak at *Dolly's,* *hot* and *hot,* without ceremony and parade."

Out into Newgate Street the pilgrim should now make his way in search of that Salutation Tavern which is precious for its associations with Coleridge and Lamb and Southey. Once more, alas! the new has usurped the place of the old, but there is some satisfaction in being able to gaze upon the lineal successor of so noted a house. The Salutation was a favourite social resort in the eighteenth century and was frequently the scene of the more formal dining occasions of the booksellers and printers. There is a poetical invitation to one such function, a booksellers' supper on January 19, 1736, which reads:

> "You're desired on Monday next to meet
> At Salutation Tavern, Newgate Street,
> Supper will be on table just at eight."

One of those rhyming invitations was sent to Samuel Richardson, the novelist, who replied in kind:

" For me I'm much concerned I cannot meet
At Salutation Tavern, Newgate Street."

Another legend credits this with being the
house whither Sir Christopher Wren resorted
to smoke his pipe while the new St. Paul's was
being built. More authentic, however, and indeed beyond dispute, are the records which
link the memories of Coleridge and Lamb and
Southey with this tavern. It was here Southey
found Coleridge in one of his many fits of de-
pression, but pleasanter far are the recollec-
tions which recall the frequent meetings of
Lamb and Coleridge, between whom there was
so much in common. They would not forget
that it was at the nearby Christ's Hospital
they were schoolboys together, the reminiscences of which happy days coloured the
thoughts of Elia as he penned that exquisite
portrait of his friend: " Come back into memory, like as thou wert in the day-spring of thy
fancies, with hope like a fiery column before
thee — the dark pillar not yet turned — Samuel
Taylor Coleridge — Logician, Metaphysician,
Bard! — How have I seen the casual passer
through the cloisters stand still, entranced with
admiration to hear thee unfold, in thy deep and
sweet intonations, the mysteries of Jamblichus,

or Plotinus, or reciting Homer in his Greek, or
Pindar — while the walls of the old Grey
Friars re-echoed to the accents of the inspired
charity-boy!'' As Coleridge was the elder by
two years he left Christ's Hospital for Cambridge before Lamb had finished his course, but
he came back to London now and then, to meet
his schoolmate in a smoky little room of the
Salutation and discuss metaphysics and poetry
to the accompaniment of egg-hot, Welsh rab-
bits, and tobacco. Those golden hours in the
old tavern left their impress deep in Lamb's
sensitive nature, and when he came to dedicate
his works to Coleridge he hoped that some of
the sonnets, carelessly regarded by the general
reader, would awaken in his friend '' remem-
brances which I should be sorry should be ever
totally extinct — the memory ' of summer days
and of delightful years,' even so far back as
those old suppers at our old Salutation Inn, —
when life was fresh and topics exhaustless —
and you first kindled in me, if not the power,
yet the love of poetry and beauty and kindli-
ness.''

Continuing westward from Newgate Street,
the explorer of the inns and taverns of old
London comes first to Holborn Viaduct, where
there is nothing of note to detain him, and then

reaches Holborn proper, with its continuation as High Holborn, which by the time of Henry III had become a main highway into the city for the transit of wood and hides, corn and cheese, and other agricultural products. It must be remembered also that many of the principal coaches had their stopping-place in this thoroughfare, and that as a consequence the inns were numerous and excellent and much frequented by country gentlemen on their visits to town. Although those inns have long been swept away, the quaint half-timbered buildings of Staple Inn remain to aid the imagination in repicturing those far-off days when the Dagger, and the Red Lion, and the Bull and Gate, and the Blue Boar, and countless other hostelries were dotted on either side of the street.

With the first of these, the Dagger Tavern, we cross the tracks of Ben Jonson once more. Twice does the dramatist allude to this house in " The Alchemist," and the revelation that Dapper frequented the Dagger would have conveyed its own moral to seventeenth century playgoers, for it was then notorious as a resort of the lowest and most disreputable kind. The other reference makes mention of " Dagger frumety," which is a reminder that this house, as was the case with another of like name, prided itself upon the excellence of its pies, which were decorated with a representation of a dagger. That these pasties were highly appreciated is the only conclusion which can be drawn from the contemporary exclamation, " I'll not take thy word for a Dagger pie," and from the fact that in " The Devil is an Ass " Jonson makes Iniquity declare that the 'prentice boys rob their masters and " spend it in pies at the Dagger and the Woolsack."

A second of these Holborn inns bore a sign which has puzzled antiquaries not a little. The name was given as the Bull and Gate, but the actual sign was said to depict the Boulogne Gate at Calais. Here, it is thought, a too phonetic pronunciation of the French word led to the contradiction of name and sign. What is more to the point, and of greater interest, is the connection Fielding established between Tom Jones and the Bull and Gate. When that hero reached London in his search after the Irish peer who brought Sophia to town, he entered the great city by the highway which is now Gray's Inn Road, and at once began his arduous search. But without success. He prosecuted his enquiry till the clock struck eleven, and then Jones " at last yielded to the advice of Partridge, and retreated to the Bull and Gate in Holborn, that being the inn where he had first alighted, and where he retired to enjoy that kind of repose which usually attends persons in his circumstances.''

No less notable a character than Oliver Cromwell is linked in a dramatic manner with the histories of the Blue Boar and the Red Lion inns. The narrative of the first incident is put in Cromwell's own mouth by Lord Broghill, that accomplished Irish peer whose conversion from royalism to the cause of the Common- wealth was accomplished by the Ironsides gen- eral in the course of one memorable interview. According to this authority, Cromwell once de- clared that there was a time when he and his party would have settled their differences with Charles I but for an incident which destroyed their confidence in that monarch. What that incident was cannot be more vividly described than by the words Lord Broghill attributed to Cromwell. '' While we were busied in these thoughts,'' he said, '' there came a letter from one of our spies, who was of the king's bed- chamber, which acquainted us, that on that day our final doom was decreed; that he could not possibly tell us what it was, but we might find it out, if we could intercept a letter, sent from the king to the queen, wherein he declared what he would do. The letter, he said, was sewed up in the skirt of a saddle, and the bearer of it would come with the saddle upon his head, about ten of the clock that night, to the Blue Boar Inn in Holborn; for there he was to take horse and go to Dover with it. This messenger knew nothing of the letter in the saddle, but some persons at Dover did. We were at Windsor, when we received this letter; and immediately upon the receipt of it, Ireton and I resolved to take one trusty fellow with us, and with troopers' habits to go to the Inn in Holborn; which accordingly we did, and set our man at the gate of the Inn, where the wicket only was open to let people in and out. Our man was to give us notice, when any one came with a saddle, whilst we in the disguise of common troopers called for cans of beer, and continued drinking till about ten o'clock: the sentinel at the gate then gave notice that the man with the saddle was come in. Upon this we immediately arose, and, as the man was leading out his horse saddled, came up to him with drawn swords and told him that we were to search all that went in and out there; but as he looked like an honest man, we would only search his saddle and so dismiss him. Upon that we ungirt the saddle and carried it into

the stall, where we had been drinking, and left
the horseman with our sentinel: then ripping
up one of the skirts of the saddle, we there
found the letter of which we had been informed: and having got it into our own hands,
we delivered the saddle again to the man, telling him he was an honest man, and bid him go
about his business. The man, not knowing
what had been done, went away to Dover. As
soon as we had the letter we opened it; in which
we found the king had acquainted the queen,
that he was now courted by both the factions,
the Scotch Presbyterians and the Army; and
which bid fairest for him should have him; but
he thought he should close with the Scots,
sooner than the other. Upon this we took
horse, and went to Windsor; and finding we
were not likely to have any tolerable terms with
the king, we immediately from that time forward resolved his ruin.''

As that scene at the Blue Boar played so important a part in the sequence of events which
were to lead to Cromwell's attainment of su-
preme power in England, so another Holborn
inn, the Red Lion, was to witness the final act
of that petty revenge which marked the down-
fall of the Commonwealth. Perplexing mystery surrounds the ultimate fate of Cromwell's

body, but the record runs that his corpse, and those of Ireton and Bradshaw, were ruthlessly torn from their graves soon after the Restoration and were taken to the Red Lion, whence, on the following morning, they were dragged on a sledge to Tyburn and there treated with the ignominy hitherto reserved for the vilest criminals. All kinds of legends surround these gruesome proceedings. One tradition will have it that some of Cromwell's faithful friends rescued his mutilated remains, and buried them in a field on the north side of Holborn, a spot now covered by the public garden in Red Lion Square. On the other hand grave doubts have been expressed as to whether the body taken to the Red Lion was really that of Cromwell. One legend asserts that it was not buried in Westminster Abbey but sunk in the Thames; another that it was interred in Naseby field; and a third that it was placed in the coffin of Charles I at Windsor.

Impatient though he may be to revel in the multifarious associations of Fleet Street, the pilgrim should turn aside into Ludgate Hill for a few minutes for the sake of that Belle Sauvage inn the name of which has been responsible for a rich harvest of explanatory theory. Addison contributed to it in his own humorous way.  An early number of the Spectator was devoted to the discussion of the advisability of an office being established for the regulation of signs, one suggestion being that when the name of a shopkeeper or innkeeper lent itself to " an ingenious sign-post " full advantage should be taken of the opportunity.  In this connection Addison offered the following explanation of the name of the Ludgate Hill inn, which, it has been shrewdly conjectured by Henry B. Wheatley, was probably intended as a joke.  " As for the bell-savage, which is the sign of a savage man standing by a bell, I was formerly very much puzzled upon the conceit of it, till I accidentally fell into the reading of an old romance translated out of the French; which gives an account of a very beautiful woman who was found in a wilderness, and is called in the French *La belle Sauvage;* and is everywhere translated by our countrymen the bell-savage."

Not quite so poetic is the most feasible explanation of this unusual name for an inn.  It seems that the original sign of the house was the Bell, but that in the middle of the fifteenth century it had an alternative designation.  A deed of that period speaks of " all that tenement or inn with its appurtenances, called Savage's inn, otherwise called the Bell on the

Hoop.'' This was evidently a case where the
name of the host counted for more than the
actual sign of the house, and the habit of speaking of Savage's Bell may easily have led to the
perversion into Bell Savage, and thence to the
Frenchified form mostly used to-day.

Leaving these questions of etymology for
more certain matters, it is interesting to recall
that it was in the yard of the Belle Sauvage
Sir Thomas Wyatt's rebellion came to an in-
glorious end. That rising was ostensibly aimed
at the prevention of Queen Mary's marriage
with a prince of Spain, and for that reason
won a large measure of support from the men
of Kent, at whose head Wyatt marched on the
capital. At London Bridge, however, his way
was blocked, and he was obliged to make a dé-
tour by way of Kingston, in the hope of entering the city by Lud Gate. But his men became
disorganized on the long march, and at each
stage more and more were cut off from the
main body by the queen's forces, until, by the
time he reached Fleet Street, the rebel had only
some three hundred followers. '' He passed
Temple Bar,'' wrote Froude, '' along Fleet
Street, and reached Ludgate. The gate was
open as he approached, when some one seeing
a number of men coming up, exclaimed, ' These

be Wyatt's antients.' Muttered curses were
heard among the by-standers; but Lord Howard was on the spot; the gates, notwithstanding the murmurs, were instantly closed; and
when Wyatt knocked, Howard's voice answered, ' Avaunt! traitor; thou shalt not
come in here.' ' I have kept touch,' Wyatt exclaimed; but his enterprise was hopeless now.
He sat down upon a bench outside the Belle
Sauvage yard.'' That was the end. His followers scattered in all directions, and in a little
while he was a prisoner, on his way to the
Tower and the block.

More peaceful are the records which tell how
the famous carver in wood, Grinling Gibbons,
and the notorious quack, Richard Rock, once
had lodgings in the Belle Sauvage Yard, and
more picturesque are the memories of those
days when the inn was the starting-place of
those coaches which lend a touch of romance
to old English life. Horace Walpole says Gibbons signalized his tenancy by carving a pot
of flowers over a doorway, so delicate in leaf
and stem that the whole shook with the motion
of the carriages passing by. The quack, into
the hands of whom and his like Goldsmith declared all fell unless they were '' blasted by
lightning, or struck dead with some sudden dis-

YARD OF BELLE SAUVAGE INN.

order,'' was a '' great man, short of stature,
fat,'' and waddled as he walked.   He was
'' usually drawn at the top of his own bills, sitting in his arm-chair, holding a little bottle
between his finger and thumb, and surrounded
with rotten teeth, nippers, pills, packets, and
gallipots.''

From the Belle Sauvage to the commence-
ment of Fleet Street is but a stone's throw, but
the pilgrim must not expect to find any memo-
rials of the past in the eastern portion of that
famous thoroughfare.   The buildings here are
practically all modern, many of them, indeed,
having been erected in the last decade.   As
these lines are being written, too, the announcement is made of a project for the further transformation of the street at the cost of half a
million pounds.   The idea is to continue the
widening of the thoroughfare further west, and
if that plan is carried out, devastation must
overtake most of the ancient buildings which
still remain.

By far the most outstanding feature of the
Fleet Street of to-day is the number and variety of its newspaper offices; two centuries ago
it had a vastly different aspect.

> " From thence, along that tipling street,
>    Distinguish'd by the name of Fleet,

> Where Tavern-Signs hang thicker far,
> Than Trophies down at Westminster;
> And ev'ry Bacchanalian Landlord
> Displays his Ensign, or his Standard,
> Bidding Defiance to each Brother,
> As if at Wars with one another."

How thoroughly the highway deserved the name of " tipling street " may be inferred from the fact that its list of taverns included but was not exhausted by the Devil, the King's Head, the Horn, the Mitre, the Cock, the Bolt-in-Tun, the Rainbow, the Cheshire Cheese, Hercules Pillars, the Castle, the Dolphin, the Seven Stars, Dick's, Nando's, and Peele's. No one would recognize in the Anderton's Hotel of to-day the lineal successor of one of these ancient taverns, and yet it is a fact that that establishment perpetuates the Horn tavern of the fifteenth century. In the early seventeenth century the house was in high favour with the legal fraternity, but its patronage of the present time is of a more miscellaneous character. The present building was erected in 1880.

Close by, a low and narrow archway gives access to Wine Office Court, a spot ever memorable for its having been for some three years the home of Oliver Goldsmith. It was in 1760, when in his thirty-second year, that he took

THE CHESHIRE CHEESE — ENTRANCE FROM FLEET STREET.

lodgings in this cramped alleyway, and here he remained, toiling as a journeyman for an astute publisher, until towards the end of 1762. So improved were Goldsmith's fortunes in these days that he launched out into supper parties, one of which, in May, 1761, was rendered memorable by the presence of Dr. Johnson, who attired himself with unusual care for the occasion. To a companion who, noting the new suit of clothes, the new wig nicely powdered, and all else in harmony, commented on his appearance, Johnson rejoined, " Why, sir, I hear that Goldsmith, who is a very great sloven, justifies his disregard of cleanliness and decency by quoting my practice, and I am desirous this night to show him a better example." The house where that supper party was held has disappeared, but in the Cheshire Cheese nearby there yet survives a building which the centuries have spared.

Exactly how old this tavern is cannot be decided. It is inevitable that there must have been a hostelry on this spot before the Great Fire of 1666, inasmuch as there is a record to show that it was rebuilt the following year. Which goes to show that the present building has attained the ripe age of nearly two and a half centuries. No one who explores its various apartments will be likely to question that fact. Everything about the place wears an air of antiquity, from the quaint bar-room to the more private chambers upstairs. The chief glory of the Cheshire Cheese, however, is to be seen downstairs on the left hand of the principal entrance. This is the genuinely old-fashioned eating-room, with its rude tables, its austere seats round the walls, its sawdust-sprinkled floor, and, above all, its sacred nook in the further right hand corner which is pointed out as the favourite seat of Dr. Johnson. Above this niche is a copy of the Reynolds portrait of the sturdy lexicographer, beneath which is the following inscription: "The Favourite Seat of Dr. Johnson. Born 18th Septr., 1709. Died 13th Decr., 1784. In him a noble understanding and a masterly intellect were united with grand independence of character and unfailing goodness of heart, which won him the admiration of his own age, and remain as recommendations to the reverence of posterity. ' No, Sir! there is nothing which has yet been contrived by man by which so much happiness has been produced as by a good tavern.' "

After all this it is surprising to learn that the authority for connecting Dr. Johnson with the Cheshire Cheese rests upon a somewhat late

THE CHESHIRE CHEESE — THE JOHNSON ROOM.

tradition. Boswell does not mention the tavern, an omission which is accounted for by noting that " Boswell's acquaintance with Johnson began when Johnson was an old man, and when he had given up the house in Gough Square, and Goldsmith had long departed from Wine Office Court. At the best," this apologist adds, " Boswell only knew Johnson's life in widely separated sections." As appeal cannot, then, be made to Boswell it is made to others. The most important of these witnesses is a Cyrus Jay, who, in a book of reminiscences published in 1868, claimed to have frequented the Cheshire Cheese for fifty-five years, and to have known a man who had frequently seen Johnson and Goldsmith in the tavern. Another writer has placed on record that he often met in the tavern gentlemen who had seen the famous pair there on many occasions.

Taking into account these traditions and the further fact that the building supplies its own evidence as to antiquity, it is not surprising that the Cheshire Cheese enjoys an enviable popularity with all who find a special appeal in the survivals of old London. As a natural consequence more recent writing in prose and verse has been bestowed upon this tavern than any other of the metropolis. Perhaps the best

of the many poems penned in its praise is that
" Ballade " written by John Davidson, the
poet whose mysterious disappearance has
added so sad a chapter to the history of literature.

> " I know a house of antique ease
>     Within the smoky city's pale,
> A spot wherein the spirit sees
>     Old London through a thinner veil.
>     The modern world so stiff and stale,
> You leave behind you when you please,
>     For long clay pipes and great old ale
> And beefsteaks in the ' Cheshire Cheese.'
>
> " Beneath this board Burke's, Goldsmith's knees
>     Were often thrust — so runs the tale —
> 'Twas here the Doctor took his ease
>     And wielded speech that like a flail
>     Threshed out the golden truth.  All hail,
> Great souls!  that met on nights like these
>     Till morning made the candles pale,
> And revellers left the ' Cheshire Cheese.'
>
> " By kindly sense and old decrees
>     Of England's use they set the sail
> *We* press to never-furrowed seas,
>     For vision-worlds we breast the gale,
>     And still we seek and still we fail,
> For still the ' glorious phantom ' flees.
>     Ah well!  no phantom are the ale
> And beefsteaks of the ' Cheshire Cheese.'

" If doubts or debts thy soul assail,
    If Fashion's forms its current freeze,
 Try a long pipe, a glass of ale,
    And supper at the ' Cheshire Cheese.' "

While the Cheshire Cheese was less fortunate than the Cock in the Fire of London, the
latter house, which escaped that conflagration,
has fallen on comparatively evil days in modern times. In other words, the exterior of the
original building, which dated from early in
the seventeenth century, was demolished in
1888, to make room for a branch establishment
of the Bank of England. Pepys knew the old
house and spent many a jovial evening beneath
its roof. It was thither, one April evening in
1667, that he took Mrs. Pierce and Mrs. Knapp,
the latter being the actress whom he thought
" pretty enough " besides being " the most excellent, mad-humoured thing, and sings the
noblest that ever I heard in my life." The trio
had a gay time; they " drank, and eat lobster,
and sang " and were " mightily merry." By
and by the crafty diarist deleted Mrs. Pierce
from the party, and went off to Vauxhall with
the fair actress, his confidence in the enterprise
being strengthened by the fact that the night
was " darkish." If she did not find out that
excursion, Mrs. Pepys knew quite enough of

her husband's weakness for Mrs. Knapp to be justified of her jealousy. And even he appears to have experienced twinges of conscience on the matter. Perhaps that was the reason why he took his wife to the Cock, and " did give her a dinner " there. Other sinners have found it comforting to exercise repentance on the scene of their offences.

Judging from an advertisement which was published in 1665, the proprietor of the Cock did not allow business to interfere with pleasure. " This is to certify," his announcement ran, " that the master of the Cock and Bottle, commonly called the Cock Alehouse, at Temple Bar, hath dismissed his servants, and shut up his house, for this Long Vacation, intending (God willing) to return at Michaelmas next."

But the tavern is prouder of its association with Tennyson than of any other fact in its history. The poet was always fond of this neighbourhood. His son records that whenever he went to London with his father, the first item on their programme was a walk in the Strand and Fleet Street. " Instead of the stuccoed houses in the West End, this is the place where I should like to live," Tennyson would say. During his early days he lodged in Norfolk Street close by, dining with his friends at the Cock and other taverns, but always having a preference for the room " high over roaring Temple-bar.'' In the estimation of the poet, as his son has chronicled, " a perfect dinner was a beef-steak, a potato, a cut of cheese, a pint of port, and afterwards a pipe (never a cigar). When joked with by his friends about his liking for cold salt beef and new potatoes, he would answer humorously, ' All fine-natured men know what is good to eat.' Very genial evenings they were, with plenty of anecdote and wit.''

All this, especially the pint of port, throws light on " Will Waterproof's Lyrical Monologue,'' which, as the poet himself has stated, was " made at the Cock.'' Its opening apostrophe is familiar enough:

> " O plump head-waiter at The Cock,
>     To which I most resort,
>   How goes the time? 'Tis five o'clock.
>     Go fetch a pint of port.''

How faithfully that waiter obeyed the poet's injunction to bring him of the best, all readers of the poem are aware:

> " The pint, you brought me, was the best
>     That ever came from pipe.''

Undoubtedly. As witness the flights of fancy which it created. Its potent vintage transformed both the waiter and the sign of the house in which he served and shaped this pretty legend.

" And hence this halo lives about
    The waiter's hands, that reach
To each his perfect pint of stout,
    His proper chop to each.
He looks not like the common breed
    That with the napkin dally;
I think he came like Ganymede,
    From some delightful valley.

" The Cock was of a larger egg
    Than modern poultry drop,
Stept forward on a firmer leg,
    And cramm'd a plumper crop;
Upon an ampler dunghill trod,
    Crow'd lustier late and early,
Sipt wine from silver, praising God,
    And raked in golden barley.

" A private life was all his joy,
    Till in a court he saw
A something-pottle-bodied boy
    That knuckled at the law:
He stoop'd and clutch'd him, fair and good,
    Flew over roof and casement:
His brothers of the weather stood
    Stock-still for sheer amazement.

" But he, by farmstead, thorpe and spire,
   And follow'd with acclaims,
A sign to many a staring shire
   Came crowing over Thames.
Right down by smoky Paul's they bore,
   Till, where the street grows straiter,
One fix'd for ever at the door,
   And one became head-waiter."

Just here the poet bethought himself. It was time to rein in his fancy. Truly it was out of place to make

" The violet of a legend blow
   Among the chops and steaks."

So he descends to more mundane things, to moralize at last upon the waiter's fate and the folly of quarrelling with our lot in life. It is interesting to learn from FitzGerald that the Cock's plump head-waiter read the poem, but disappointing to know that his only remark on the performance was, " Had Mr. Tennyson dined oftener here, he would not have minded it so much." From which poets may learn the moral that to trifle with Jove's cupbearer in the interests of a tavern waiter is liable to lead to misunderstanding. But it is, perhaps, of more importance to note that, notwithstanding the destruction of the exterior of the Cock in

1888, one room of that ancient building was preserved intact and may be found on the first floor of the new house. There, for use as well as admiration, are the veritable mahogany boxes which Tennyson knew, —

> " Old boxes, larded with the steam
> Of thirty thousand dinners — "

and not less in evidence is the stately old fire-place which Pepys was familiar with.

Not even a seat or a fireplace has survived of the Mitre tavern of Shakespeare's days, or the Mitre tavern which Boswell mentions so often.  They were not the same house, as has sometimes been stated, and the Mitre of to-day is little more than a name-successor to either. Ben Jonson's plays and other literature of the seventeenth century make frequent mention of the old Mitre, and that was no doubt the tavern Pepys patronized on occasion.

No one save an expert indexer would have the courage to commit himself to the exact number of Boswell's references to the Mitre. He had a natural fondness for the tavern as the scene of his first meal with Johnson, and with Johnson himself, as his biographer has explained, the place was a first favourite for many years.  '' I had learned,'' says Boswell

in recording the early stages of his acquaintance with his famous friend, "that his place
of frequent resort was the Mitre Tavern in
Fleet Street, where he loved to sit up late, and
I begged I might be allowed to pass an evening
with him there, which he promised I should.
A few days afterwards I met him near Temple-
bar, about one o'clock in the morning, and
asked if he would then go to the Mitre. ' Sir,'
said he, ' it is too late; they won't let us in.
But I'll go with you another night with all my
heart.' " That other night soon came. Boswell
called for his friend at nine o'clock, and the
two were soon in the tavern. They had a good
supper, and port wine, but the occasion was
more than food and drink to Boswell. " The
orthodox high-church sound of the Mitre, —
the figure and manner of the celebrated Samuel
Johnson, — the extraordinary power and pre-
cision of his conversation, and the pride arising
from finding myself admitted as his companion,
produced a variety of sensations, and a pleas-
ing elevation of mind beyond what I had ever
before experienced."

On the next occasion Goldsmith was of the
company, and the visit after that was brought
about through Boswell's inability to keep his
promise to entertain Johnson at his own rooms.

The little Scotsman had a squabble with his landlord, and was obliged to take his guest to the Mitre. '' There is nothing,'' Johnson said, '' in this mighty misfortune; nay, we shall be better at the Mitre.'' And Boswell was characteristically oblivious of the slur on his gifts as a host. But that, perhaps, is a trifle compared with the complacency with which he records further snubbings administered to him at that tavern. For example, there was that rainy night when Boswell made some feeble complaints about the weather, qualifying them with the profound reflection that it was good for the vegetable creation. '' Yes, sir,'' Johnson rejoined, '' it is good for vegetables, and for the animals who eat those vegetables, and for the animals who eat those animals.'' Then there was that other occasion when the note-taker talked airily about his interview with Rousseau, and asked Johnson whether he thought him a bad man, only to be crushed with Johnson's, '' Sir, if you are talking jestingly of this, I don't talk with you. If you mean to be serious, I think him one of the worst of men.'' Severer still was the rebuke of another conversation at the Mitre. The ever-blundering Boswell rated Foote for indulging his talent of ridicule at the expense of his visitors, '' making fools of his

DR. SAMUEL JOHNSON.

company," as he expressed it. " Sir," Johnson said, " he does not make fools of his company; they whom he exposes are fools already: he only brings them into action."

But, if only in gratitude for what Boswell accomplished, last impressions of the Mitre should not be of those castigations. A far prettier picture is that which we owe to the reminiscences of Dr. Maxwell, who, while assistant preacher at the Temple, had many opportunities of enjoying Johnson's company. Dr. Maxwell relates that one day when he was paying Johnson a visit, two young ladies from the country came to consult him on the subject of Methodism, to which they were inclined. " Come," he said, " you pretty fools, dine with Maxwell and me at the Mitre, and we will take over that subject." Away they went, and after dinner Johnson " took one of them upon his knee, and fondled her for half an hour together." Dante Gabriel Rossetti chose that incident for a picture, but neither his canvas nor Dr. Maxwell's record enlightens us as to whether the " pretty fools " were preserved to the Church of England. But it was a happy evening — especially for Dr. Johnson.

As with the Cock, a part of the interior of the Rainbow Tavern dates back more than a

couple of centuries. The chief interest of the
Rainbow, however, lies in the fact that it was
at first a coffee-house, and one of the earliest
in London. It was opened in 1657 by a barber
named James Farr who evidently anticipated
more profit in serving cups of the new beverage
than in wielding his scissors and razor. He
succeeded so well that the adjacent tavern-
keepers combined to get his coffee-house suppressed, for, said they, the " evil smell " of the
new drink " greatly annoyed the neighbourhood." But Mr. Farr prospered in spite of
his competitors, and by and by he turned the
Rainbow into a regular tavern.

No one who gazes upon the century-old print
of the King's Head can do other than regret the
total disappearance of that picturesque building. This tavern stood at the west corner of
Chancery Lane and is believed by antiquaries
to have been built in the reign of Edward VI.
It figures repeatedly in ancient engravings of
the royal processions of long-past centuries, and
contributed a notable feature to the progress
of Queen Elizabeth as she was on her way to
visit Sir Thomas Gresham. The students of
the Temple hit upon the effective device of having several cherubs descend, as it were, from
the heavens, for the purpose of presenting the

queen with a crown of gold and laurels, together
with the inevitable verses of an Elizabethan
ceremony, and the roof of the King's Head was
chosen as the heaven from whence these visitants came down.  Only the first and second
floors were devoted to tavern purposes; on the
ground floor were shops, from one of which the
first edition of Izaak Walton's " Complete Angler " was sold, while another provided accommodation for the grocery business of Abraham
Cowley's father.

From 1679 the King's Head was the common
headquarters of the notorious Green Ribbon
Club, which included a precious set of scoun-
drels among its members, chief of them all being that astounding perjurer, Titus Oates.
Hence the tavern's designation as a " Protest-
ant house."  It was pulled down in 1799.

Another immortal tavern of Fleet Street, the
most immortal of them all, Ben Jonson's Devil,
has also utterly vanished.  Its full title was
The Devil and St. Dunstan, aptly represented
by the sign depicting the saint holding the
tempter by the nose, and its site, appropriately
enough, was opposite St. Dunstan's Church, on
the south side of Fleet Street and close to Temple-bar.  One of Hogarth's illustrations to
" Hudibras " gives a glimpse of the tavern, but

on the wrong side of the street, as is so common in the work of that artist.

No doubt the Devil had had a protracted existence prior to Jonson's day, but its chief title to fame dates from the time when the convivial dramatist made it his principal rendezvous. The exact date of that event is difficult to determine. Nor is it possible to explain why Jonson removed his patronage from the Mermaid in Cheapside to the Devil in Fleet Street. The fact remains, however, that while the earlier period of his life has its focus in Cheapside the later is centred in the vicinity of Temple-bar.

Perhaps Jonson may have found the accommodation of the Devil more suited to his needs. After passing through those years of opposition which all great poets have to face, there came to him the crown of acknowledged leadership among the writers of his day. He accepted it willingly. He seems to have been temperamentally fitted to the post. He was, in fact, never so happy as when in the midst of a group of men who owned his pre-eminence. What was more natural, then, than that he should have conceived the idea of forming a club? And in the great Apollo room at the Devil he found the most suitable place of meeting. Over the door of this room, inscribed in gold letters

TABLET AND BUST FROM THE DEVIL TAVERN.

on a black ground, this poetical greeting was
displayed.

> " Welcome all who lead or follow
> To the Oracle of Apollo —
> Here he speaks out of his pottle,
> Or the tripos, his tower bottle:
> All his answers are divine,
> Truth itself doth flow in wine.
> Hang up all the poor hop-drinkers,
> Cries old Sam, the king of skinkers;
> He the half of life abuses,
> That sits watering with the Muses.
> Those dull girls no good can mean us;
> Wine it is the milk of Venus,
> And the poet's horse accounted:
> Ply it, and you all are mounted.
> 'Tis the true Phœbian liquor,
> Cheers the brains, makes wit the quicker.
> Pays all debts, cures all diseases,
> And at once three senses pleases.
> Welcome all who lead or follow,
> To the Oracle of Apollo."

That relic of the Devil still exists, carefully
preserved in the banking establishment which
occupies the site of the tavern; and with it,
just as zealously guarded, is a bust of Jonson
which stood above the verses. Inside the
Apollo room was another poetical inscription,
said to have been engraved in black marble.

These verses were in the dramatist's best Latin, and set forth the rules for his tavern academy. Much of their point is lost in the English version, which, however, deserves quotation for the sake of the inferences it suggests as to the conduct which was esteemed " good form " in Jonson's club.

" As the fund of our pleasure, let each pay his shot,
    Except some chance friend, whom a member brings in.
Far hence be the sad, the lewd fop, and the sot;
    For such have the plagues of good company been.

" Let the learned and witty, the jovial and gay,
    The generous and honest, compose our free state;
And the more to exalt our delight whilst we stay,
    Let none be debarred from his choice female mate.

" Let no scent offensive the chamber infest.
    Let fancy, not cost, prepare all our dishes.
Let the caterer mind the taste of each guest,
    And the cook, in his dressing, comply with their wishes.

" Let's have no disturbance about taking places,
    To show your nice breeding, or out of vain pride.
Let the drawers be ready with wine and fresh glasses,
    Let the waiters have eyes, though their tongues must be ty'd.

" Let our wines without mixture or stum, be all fine,
    Or call up the master, and break his dull noddle.

Let no sober bigot here think it a sin,
   To push on the chirping and moderate bottle.

" Let the contests be rather of books than of wine,
   Let the company be neither noisy nor mute,
Let none of things serious, much less of divine,
   When belly and head's full profanely dispute.

" Let no saucy fidler presume to intrude,
   Unless he is sent for to vary our bliss.
With mirth, wit, and dancing, and singing conclude,
   To regale every sense, with delight in excess.

" Let raillery be without malice or heat.
   Dull poems to read let none privilege take.
Let no poetaster command or intreat
   Another extempore verses to make.

" Let argument bear no unmusical sound,
   Nor jars interpose, sacred friendship to grieve.
For generous lovers let a corner be found,
   Where they in soft sighs may their passions relieve.

" Like the old Lapithites, with the goblets to fight,
   Our own 'mongst offences unpardoned will rank,
Or breaking of windows, or glasses, for spight,
   And spoiling the goods for a rakehelly prank.

" Whoever shall publish what's said, or what's done,
   Be he banished for ever our assembly divine.
Let the freedom we take be perverted by none
   To make any guilty by drinking good wine."

By the testimony of those rules alone it is easy to see how thoroughly the masterful spirit of Jonson ruled in the Apollo room. His chair was a throne, his word a sceptre that must be obeyed. This impression is confirmed by many records and especially by Drummond's character sketch. The natural consequence was that membership in the Apollo Club came to be regarded as an unusual honour. There appears to have been some kind of ceremony at the initiation of each new member, which gave all the greater importance to the rite of being '' sealed of the tribe of Ben.'' Long after the dramatist was dead, his '' sons '' boasted of their intimacy with him, much to the irritation of Dryden and others. While he lived, too, they were equally elated at being admitted to the inner circle at the Devil, and, after the manner of Marmion, sung the praises of their '' boon Delphic god,'' surrounded with his '' incense and his altars smoking.''

Incense was an essential if Jonson was to be kept in good humour. Many anecdotes testify to that fact. There is the story of his loss of patience with the country gentleman who was somewhat talkative about his lands, and his interruption, '' What signifies to us your dirt and your clods? Where you have an acre

BEN JONSON.

of land, I have ten acres of wit.'' And Howell
tells of that supper party which, despite good
company, excellent cheer and choice wines, was
turned into a failure by Jonson engrossing all
the conversation and '' vapouring extremely of
himself and vilifying others.'' Yet there were
probably few of his own circle, the '' sons of
Ben,'' who would have had it otherwise. Few
indeed and fragmentary are the records of his
conversation in the Apollo room, but they are
sufficient to prove how ready a wit the poet
possessed. Take, for example, the story of that
convivial gathering when the tavern keeper
promised to forgive Jonson the reckoning if
he could tell what would please God, please the
devil, please the company, and please him. The
poet at once replied:

" God is pleased, when we depart from sin,
    The devil's pleas'd, when we persist therein;
    Your company's pleas'd, when you draw good wine,
    And thou'd be pleas'd, if I would pay thee thine."

Some austere biographers have chided the
memory of the poet for spending so much of
his time at the Devil. They forget, or are ignorant of the fact that there is proof the time
was well spent. In a manuscript of Jonson
which still exists there are many entries which

go to show that some of his finest work was inspired by the merry gatherings in the Apollo room.

For many years after Jonson's death the Devil, and especially the Apollo room, continued in high favour with the wits of London and the men about town. Pepys knew the house, of course, and so did Evelyn, and Swift dined there, and Steele, and many another genius of the eighteenth century. It was in the Apollo room, too, that the official court-day odes of the Poets Laureate were rehearsed, which explains the point of the following lines:

" When Laureates make odes, do you ask of what sort?
  Do you ask if they're good or are evil?
You may judge — From the Devil they come to the
  Court,
  And go from the court to the Devil."

But the Apollo room is not without its idyliic memory. It was created by the ever-delightful pen of Steele. Who can forget the picture he draws of his sister Jenny and her lover Tranquillus and their wedding morning? '' The wedding,'' he writes, '' was wholly under my care. After the ceremony at church, I resolved to entertain the company with a dinner suitable to the occasion, and pitched upon the Apollo, at the Old Devil at Temple-bar, as a place sacred to mirth tempered with discretion, where Ben Jonson and his sons used to make their liberal meetings.'' The mirth of that assembly was threatened by the indiscretion of that double-meaning speaker who is usually in evidence at such gatherings to the confusion of the bride, but happily his career was cut short by the plain sense of the soldier and sailor, as may be read in the pages of the '' Tatler.''

Within easy hail of the Devil, on the site now occupied by St. Clement's Chambers, Dane's Inn, there stood until 1853 a quaint old hostelry known as the Angel Inn. It dated from the opening years of the sixteenth century at least, for it is specifically named in a letter of February 6th, 1503. In the middle of that century, too, it figures in the progress of Bishop Harper to the martyr's stake, for it was from this inn that prelate was taken to Gloucester to be burnt. The Angel cannot hope to compete with the neighbouring taverns of Fleet Street on the score of literary associations, but the fact that seven or eight mail coaches started from its yard every night will indicate how large a part it played in the life of old London.

# CHAPTER IV

EVEN one short generation ago it would have been difficult to recognize in the Strand of that period any resemblance to the picture of that highway given by Stow at the dawn of the seventeenth century. Much less would it have been possible to recall its aspect in those earlier years when it was literally a strand, that is, a low-lying road by the side of the Thames, stretching from Temple-bar to Charing Cross. On the south side of the thoroughfare were the mansions of bishops and nobles dotted at sparse intervals; on the north was open country. To-day there are even fewer survivals of the past than might have been seen thirty years ago. The wholesale clearance of Holywell Street and the buildings to the north has completely transformed the neighbourhood, while along the southern line of the highway, changes almost equally revolutionary have been carried out. As a consequence the inns and taverns of the Strand and the streets leading therefrom have nearly all been swept away, leaving a modern representative only here and there.

Utterly vanished, for example, leaving not a wreck behind, are the Spotted Dog and the Craven Head, two houses more or less associated with the sporting fraternity. The former, indeed, was a favourite haunt of prize-fighters and their backers; the latter was notorious for its host, Robert Hales by name, whose unusual stature — he stood seven feet six inches — enabled him '' to look down on all his customers, although he was always civil to them.'' When the novelty of Hales' physical proportions wore off, and trade declined, a new attraction was provided in the form of a couple of buxom barmaids attired in bloomer costume — importations, so the story goes, from the United States.

A far more ancient and reputable house was the Crown and Anchor which had entrances both on the Strand and Arundel Street. It is referred to by Strype in his edition of Stow, published in 1720, as '' a large and curious house, with good rooms and other conveniences,'' and could boast of associations with Johnson, and Boswell, and Reynolds. Perhaps there was something in the atmosphere of the place which tended to emphasize Johnson's natural argumentativeness; at any rate the Crown and Anchor was the scene of his dispute with Reynolds as to the merits of wine in assisting conversation, and it was here too that he had his famous bout with Dr. Percy. Boswell describes him as being in '' remarkable vigour of mind, and eager to exert himself in conversation '' on that occasion, and then transcribes the following proof. '' He was vehement against old Dr. Mounsey, of Chelsea College, as ' a fellow who swore and talked bawdy.' ' I have been often in his company,' said Dr. Percy, ' and never heard him swear or talk bawdy.' Mr. Davies, who sat next to Dr. Percy, having after this had some conversation with him, made a discovery which in his zeal to pay court to Dr. Johnson, he eagerly proclaimed aloud from the foot of the table: ' Oh, sir, I have found out a very good reason why Dr. Percy never heard Mounsey swear or talk bawdy, for he tells me he never saw him but at the Duke of Northumberland's table.' ' And so, sir,' said Dr. Johnson loudly to Dr. Percy, ' you would shield this man from the charge of swearing and talking bawdy, because he did not do so at the Duke of Northumberland's table. Sir, you might as well tell us that you had seen him hold up his hand at the Old Bailey, and

he neither swore nor talked bawdy; or that
you had seen him in the cart at Tyburn, and
he neither swore nor talked bawdy. And is it
thus, sir, that you presume to controvert what
I have related? ' Dr. Johnson's animadversion
was uttered in such a manner, that Dr. Percy
seemed to be displeased, and soon after left the
company, of which Johnson did not at that time
take any notice.'' Nor did the following morning bring any regret. '' Well,'' said he when
Boswell called, '' we had good talk.'' And
Boswell's '' Yes, sir; you tossed and gored
several persons '' no doubt gave him much
pleasure.

When the Crown and Anchor was rebuilt in
1790 the accommodation of the tavern was materially increased by the erection of a large
room suitable for important public occasions
and capable of seating upwards of two thousand persons. That room was but eight years
old when it was the scene of a remarkable gathering. Those were stirring times politically,
largely owing to Fox's change of party and to
his adhesion to the cause of electoral reform.
Hence the banquet which took place at the
Crown and Anchor on January 24th, 1798, in
honour of Fox's birthday. The Duke of Norfolk presided over a company numbering fully

two thousand persons, and the notable men present included Sheridan and Horne Tooke. The record of the function tells how " Captain Morris " — elder brother of the author of " Kitty Crowder," and a song-writer of some fame in his day — " produced three new songs on the occasion," and how " Mr. Hovell, Mr. Robinson, Mr. Dignum, and several other gentlemen, in the different rooms sang songs applicable to the *fête*." But the ducal chairman's speech and the toasts which followed were the features of the gathering. The former was commendably brief. " We are met," he said, " in a moment of most serious difficulty, to celebrate the birth of a man dear to the friends of freedom. I shall only recall to your memory, that, not twenty years ago, the illustrious George Washington had not more than two thousand men to rally round him when his country was attacked. America is now free. This day full two thousand men are assembled in this place. I leave you to make the application. I propose to you the health of Charles Fox."

Then came the following daring toasts:

" The rights of the people."

" Constitutional redress of the wrongs of the people."

" A speedy and effectual reform in the representation of the people in Parliament.''

" The genuine principles of the British constitution.''

" The people of Ireland; and may they be speedily restored to the blessings of law and liberty.''

And when the chairman's health had been drunk " with three times three,'' that nobleman concluded his speech of thanks with the words: " Before I sit down, give me leave to call on you to drink our sovereign's health: ' The majesty of the people.' "

Such " seditious and daring tendencies,'' as the royalist chronicler of the times described them, could not be overlooked in high quarters, and the result of that gathering at the Crown and Anchor was that the Duke of Norfolk was dismissed from the lord-lieutenancy of the west riding of Yorkshire, and from his regiment in the militia. It would have been a greater punishment could George III have ordered a bath for the indiscreet orator. That particular member of the Howard family had a horror of soap and water, and appears to have been washed only when his servants found him helpless in a drunken stupor. He it was also who complained to Dudley North that he had vainly tried every remedy for rheumatism, to receive the answer, " Pray, my lord, did you ever try a clean shirt ? "

In that district of the Strand known as the Adelphi — so called from the pile of buildings erected here in 1768 by the brothers Adam — there still exists an Adelphi Hotel which may well perpetuate the building in which Gibbon found a temporary home in 1787. Ten years earlier it was known as the Adelphi Tavern, and on the thirteenth of January was the scene of an exciting episode. The chief actors in this little drama, which nearly developed into a tragedy, were a Captain Stony and a Mr. Bates, the latter being the editor of *The Morning Post*. It appears that that journal had recently published some paragraphs reflecting on the character of a lady of rank, whose cause, as the sequel will show, Captain Stony had good reason for making his own. Whether the offending editor had been lured to the Adelphi ignorant of what was in store, or whether the angry soldier met him there by accident, does not transpire; the record implies, however, that the couple had a room to themselves in which to settle accounts. The conflict opened with each discharging his pistol at the other, but without effect, which does not speak well for

the marksmanship of either. Then they took
to their swords, with the result of the captain
receiving wounds in the breast and arm and
Mr. Bates a thrust in the thigh, clearly demon-
strating that at this stage the man of the pen
had the better of the man of the sword. And
he maintained the advantage. For a little later
the editor's weapon " bent and slanted against
the captain's breast-bone." On having his attention called to the fact the soldier agreed that
Mr. Bates should straighten his blade. At this
critical moment, however, while, indeed, the
journalist had his sword under his foot, the
door of the room was broken open and the
combatants separated. " On the Sunday following," so the sequel reads, " Captain Stony
was married to the lady in whose behalf he
had thus hazarded his life."

Duels were so common in those days that
Gibbon probably heard nothing about the fight
in the Adelphi when he took rooms there one
hot August day in 1787. Besides, he had more
important matters to occupy his thoughts.
Only six weeks had passed since, between the
hours of eleven and twelve at night, he had,
in the summer house of his garden at Laus-
sanne, written the last sentence of " The Decline and Fall of the Roman Empire," and now

he had arrived in London with the final instalment of the manuscript on which he had be-
·stowed the labour of nearly twenty years. The heightened mood he experienced on the completion of his memorable task may well have persisted to the hour of his arrival in London. Some reflection of that feeling perhaps underlay the jocular announcement of his letter from the Adelphi to Lord Sheffield, wherein he wrote: '' INTELLIGENCE EXTRAORDINARY. This day (August the seventh) the celebrated E. G. arrived with a numerous retinue (one servant). We hear that he has brought over from Lausanne the remainder of his History for immediate publication.'' Gibbon remained at the Adelphi for but a few days, after which the story of the tavern lapses into the happiness which is supposed to accrue from a lack of history.

Before retracing his steps to explore the many interesting thoroughfares which branch off from the Strand, the pilgrim should continue on that highway to its western extremity at Charing Cross. The memory of several famous inns is associated with that locality, including the Swan, the Golden Cross, Locket's, and the Rummer. The first named dated from the fifteenth century. It survived sufficiently

long to be frequented by Ben Jonson and is the
subject of an anecdote told of that poet. Being
called upon to make an extemporary grace before King James, and having ended his last
line but one with the word " safe," Jonson finished with the words, " God blesse me, and
God blesse Raph." The inquisitive monarch
naturally wanted to know who Ralph was, and
the poet replied that he was " the drawer at
the Swanne Taverne by Charing Crosse, who
drew him good Canarie." It is feasible to conclude that no small portion of the hundred
pounds with which the king rewarded Jonson
was expended on that " good Canarie." And
perhaps Ralph was not forgotten.

By name, at any rate, the Golden Cross is still
in existence, but the present building dates no
farther back than 1832. Of Locket's ordinary,
however, no present-day representative exists.
When Leigh Hunt wrote " The Town " he declared that it was no longer known where it
exactly stood, but more recent investigators
have discovered that Drummond's banking
house covers its site.

As was the case with Pontack's in the city,
Locket's was pre-eminently the resort of the
" smart set." The prices charged are proof
enough of that, even though they were not al-

ways paid. The case of Sir George Ethrege
is one in point. That dissolute dramatist and
diplomat of the Restoration period was a
frequent customer at Locket's until his debt
there became larger than his means to discharge it. Before that catastrophe overtook
him he was the principal actor in a lively scene
at the tavern. Something or other caused an
outbreak of fault-finding one evening, and the
commotion brought Mrs. Locket on the scene.
" We are all so provoked," said Sir George to
the lady, " that even I could find in my heart
to pull the nosegay out of your bosom, and
throw the flowers in your face."

Nor was that the only humourous threat
against Mrs. Locket from the same mouth.
Probably because he was so good a customer
and an influential man about town, his indebt-
edness to the ordinary was allowed to mount
up until it reached a formidable figure. And
then Sir George stopped his visits. Mrs.
Locket, however, sent some one to dun him for
the money and to threaten him with prosecu-
tion. But that did not daunt the wit. He bade
the messenger tell Mrs. Locket that he would
kiss her if she stirred in the matter. Sir
George's command was duly obeyed. It stirred
Mrs. Locket to action. Calling for her hood

and scarf, and declaring that she would see if
" there was any fellow alive that had the im-
pudence," she was about to set out to put the
matter to the test when her husband restrained
her with his " Pr'ythee, my dear, don't be so
rash, you don't know what a man may do in
his passion."

It is not difficult to understand how the bill
of Sir George Ethrege reached such alarming
proportions.   " They shall compose you a
dish," is a contemporary reference, " no bigger
than a saucer, shall come to fifty shillings."
And again,

> " At Locket's, Brown's, and at Pontack's enquire
> What modish kickshaws the nice beaux desire,
> What fam'd ragouts, what new invented sallat,
> Has best pretensions to regale the palate."

Adam Locket, the founder of the house, lived
until about 1688, and was succeeded by his son
Edward who was at the head of affairs until
1702. All through the reign of Queen Anne the
ordinary flourished, but after her death references to it become scanty and finally it disappeared so completely that Leigh Hunt, as has
been said, was in ignorance as to its site.

And Hunt also owned to not knowing the
site of another Charing Cross tavern, the Rum-

mer.  As a matter of fact that, to modern ear, curiously-named tavern was at first located almost next door to Locket's, whence it was removed to the waterside in 1710 and burnt down in 1750.  The memory of the tavern would probably have sunk into oblivion with its charred timbers, save for the accident of its connection with Matthew Prior.  For the Rummer was kept by an uncle of the future poet, into whose keeping he is supposed to have fallen on the death of his father.  One cannot resist the suspicion that this uncle, Samuel Prior by name, was of a shifty nature.  He had serious enemies, that is certain.  The best proof of that fact is the announcement he inserted in the *London Gazette* offering a reward of ten guineas for the discovery of the persons who spread the report that he was in league with the clippers of coin.  Then there is the nephew's portrait, which implies that his tavern-keeping relative was an adept in the tricks of his trade.

> " My uncle, rest his soul ! when living,
>   Might have contrived me ways of thriving;
>   Taught me with cider to replenish
>   My vats, or ebbing tide of Rhenish;
>   So, when for hock I drew pricked white-wine,
>   Swear't had the flavour, and was right-wine."

Destiny, however, had decided the nephew's
fate otherwise. The Earl of Dorset, so the
story goes, was at the Rummer with a party
one day when a dispute arose over a passage
in Horace. Young Prior, then a scholar of
Westminster, was called in to decide the point,
and so admirably did he do it that the earl immediately undertook to pay his expenses at
Cambridge. He, in fact, '' spoiled the youth
to make a poet.'' Annotators of Hogarth have
pointed out that the scene of his '' Night '' picture was laid in that district of Charing Cross
where Locket's and the Rummer were situated.

Harking back now to Drury Lane the explorer finds himself in the midst of the memories of many daring adventures. The Jacobites who aimed at the dethroning of William
III were responsible for one of those episodes.
During the absence of that monarch they tried
to raise a riot in London on the birthday of the
Prince of Wales. Macaulay tells the rest of
the story. '' They met at a tavern in Drury
Lane, and, when hot with wine, sallied forth
sword in hand, headed by Porter and Goodman,
beat kettledrums, unfurled banners, and began
to light bonfires. But the watch, supported by
the populace, was too strong for the revellers.

They were put to rout: the tavern where they had feasted was sacked by the mob: the ring-leaders were apprehended, tried, fined, and imprisoned, but regained their liberty in time to bear a part in a far more criminal design.''

Noisy brawls and dark deeds became common in Drury Lane. It was the haunt of such quarrelsome persons as that Captain Fantom, who, coming out of the Horseshoe Tavern late one night, was offended by the loud jingling spurs of a lieutenant he met, and forthwith challenged him to a duel and killed him. And the tavern-keepers of Drury Lane were not always model citizens. There was that Jack Grimes, for example, whose death in Holland in 1769 recalled the circumstance that he was known as '' Lawyer Grimes,'' and formerly kept the Nag's Head Tavern in Princes' Street, Drury Lane, '' and was transported several years ago for fourteen years, for receiving fish, knowing them to be stolen.'' There is, however, one relieving touch in the tavern history of this thoroughfare. One of its houses of public entertainment was the meeting-place of a club of virtuosi, for whose club-room Louis Laguerre, the French painter who settled in London in 1683, designed and executed a Bacchanalian procession. This was the artist who was coupled with Verrio in Pope's depreciatory line,

"Where sprawl the Saints of Verrio and Laguerre."

Poets and prose writers alike were wont to agree in giving Catherine Street an unenviable reputation. Gay is specially outspoken in his description of that thoroughfare and the class by which it used to be haunted. It was in this street, too, that Jessop's once flourished, "the most disreputable night house of London." That nest of iniquity, however, has long been cleared away, and there are no means of identifying that tavern of which Boswell speaks. He describes it, on the authority of Dr. Johnson, as a "pretty good tavern, where very good company met in an evening, and each man called for his own half-pint of wine, or gill if he pleased; they were frugal men, and nobody paid but for what he himself drank. The house furnished no supper; but a woman attended with mutton pies, which anybody might purchase."

If the testimony of Pope is to be trusted, the cuisine of the Bedford Head, which was described in 1736 as "a noted tavern for eating, drinking, and gaming, in Southampton Street, Covent Garden," was decidedly out of the or-

dinary. In his imitation of the second satire
of Horace he makes Oldfield, the notorious
glutton who exhausted a fortune of fifteen hundred pounds a year in the " simple luxury of
good eating," declare,

> " Let me extol a Cat, on oysters fed,
> I'll have a party at the Bedford-head."

And in another poem he asks,

> " When sharp with hunger, scorn you to be fed,
> Except on pea-chicks at the Bedford-head? "

There is an earlier reference to this house than
the one cited above, for an advertisement of
June, 1716, alludes to it as " the Duke of Bedford's Head Tavern in Southampton Street,
Covent Garden." Perhaps the most notable
event in its history was it being the scene of
an abortive attempt to repeat in 1741 that glori-
fication of Admiral Vernon which was a great
success in 1740. That seaman, it will be remembered, had in 1739 kept his promise to capture Porto Bello with a squadron of but six
ships. That the capture was effected with the
loss of but seven men made the admiral a popular hero, and in the following year his birthday was celebrated in London with great ac-

claim. But in 1740 his attempt to seize Carta-
gena ended in complete failure, and another
enterprise against Santiago came to a similar
result. All this, however, did not daunt his
personal friends, who wished to engineer
another demonstration in Vernon's honour.
Horace Walpole tells how the attempt failed.
" I believe I told you," he wrote to one of
his friends, " that Vernon's birthday passed
quietly, but it was not designed to be pacific;
for at twelve at night, eight gentlemen dressed
like sailors, and masked, went round Covent
Garden with a drum beating for a volunteer
mob; but it did not take; and they retired to
a great supper that was prepared for them at
the Bedford Head, and ordered by Whitehead,
the author of ' Manners.' " At a later date it
was the meeting-place of a club to which John
Wilkes belonged.

In all London there is probably no thoroughfare of equal brief length which can boast so
many deeply interesting associations as Maiden
Lane, which stretches between Southampton
and Bedford Streets in the vicinity of Covent
Garden. Andrew Marvell had lodgings here in
1677; Voltaire made it his headquarters on his
visit to London in 1727; it was the scene of the
birth of Joseph Mallord William Turner in

1775; and while one tavern was the rendezvous
of the conspirators against the life of William
III, another was the favourite haunt of Richard Porson, than whom there is hardly a more
illustrious name in the annals of English classical scholarship.

While the name of the conspirators' tavern
is not mentioned by Macaulay, that frequented
by Porson had wide fame under the sign of the
Cider Cellars. It had been better for the great
scholar's health had nothing but cider been
sold therein. But that would hardly have
suited his tastes. It is a kindly judgment which
asserts that he would have achieved far more
than he actually did " if the sobriety of his life
had been equal to the honesty and truthfulness
of his character." All accounts agree that the
charms of his society in such gatherings as
those at the Cider Cellars were irresistible.
" Nothing," was the testimony of one friend,
" could be more gratifying than a tête-à-tête
with him; his recitations from Shakespeare,
and his ingenious etymologies and dissertations
on the roots of the English language were a
high treat." And another declares that nothing " came amiss to his memory; he would set
a child right in his twopenny fable-book, repeat
the whole of the moral tale of the Dean of

Badajos, or a page of Athenæus on cups, or
Eustathius on Homer.'' One anecdote tells of
his repeating the '' Rape of the Lock,'' making
observations as he went on, and noting the
various readings. And an intimate friend records the following incident connected with the
tavern he held most in regard. '' I have heard
Professor Porson at the Cider Cellars in
Maiden Lane recite from memory to delighted
listeners the whole of Anstey's ' Pleaders'
Guide.' He concluded by relating that when
buying a copy of it and complaining that the
price was very high, the bookseller said, ' Yes,
sir, but you know Law books are always very
dear.' ''

Somewhat earlier than Porson's day another
convivial soul haunted this neighbourhood.
This was George Alexander Stevens, the strolling player who eventually attained a place in
the company of Covent Garden theatre. He
was an indifferent actor but an excellent lecturer. One of his discourses, a lecture on
Heads, was immensely popular in England, and
not less so in Boston and Philadelphia. Prior
to the affluence which he won by his lecture
tours he had frequently to do '' penance in
jail for the debts of the tavern.'' He was, as
Campbell says, a leading member of all the

great Bacchanalian clubs of his day, and had
no mean gift in writing songs in praise of hard
drinking. One of these deserves a better fate
than the oblivion into which it has fallen, and
may be cited here as eminently descriptive of
the scenes enacted nightly in such a resort as
the Cider Cellars.

" Contented I am, and contented I'll be,
    For what can this world more afford,
Than a lass that will sociably sit on my knee,
    And a cellar as sociably stored,
                        My brave boys.

" My vault door is open, descend and improve,
    That cask, — ay, that will we try.
'Tis as rich to the taste as the lips of your love,
    And as bright as her cheeks to the eye:
                        My brave boys.

" In a piece of slit hoop, see my candle is stuck,
    'Twill light us each bottle to hand;
The foot of my glass for the purpose I broke,
    As I hate that a bumper should stand,
                        My brave boys.

" Astride on a butt, as a butt should be strod,
    I gallop the brusher along;
Like a grape-blessing Bacchus, the good fellow's god,
    And a sentiment give, or a song,
                        My brave boys.

" We are dry where we sit, though the coying drops
    seem
    With pearls the moist walls to emboss;
From the arch mouldy cobwebs in gothic taste stream,
    Like stucco-work cut out of moss:
                My brave boys.


" When the lamp is brimful, how the taper flame shines,
    Which, when moisture is wanting, decays;
Replenish the lamp of my life with rich wines,
    Or else there's an end of my blaze,
                My brave boys.


" Sound those pipes, they're in tune, and those bins
    are well fill'd;
    View that heap of old Hock in your rear;
Yon bottles are Burgundy! mark how they're pil'd,
    Like artillery, tier over tier,
                My brave boys.


" My cellar's my camp, and my soldiers my flasks,
    All gloriously rang'd in review;
When I cast my eyes round, I consider my casks
    As kingdoms I've yet to subdue,
                My brave boys.


" Like Macedon's Madman, my glass I'll enjoy,
    Defying hyp, gravel, or gout;
He cried when he had no more worlds to destroy,
    I'll weep when my liquor is out,
                My brave boys.

"On their stumps some have fought, and as stoutly
   will I,
  When reeling, I roll on the floor;
Then my legs must be lost, so I'll drink as I lie,
  And dare the best Buck to do more,
                    My brave boys.

"'Tis my will when I die, not a tear shall be shed,
  No *Hic Jacet* be cut on my stone;
But pour on my coffin a bottle of red,
  And say that his drinking is done,
                    My brave boys."

Although to-day celebrated chiefly for being
the central clearing-house for the flower, fruit
and vegetable supply of London, Covent Garden as a whole can vie with any other district
of the British capital in wealth of interesting
association. The market itself dates from the
middle of the seventeenth century, but the area
was constituted a parish a few years earlier.
By that time, however, it could boast many
town residences of the nobility, and several
inns. One of these has its name preserved only
in the records of the House of Lords, in a letter from a John Dutton at Amsterdam, who
wrote to his brother "with Mr. Wm. Wayte,
at the sign of the Horseshoe, Covent Garden."
But the taverns of greater note, such as Chatelaine's, the Fleece, the Rose, the Hummums,

and Macklin's ill-fated ordinary, belong to more recent times.

Which of these houses was first established it would be hard to say. There can be no question, however, that Chatelaine's ordinary was in great repute during the reign of Charles II, and that it continued in high favour throughout the latter years of the seventeenth century. Pepys alludes to it in 1667 and again in his entries of the following year. On the second occasion his visit interfered with toothsome purchases he was making for a dinner at his own house. '' To the fishmonger's, and bought a couple of lobsters, and over to the 'sparagus garden, thinking to have met Mr. Pierce, and his wife, and Knipp; but met their servant coming to bring me to Chatelin's, the French house, in Covent Garden, and there with musick and good company, Manuel and his wife, and one Swaddle, a clerk of Lord Arlington's, who dances, and speaks French well, but got drunk, and was then troublesome, and here mighty merry till ten at night. This night the Duke of Monmouth and a great many blades were at Chatelin's, and I left them there, with a hackney-coach attending him.'' This was a different experience than fell to the lot of Pepys on the previous occasion, for he tells how the dinner cost the party eight shillings and sixpence apiece, and it was " a base dinner, which did not please us at all." The ordinary was evidently in the same class as Pontack's and Locket's, as may be inferred from it being classed with the latter in one contemporary reference:

"Next these we welcome such as firstly dine
At Locket's, at Gifford's, or with Shataline."

Allusions in the plays of the period also show it was the resort of those who thought quite as much of spending money as of eating. Thus Shadwell makes one of his characters say of another who had risen in life that he was " one that the other day could eat but one meal a day, and that at a threepenny ordinary, now struts in state and talks of nothing but Shattelin's and Lefrond's." And another dramatist throws some light on the character of its frequenters by the remark, " Come, prettie, let's go dine at Chateline's, and there I'll tell you my whole business."

Far less fashionable was the Fleece tavern, where Pepys found pleasant entertainment on several occasions. His earliest reference to the house is in his account of meeting two gentlemen who told him how a Scottish knight was "killed basely the other day at the Fleece," but that tale did not prevent him from visiting the tavern himself. Along with a "Captain Cuttle" and two others he went thither to drink, and "there we spent till four o'clock, telling stories of Algiers, and the manner of life of slaves there." And then he tells how one night he dropped in at the Opera for the last act "and there found Mr. Sanchy and Mrs. Mary Archer, sister to the fair Betty, whom I did admire at Cambridge, and thence took them to the Fleece in Covent Garden; but Mr. Sanchy could not by any argument get his lady to trust herself with him into the taverne, which he was much troubled at."

Equally lively reputations were enjoyed by the Rose and the Hummums. The former was conveniently situated for first-nighters at the King's Playhouse, as Pepys found on a May midday in 1668. Anxious to see the first performance of Sir Charles Sedley's new play, which had been long awaited with great expectation, he got to the theatre at noon, only to find the doors not yet open. Gaining admission shortly after he seems to have been content to sit for a while and watch the gathering audience. But eventually the pangs of hunger mastered him, and so, getting a boy to keep his place, he slipped out to '' the Rose Tavern, and there got half a breast of mutton off the spit, and dined all alone.'' Twenty years later the vicinity of the Rose gained an unenviable reputation. '' A man could not go from the Rose Tavern to the Piazza once, but he must venture his life twice.'' And it maintained that reputation well into the next century, growing ever more and more in favour with the gamblers and rufflers of the times. It was at the bar of this house that Hildebrand Horden, an actor of talent and one who promised to win a great name, was killed in a brawl. Colley Cibber tells that he was exceedingly handsome, and that before he was buried '' it was observable that two or three days together several of the fair sex, well dressed, came in masks, and some in their own coaches, to visit the theatrical hero in his shroud.''

To the student of etymology the name of the Hummums tells its own tale. The word is a near approach to the Arabic '' Hammam,'' meaning a hot bath, and hence implies an establishment for bathing in the Oriental manner. The tavern in Covent Garden bearing that name was one of the first bathing establishments founded in England, and the fact that it introduced a method of ablution which

had its origin in a country of slavery prompted
Leigh Hunt to reflect that Englishmen need
not have wondered how Eastern nations could
endure their servitude. " This is one of the
secrets by which they endure it. A free man
in a dirty skin is not in so fit a state to endure
existence as a slave with a clean one; because
nature insists that a due attention to the clay
which our souls inhabit shall be the first requisite to the comfort of the inhabitant. Let us
not get rid of our freedom; let us teach it
rather to those that want it; but let such of
us as have them, by all means get rid of our
dirty skins. There is now a moral and intellectual commerce among mankind, as well as
an interchange of inferior goods; we should
send freedom to Turkey as well as clocks and
watches, and import not only figs, but a fine
state of pores."

John Wolcot, the satirist to whom, as Peter
Pindar, nothing was sacred, and who surely
had more accomplishments to fall back upon
than ever poet had before, having been in turns
doctor, clergyman, politician and painter, found
a congenial resort at the Hummums when he
established himself in London. He preserved
the memory of the house in verse, but it is an
open question whether his reflections on the

horrible sounds of which he complains should be referred to Covent Garden or to the city he had abandoned.

"In Covent Garden at the Hummums, now
  I sit, but after many a curse and vow,
    Never to see the madding City more;
  Where barrows truckling o'er the pavement roll:
  And, what is sorrow to a tuneful soul,
    Where asses, asses greeting, love songs roar:
  Which asses, that the Garden square adorn,
  Must lark-like be the heralds of my morn."

Those love songs have not ceased in Covent Garden; the amorous duets are to be heard to this day from the throats of countless costermongers' donkeys. But they disturb Peter Pindar's tuneful soul no more as he lies in his grave near by.

It would be a grave injustice to the Hummums to overlook the fact that it possessed a ghost-story of its own. Its subject was Dr. Johnson's cousin, the Parson Ford "in whom both talents and good dispositions were disgraced by licentiousness," and the story was told to Boswell by Johnson himself. "A waiter at the Hummums," Johnson said, "in which house Ford died, had been absent for some time, and returned, not knowing that

Ford was dead. Going down to the cellar, according to the story, he met him; going down again, he met him a second time. When he came up he asked some of the people of the house what Ford could be doing there. They told him Ford was dead. The waiter took a fever, in which he lay for some time. When he recovered, he said he had a message to deliver to some women from Ford; but he was not to tell what or to whom. He walked out; he was followed; but somewhere about St. Paul's they lost him. He came back and said he had delivered it, and the women exclaimed, ' Then we are all undone! ' Dr. Pellet, who was not a credulous man, inquired into the truth of this story, and he said the evidence was irresistible.'' A tantalizing ghost-story this, and one that begets regret that the Society for Psychical Research did not enter on its labours a century or so earlier.

One other tavern, or ordinary, of unusual interest spent its brief career of less than a year under the Piazza of Covent Garden. It was the experiment of Charles Macklin, an eighteenth century actor of undoubted talent and just as undoubted conceit and eccentricity. He had reached rather more than the midway of his long life — he was certainly ninety-seven

when he died and may have been a hundred —
when he resolved to leave the stage and carry
out an idea over which he had long ruminated.
This was nothing less than the establishment
of what he grandiloquently called the British
Institution.

So much in earnest was Macklin that he accepted a farewell benefit at Drury Lane theatre, at which he recited a good-bye prologue
commending his daughter to the favour of playgoers. In the greenroom that night, when re-
grets were expressed at the loss of so admirable
an actor, Foote remarked, " You need not fear;
he will first break in business, and then break
his word." And Foote did not a little to make
his prophecy come true. For a part of Macklin's scheme, whereby he was to instruct the
public and fill his own pockets at the same time,
was a lecture-room on the " plan of the ancient
Greek, Roman, and Modern French and Italian
Societies of liberal investigation." Macklin
appointed himself the instructor in chief, and
there was hardly a subject under the sun upon
which he was not prepared to enlighten the
British public at the moderate price of " one
shilling each person." The first two or three
lectures were a success. Then the novelty wore

off and opposition began. Foote set up a rival oratory and devoted himself to the simple task of burlesquing that of Macklin. He would impersonate Macklin in his armchair, examining a pupil in classics after this fashion.

" Well, sir, did you ever hear of Aristophanes? "

" Yes, sir; a Greek Dramatist, who wrote — "

" Ay; but I have got twenty comedies in these drawers, worth his *Clouds* and stuff. Do you know anything of Cicero? "

" A celebrated Orator of Rome, who in the polished and persuasive is considered a master in his art."

" Yes, yes; but I'll be bound he couldn't teach Elocution."

Of course all this raillery was more attractive to the public than Macklin's serious and pedagogic dissertations. The result may be imagined. Foote's oratory was crowded; Macklin's empty.

But that was not the worst. Another feature of the British Institution was the establishment of the ordinary aforesaid. The prospectus of the Institution bore this notice: " There is a public ordinary every day at four

o'clock, price three shillings. Each person to
drink port, claret, or whatever liquor he shall
choose." A disastrous precursor of the free
lunch this would seem. And so it proved. But
not immediately. Attracted by the novelty of
having a famous actor for host, the ordinary
went swimmingly for a time. Macklin presided
in person. As soon as the door of the room
was shut — a bell rang for five minutes, a further ten minutes' grace was given, and then
no more were admitted — the late actor bore
in the first dish and then took his place at the
elaborate sideboard to superintend further operations. Dinner over, and the bottles and
glasses placed on the table, " Macklin, quitting
his former situation, walked gravely up to the
front of the table and hoped ' that all things
were found agreeable; ' after which he passed
the bell-rope round the chair of the person who
happened to sit at the head of the table, and,
making a low bow at the door, retired." He
retired to read over the notes of the lecture
he had prepared for these same guests, and
during his absence for the rest of the evening
his waiters and cooks seized the opportunity
to reap their harvest. The sequel of the tale
was soon told in the bankruptcy court, and
Macklin went back to the stage, as Foote said

he would.   And now he lies peacefully enough
in his grave in the Covent Garden St. Paul's,
within stone's throw of the scene where he
tried to be a tavern-keeper and failed.

# CHAPTER V

OUTSIDE the more or less clearly defined limits of the city, the neighbourhood of St. Paul's, Fleet Street, the Strand and Covent Garden, the explorer of the inns and taverns of old London may encircle the metropolis from any given point and find something of interest everywhere. Such a point of departure may be made, for example, in the parish of Lambeth, where, directly opposite the Somerset House of to-day, once stood the Feathers Tavern connected with Cuper's Gardens. The career of that resort was materially interfered with by the passing of an act in 1752 for the regulation of places of entertainment " and punishing persons keeping disorderly houses." The act stipulated that every place kept for public dancing, music, or other entertainment, within twenty miles of the city, should be under a license.

Evidently it was found impossible to secure a license for Cuper's Gardens, for in a public

FEATHERS TAVERN.

print of May 22nd, 1754, the Widow Evans advertises that "having been deny'd her former Liberty of opening her Gardens as usual, through the malicious representations of ill-meaning persons, she therefore begs to acquaint the Public that she hath open'd them as a Tavern till further notice. Coffee and Tea at any hour of the day." There is no record of the Widow Evans ever recovering her former "Liberty," and hence the necessity of continuing the place as a tavern merely, with its seductive offer of "coffee and tea at any hour." Even without a license, however, a concert was announced for the night of August 30th, 1759, the law being evaded by the statement that the vocal and instrumental programme was to be given by "a select number of gentlemen for their own private diversion." As there is no record of any other entertainment having been given at the Feathers, it is probable that this attempt to dodge the law met with condign punishment, and resulted in the closing of the place for good. After it had stood unoccupied for some time Dr. Johnson passed it in the company of Beauclerk, Langton, and Lady Sydney Beauclerk, and made a sportive suggestion that he and Beauclerk and Langton should take it. " We amused ourselves,'' he said, '' with scheming how we should all do our parts. Lady Sydney grew angry and said, ' An old man should not put such things in young people's heads.' She had no notion of a joke, sir; had come late into life, and had a mighty unpliable understanding.'' Though Johnson did not carry his joke into effect, the Feathers has not lacked for perpetuation, as is shown by the modern public-house of that name in the vicinity of Waterloo Bridge.

From Lambeth to Westminster is an easy journey, but unhappily there are no survivals of the numerous inns which figure in records of the sixteenth and seventeenth centuries. One of those hostelries makes its appearance in the expense sheet of a Roger Keate who went to London in 1575 on the business of his town of Weymouth. He notes that on Friday the tenth day of February, '' in the companie of certain courtiars, and of Mr. Robert Gregorie, at Westminster, at the Sarrazin's Head '' he spent the sum of five shillings. This must have been a particularly festive occasion, for a subsequent dinner cost Mr. Keate but twenty pence, and '' sundrie drinkinges '' another day left him the poorer by but two shillings and twopence.

Another document, this time of date 1641, perpetuates the memory of a second Westminster inn in a lively manner. This is a petition of a constable of St. Martin's-in-the-Fields to the House of Commons, and concerned the misdoings of certain apprentices at the time of the riot caused by Colonel Lunsford's assault on the citizens of Westminster. The petitioner, Peter Scott by name, stated that he tried to appease the 'prentices by promising to release their fellows detained as prisoners in the Mermaid tavern. When he and another constable approached the door of the house, his colleague was thrust in the leg with a sword from within, which so enraged the 'prentices — though why is not explained — that they broke into the tavern, and the keeper had since prosecuted the harmless Peter Scott for causing a riot.

Numerous as were the taverns of Westminster, it is probable that the greater proportion of them were to be found in one thoroughfare, to wit, King Street. It was the residence and place of business of one particularly aggressive brewer in the closing quarter of the seventeenth century. This vendor of ale, John England by name, had the distinction of being the King's brewer, and he appears to have thought that that position gave him more rights than were possessed by ordinary mortals. So when an order was made prohibiting the passing of drays through King Street during certain hours of the day, he told the constables that he, the King's brewer, cared nothing for the order of the House of Lords. The example proved infectious. Other brewers' draymen became obstreperous too, one calling the beadle that stopped him "a rogue" and another vowing that if he knew the beadle "he would have a touch with him at quarterstaff." But all these fiery spirits of King Street were brought to their senses, and are found expressing sorrow for their offence and praying for their discharge.

According to the legend started by Ben Jonson, this same King Street was the scene of poet Spenser's death of starvation. "He died," so Jonson said, "for want of bread in King Street; he refused twenty pieces sent him by my Lord Essex, and said he was sure he had no time to spend them." This myth is continually cropping up, but no evidence has been adduced in its support. The fact that he died in a tavern in King Street tells against the story. That thoroughfare, then the only highway between the Royal Palace of Whitehall and the Parliament House, was a street of considerable importance, and Spenser's presence there is explained by Stow's remark that " for the accommodation of such as come to town in the terms, here are some good inns for their reception, and not a few taverns for entertainment, as is not unusual in places of great confluence." There are ample proofs, too, that King Street was the usual resort of those who were messengers to the Court, such as Spenser was at the time of his death.

It is strange, however, that not many of the names of these taverns have survived. Yet there are two, the Leg and the Bell, to which there are allusions in seventeenth century records. There is one reference in that " Parliamentary Diary " supposed to have been written by Thomas Burton, the book which Carlyle characterized as being filled " with mere dim inanity and moaning wind." This chronicler, under date December 18th, 1656, tells how he dined with the clothworkers at the Leg, and how " after dinner I was awhile at the Leg with Major-General Howard and Mr. Briscoe." Being so near Whitehall in one direction and the Parliament House in the other, it is not surprising to learn that the nimble Pepys was a frequent visitor at the tavern. After a morning at Whitehall " with

my lord '' in June, 1660, he dined there with
a couple of friends. Nearly a year later business took him to the House of Lords, but as
he failed to achieve the purpose he had in view
he sought consolation at the Leg, where he
'' dined very merry.'' A more auspicious occasion took place three years after. '' To the
Exchequer, and there got my tallys for £17,500,
the first payment I ever had out of the Exchequer, and at the Legg spent 14s. upon my
old acquaintance, some of them the clerks, and
away home with my tallys in a coach, fearful
every moment of having one of them fall out,
or snatched from me.'' He was equally glowing with satisfaction when he visited the tavern
again in 1667. All sorts of compliments had
been paid him that day, and he had been con-
gratulated even by the King and the Duke of
York. '' I spent the morning thus walking in
the Hall, being complimented by everybody
with admiration: and at noon stepped into the
Legg with Sir William Warren.''

Then there was that other house in King
Street, the Bell, upon which the diarist bestowed some of his patronage. On his first
visit he was caught in a neat little trap. '' Met
with Purser Washington, with whom and a
lady, a friend of his, I dined at the Bell Tavern

in King Street, but the rogue had no more manners than to invite me, and to let me pay my
club." Which was too bad of the Purser, when
Pepys' head and heart were full of " infinite
business." The next call, however, was more
satisfactory and less expensive. He merely
dropped in to see " the seven Flanders mares
that my Lord has bought lately." But the Bell
had a history both before and after Pepys'
time. It is referred to so far back as the middle of the fifteenth century, and it was in high
favour as the headquarters of the October Club
in the reign of Queen Anne.

During the eighteenth century many fashionable resorts were located in Pall Mall and
neighbouring streets. In Pall Mall itself was
the famous Star and Garter, and close by was
St. Alban's Tavern, celebrated for its political
gatherings and public dinners. Horace Walpole has several allusions to the house and tells
an anecdote which illustrates the wastefulness
of young men about town. A number of these
budding aristocrats were dining at St. Alban's
Tavern and found the noise of the coaches outside jar upon their sensitive nerves. So they
promptly ordered the street to be littered with
straw, and probably cared little that the freak
cost them fifty shillings each.

No doubt the charges at the St. Alban's were in keeping with the exclusive character of the house, and it might be inferred that the same would have held good at the Star and Garter. But that was not the case. Many testimonies to the moderate charges of that house have been cited. Perhaps the most conclusive evidence on this point is furnished by Swift, who was always a bit of a haggler as to the prices he paid at taverns. It was at his suggestion that the little club to which he belonged discarded the tavern they had been used to meeting in and went to the Star and Garter for their dinner. "The other dog," Swift wrote in one of his little letters to Stella, "was so extravagant in his bills that for four dishes, and four, first and second course, without wine or dessert, he charged twenty-one pounds, six shillings and eightpence." That the bill at the Star and Garter was more reasonable is a safe inference from the absence of any complaint on the part of Swift.

Several clubs were wont to meet under this roof. Among these was the Nottinghamshire Club, an association of gentlemen who had estates in that county and were in the habit of dining together when in town. One such gathering, however, had a tragic termination.

It took place on January 26th, 1765, and among
those present were William Chaworth, John
Hewett, Lord Byron, a great-uncle of the poet,
and seven others. Perfect harmony prevailed
until about seven o'clock, when the wine was
brought in and conversation became general.
At this juncture one member of the company
started a conversation about the best method
of preserving game, and the subject was at once
taken up by Mr. Chaworth and Lord Byron,
who seem to have held entirely opposite views.
The former was in favour of severity against
all poachers, the latter declaring that the best
way to have most game was to take no care
of it all. Nettled by this opposition, Mr. Chaworth ejaculated that he had more game on five
acres than Lord Byron had on all his manors.
Retorts were bandied to and fro, until finally
Mr. Chaworth clenched matters by words which
were tantamount to a challenge to a duel.

Nothing more was said, however, and the
company was separating when Mr. Chaworth
and Lord Byron happened to meet on a landing. What transpired at first then is not
known, but evidently the quarrel was resumed
in some form or other, for the two joined in
calling a waiter and asking to be shown into
an empty room. The waiter obeyed, opening

the door and placing a small tallow candle on
the table before he retired. The next news
from that room was the ringing of a bell, and
when it was answered it was found that Mr.
Chaworth was mortally wounded. What had
happened was explained by Mr. Chaworth, who
said that he could not live many hours; that
he forgave Lord Byron, and hoped the world
would; that the affair had passed in the dark,
only a small tallow candle burning in the room;
that Lord Byron asked him if he meant the
conversation on the game to Sir Charles Sedley or to him? To which he replied, if you have
anything to say, we had better shut the door;
that while he was doing this, Lord Byron bid
him draw, and, in turning, he saw his lordship's
sword half drawn, on which he whipped out
his own, and made the first pass; the sword
being through his lordship's waistcoat, he
thought he had killed him, and asking whether
he was not mortally wounded, Lord Byron,
while he was speaking, shortened his sword,
and stabbed him in the abdomen. Mr. Chaworth survived but a few hours. There was
a trial, of course, but it ended in Lord Byron's
acquittal on the ground that he had been guilty
of but manslaughter. And the poet, the famous
grand-nephew, rounds off this story of the Star

and Garter by declaring that his relative, so
far from feeling any remorse for the death of
Mr. Chaworth, always kept the sword he had
used with such fatal effect and had it hanging
in his bedroom when he died.

Although the neighbouring Suffolk Street is
a most decorous thoroughfare at the present
time, and entirely innocent of taverns, it was
furnished with two, the Cock and The Golden
Eagle, in the latter portion of the seventeenth
century. At the former Evelyn dined on one
occasion with the councillors of the Board of
Trade; at the latter, on January 30th, 1735,
occurred the riot connected with the mythical
Calf's Head Club. How the riot arose is something of a mystery. It seems, however, that
a mob was gathered outside the tavern by the
spreading of the report that some young nobles
were dining within on a calf's head in ridicule
of the execution of Charles I, and a lurid account was afterwards circulated as to how a
bleeding calf's head, wrapped in a napkin, was
thrown out of the window, while the merry-
makers within drank all kinds of confusion to
the Stuart race. According to the narrative
of one who was in the tavern, the calf's head
business was wholly imaginary. Nor was the
date of the dinner a matter of prearrangement.

It seems that the start of the commotion was occasioned by some of the company inside observing that some boys outside had made a bonfire, which, in their hilarity, they were anxious to emulate. So a waiter was commissioned to make a rival conflagration, and then the row began. It grew to such proportions that the services of a justice and a strong body of guards were required ere peace could be restored to Suffolk Street.

Rare indeed is it to find a tavern in this district which can claim a clean record in the matter of brawls, and duels, and sudden deaths. Each of the two most famous houses of the Haymarket, that is, Long's and the Blue Posts Tavern, had its fatality. It was at the former ordinary, which must not be confused with another of the same name in Covent Garden, that Philip Herbert, the seventh Earl of Pembroke, committed one of those murderous assaults for which he was distinguished. He killed a man in a duel in 1677, and in the first month of the following year was committed to the Tower "for blasphemous words." That imprisonment, however, was of brief duration, for in February a man petitioned the House of Lords for protection from the earl's violence. And the day before, in a drunken scuffle at Long's he had killed a man named Nathaniel Cony. This did not end his barbarous conduct, for two years later he murdered an officer of the watch, when returning from a drinking bout at Turnham Green. Mercifully for the peace of the community this blood-thirsty peer died at the age of thirty. At the Blue Posts Tavern the disputants were a Mr. Moon and a Mr. Hunt, who began their quarrel in the house, " and as they came out at the door they drew their swords, and the latter was run through and immediately died." There was another Blue Posts in Spring Gardens close by, which became notorious from being the resort of the Jacobites. This, in fact, was the house in which Robert Charnock and his fellow conspirators were at breakfast when news reached them which proved that their plot had been discovered.

A more refined atmosphere hangs around the memory of the Thatched House, that St. James's Street tavern which started on its prosperous career in 1711 and continued it until 1865, at which date the building was taken down to make room for the Conservative Clubhouse. Its title would have led a stranger to expect a modest establishment, but that seems to have been bestowed on the principle which still prevails when a mansion is designated a cottage. It reminds one of Coleridge and his

> " the Devil did grin, for his darling sin
> Is the pride that apes humility."

Swift was conscious of the incongruity of the name, as witness the lines,

> " The Deanery House may well be match'd,
> Under correction, with the Thatch'd."

As a matter of fact the tavern was of the highest class and greatly in repute with the leaders of society and fashion. And its frequenters were not a little proud of being known among its patrons. Hence the delightful retort of the Lord Chancellor Thurlow recorded by Lord Campbell. " In the debates on the Regency, a prim peer, remarkable for his finical delicacy and formal adherence to etiquette, having cited pompously certain resolutions which he said had been passed by a party of noblemen and gentlemen of great distinction at the Thatched House Tavern, the Lord Chancellor Thurlow, in adverting to these said, ' As to what the noble lord in the red ribbon told us he had heard at the ale-house.' "

Town residences of a duke and several earls

are now the most conspicuous buildings in the
Mayfair Stanhope Street, but in the closing
years of the eighteenth century there was a
tavern here of the name of Pitt's Head. On
a June night in 1792 this house was the scene
of a gathering which had notable results. The
host conceived the idea of inviting a number
of the servants of the neighbourhood to a fes-
tivity in honour of the King's birthday, one
feature of which was to be a dance. The company duly assembled to the number of forty,
but some busybody carried news of the gathering to a magistrate who, with fifty constables,
quickly arrived on the scene to put an end to
the merrymaking. Every servant in the tavern was taken into custody and marched off
to a watch-house in Mount Street. News of
what had happened spread during the night,
and early in the morning the watch-house was
surrounded by a furious mob. A riot followed,
which was not easily suppressed. But another
consequence followed. During the riot the
Earl of Lonsdale was stopped in his carriage
while passing to his own house, and annoyed
by that experience he addressed some curt
words to a Captain Cuthbert who was on duty
with the soldiers. Of course a duel was the
next step. After failing to injure each other

at two attempts, the seconds intervened, and insisted that, as their quarrel had arisen through a mutual misconception, and as neither of them would make the first concession, they should advance towards each other, step for step, and both declare, in the same breath, that they were sorry for what had happened.

In pre-railway days Piccadilly could boast of the White Horse Cellar, which Dickens made famous as the starting-point of Mr. Pickwick for Bath after being mulct in seven hundred and fifty pounds damages by the fair widow Bardell. The fact that it was an important coaching depot appears to have been its chief attraction in those and earlier days, for the novelist's description of the interior would hardly prove seductive to travellers were the house existing in its old-time condition. " The travellers' room at the White Horse Cellar," wrote Dickens, " is of course uncomfortable; it would be no travellers' room if it were not. It is the right-hand parlour, into which an aspiring kitchen fireplace appears to have walked, accompanied by a rebellious poker, tongs, and shovel. It is divided into boxes, for the solitary confinement of travellers, and is furnished with a clock, a looking-glass, and a live waiter: which latter article is kept in

a small kennel for washing glasses, in a corner
of the apartment.'' Pierce Egan, in the closing
pages of his lively account of Jerry Haw-
thorn's visit to London, gives an outside view
of the tavern only. And that more by suggestion than direct description. It is the bustle
of the place rather than its architectural features Egan was concerned with, and in that he
was seconded by his artist, George Cruikshank,
whose picture of the White Horse Cellar is
mostly coach and horses and human beings.

Few if any London taverns save the Adam
and Eve can claim to stand upon ground once
occupied by a King's palace. This tavern,
which has a modern representative of identical
name, was situated at the northern end of Tot-
tenham Court Road, at the junction of the road
leading to Hampstead. It was built originally
on the site of a structure known as King John's
Palace, which subsequently became a manor
house, and then gave way to the Adam and
Eve tavern and gardens. This establishment
had a varied career. At one time it was highly
respectable; then its character degenerated to
the lowest depths; afterwards taking an up-
ward move once more.

Something in the shape of a place for refreshments was standing on this spot in the

mid seventeenth century, for the parish books of St. Giles in the Fields record that three serving maids were in 1645 fined a shilling each for " drinking at Totenhall Court on the Sabbath daie." In the eighteenth century the resort was at the height of its popularity. It had a large room with an organ, skittle-alleys, and cosy arbours for those who liked to consume their refreshments out of doors. At one time also its attractions actually embraced " a monkey, a heron, some wild fowl, some parrots, and a small pond for gold-fish." It was at this stage in its history, when its surroundings were more rural than it is possible to imagine to-day, that the tavern was depicted by Hogarth in his " March to Finchley " plate. Early in the last century, however, it " became a place of more promiscuous resort, and persons of the worst character and description were in the constant habit of frequenting it; highwaymen, footpads, pickpockets, and common women formed its leading visitants, and it became so great a nuisance to the neighbourhood, that the magistrates interfered, the organ was banished, the skittle-grounds destroyed, and the gardens dug up." A creepy story is told of a subterraneous passage having existed in connection with the manor house which formerly stood on

ADAM AND EVE TAVERN.

this spot, a passage which many set out to explore but which has kept its secret hidden to this day.

Record has already been made of the fact that there was one '' Sarrazin's '' Head tavern at Westminster; it must be added that there was another at Snow Hill, which disappeared when the Holborn Viaduct was built. Dickens, who rendered so many valuable services in describing the buildings of old London, has left a characteristic pen-picture of this tavern. '' Near to the jail, and by consequence near to Smithfield, and on that particular part of Snow Hill where omnibuses going eastward seriously think of falling down on purpose, and where horses in hackney cabriolets going westward not unfrequently fall by accident, is the coachyard of the Saracen's Head Inn; its portals guarded by two Saracens' heads and shoulders frowning upon you from each side of the gateway. The Inn itself garnished with another Saracen's head, frowns upon you from the top of the yard. When you walk up this yard you will see the booking-office on your left, and the tower of St. Sepulchre's Church darting abruptly up into the sky on your right, and a gallery of bedrooms upon both sides. Just before you, you will observe a long

window with the words ' Coffee Room ' legibly
painted above it.'' That allusion to St. Sepulchre's Church recalls the fact that in that building may be seen the brass to the memory of
the redoubtable Captain John Smith, who was
to win the glory of laying the first abiding
foundations of English life in America. The
brass makes due record of the fact that he was
'' Admiral of New England,'' and it also bears
in the coat of arms three Turks' heads, in memory of Smith's alleged single-handed victory
over that number of Saracens. As Selden
pointed out, when Englishmen came home from
fighting the Saracens, and were beaten by them,
they, to save their own credit, pictured their
enemy with big, terrible faces, such as frowned
at Dickens from so many coigns of vantage in
the old Saracen's Head.

During the closing decade of the famous Bartholomew Fair — an annual medley of commerce and amusement which had its origin in
the days when it was the great cloth exchange
of all England and attracted clothiers from all
quarters — the scene of what was known as the
Pie-Powder Court was located in a tavern
known as the Hand and Shears. Concerning
this court Blackstone offered this interesting
explanation: '' The lowest, and, at the same

A TRIAL BEFORE THE PIE-POWDER COURT AT THE HAND AND SHEARS TAVERN.

time, the most expeditious court of justice
known to the law of England, is the Court of
Pie-Powder, *curia pedis pulverizati,* so called
from the dusty feet of the suitors.'' Another
explanation of the name is that the court was
so called '' because justice is there done as
speedily as dust can fall from the foot.''
Whatever be the correct solution, the curious
fact remains that this court was a serious affair, and had the power to enforce law and deal
out punishment within the area of the Fair.
There is an excellent old print of the Hand
and Shears in which the court was held, and
another not less interesting picture showing
the court engaged on the trial of a case. It
is evident from the garb of the two principal
figures that plaintiff and defendant belonged
to the strolling-player fraternity, who always
contributed largely to the amusements of the
Fair. This curious example of swift justice,
recalling the Old Testament picture of the
judge sitting at the gate of the city, became
entirely a thing of the past when Bartholomew
Fair was abolished in 1854.

There are two other inns, one to the north,
the other to the south, the names of which can
hardly escape the notice of the twentieth century visitor to London. These are the Angel

at Islington, and the Elephant and Castle at Walworth. The former is probably the older of the two, though both were in their day famous as the starting-places of coaches, just as they are conspicuous to-day as traffic centres of omnibuses and tram-cars. The Angel dates back to before 1665, for in that year of plague in London a citizen broke out of his house in the city and sought refuge here. He was refused admission, but was taken in at another inn and found dead in the morning. In the seventeenth century and later, as old pictures testify, the inn presented the usual features of a large old country hostelry. As such the courtyard is depicted by Hogarth in his print of the "Stage Coach." Its career has been uneventful in the main, though in 1767 one of its guests ended his life by poison, leaving behind this message: "I have for fifteen years past suffered more indigence than ever gentleman before submitted to, I am neglected by my acquaintance, traduced by my enemies, and insulted by the vulgar."

If he would complete the circle of his tour on the outskirts of London proper, the pilgrim, on leaving the Elephant and Castle, should wend his way to Bankside, though not in the expectation of finding any vestige left of that

FALCON TAVERN, BANKSIDE.

Falcon tavern which was the daily resort of Shakespeare and his theatrical companions. Not far from Blackfriars Bridge used to be Falcon Stairs and the Falcon Glass Works, and other industrial buildings bearing that name, but no Falcon tavern within recent memory. It has been denied that Shakespeare frequented the Falcon tavern which once did actually exist. But so convivial a soul must have had some " house of call," and there is no reason to rob the memory of the old Falcon of what would be its greatest honour. Especially does it seem unnecessary in view of the fact that the Falcon and many another inn and tavern of old London, has vanished and left " not a rack behind."

# II

# COFFEE - HOUSES OF OLD LONDON

# CHAPTER I

COFFEE - HOUSES still exist in London, but it would be difficult to find one answering to the type which was so common during the last forty years of the seventeenth century and the first half of the eighteenth. The establishment of to-day is nothing more than an eating-house of modest pretensions, frequented mostly by the labouring classes. In many cases its internal arrangements follow the old-time model, and the imitation extends to the provision of a daily newspaper or two from which customers may glean the news of the day without extra charge. Here and there, too, the coffee-house of the present perpetuates the convenience of its prototype by allowing customers' letters to be sent to its address. But the more exalted type of coffee-house has lost its identity in the club.

It is generally agreed that 1652 was the date of the opening of the first coffee-house in London. There are, however, still earlier references to the drink itself. For example, Sir Henry Blount wrote from Turkey in 1634 to the effect that the natives of that country had a " drink called *cauphe* . . . in taste a little bitterish," and that they daily entertained themselves " two or three hours in *cauphe-*houses, which, in Turkey, abound more than inns and alehouses with us." Also it will be remembered that Evelyn, under date 1637, recorded how a Greek came to Oxford and " was the first I ever saw drink coffee."

Whether the distinction of opening the first coffee-house in London belongs to a Mr. Bowman or to a Pasqua Rosee cannot be decided. But all authorities are as one in locàting that establishment in St. Michael's Alley, Cornhill, and that the date was 1652. The weight of evidence seems to be in favour of Rosee, who was servant to a Turkey merchant named Edwards. Having acquired the coffee-drinking habit in Turkey, Mr. Edwards was accustomed to having his servant prepare the beverage for him in his London house, and the new drink speedily attracted a levee of curious onlookers and tasters. Evidently the company grew too large to be convenient, and at this juncture Mr. Edwards suggested that Rosee should set up as a vendor of the drink. He did so, and a copy of the prospectus he issued on the occasion still exists. It set forth at great length " the virtue of the Coffee Drink First publiquely made and sold in England by Pasqua Rosee," the berry of which was described as " a simple innocent thing " but yielding a liquor of countless merits. But Rosee was frank as to its drawbacks; " it will prevent drowsiness," he continued, " and make one fit for business, if one have occasion to watch; and therefore you are not to drink it after supper, unless you intend to be watchful, for it will hinder sleep for three or four hours."

That Pasqua Rosee prospered amazingly in St. Michael's Alley, " at the Signe of his own Head," is the only conclusion possible from the numerous rival establishments which were quickly set up in different parts of London. By the end of the century it was computed that the coffee-houses of London numbered nearly three thousand.

But there were days of tribulation to be passed through before that measure of success was attained. In eight years after Rosee had opened his establishment the consumption of coffee in England had evidently increased to a notable extent, for in 1660 the House of Commons is found granting to Charles II for life

the excise duty on coffee " and other outlandish drinks." But it is a curious fact that while
the introduction of tea was accepted with equa-
nimity by the community, the introduction of
coffee was strenuously opposed for more than
a decade. Poets and pamphleteers combined to
decry the new beverage. The rhyming author
of " A Cup of Coffee, or Coffee in its Colours,"
published in 1663, voiced his indignation thus:

" For men and Christians to turn Turks and think
   To excuse the crime, because 'tis in their drink!
   Pure English apes! ye might, for aught I know,
   Would it but mode — learn to eat spiders too.
   Should any of your grandsires' ghosts appear
   In your wax-candle circles, and but hear
   The name of coffee so much called upon,
   Then see it drank like scalding Phlegethon;
   Would they not startle, think ye, all agreed
   'Twas conjuration both in word and deed?"

By way of climax this opponent of the new
drink appealed to the shades of Ben Jonson
and other libation-loving poets, and recalled
how they, as source of inspiration, " drank
pure nectar as the Gods drink too."

Three years later a dramatist seems to have
tried his hand at depicting the new resort on
the stage, for Pepys tells how in October, 1666,
he saw a play called " The Coffee-House." It

was not a success; " the most ridiculous, insipid play that ever I saw in my life," was
Pepys' verdict. But there was nothing insipid
about the pamphlet which, under the title of
" The Character of a Coffee-House," issued
from the press seven years later. The author
withheld his name, and was wise in so doing,
for his cuts and thrusts with his pen would
have brought down upon him as numerous cuts
and thrusts with a more dangerous weapon
had his identity been known. " A coffee-
house," he wrote, " is a lay-conventicle, good-
fellowship turned puritan, ill-husbandry in
masquerade; whither people come, after toping
all day, to purchase, at the expense of their last
penny, the repute of sober companions: a rota-
room, that, like Noah's ark, receives animals
of every sort, from the precise diminutive
band, to the hectoring cravat and cuffs in folio;
a nursery for training up the smaller fry of
virtuosi in confident tattling, or a cabal of kit-
tling critics that have only learned to spit and
mew; a mint of intelligence, that, to make
each man his penny-worth, draws out into
petty parcels what the merchant receives in
bullion. He, that comes often, saves two-pence
a week in Gazettes, and has his news and his
coffee for the same charge, as at a three-penny

ordinary they give in broth to your chop of mutton; it is an exchange where haberdashers of political smallwares meet, and mutually abuse each other, and the public, with bottomless stories, and headless notions; the rendezvous of idle pamphlets, and persons more idly employed to read them; a high court of justice, where every little fellow in a camlet cloke takes upon him to transpose affairs both in church and state, to shew reasons against acts of parliament, and condemn the decrees of general councils.''

Having indulged in that trenchant generalization, this vigorous assailant proceeded to describe a coffee-house in detail. The room '' stinks of tobacco worse than hell of brimstone; '' the coffee itself had the appearance of '' Pluto's diet-drink, that witches tipple out of dead men's skulls; '' and the company included '' a silly fop and a worshipful justice, a griping rook and a grave citizen, a worthy lawyer and an errant pickpocket, a reverend nonconformist and a canting mountebank, all blended together to compose an oglio of impertinence.'' There is a delightful sketch of one named '' Captain All-man-sir,'' as big a boaster as Falstaff, and a more delicately etched portrait of the Town Wit, who is summed up as the "jack-pudding of society" in the judgment of all wise men, but an incomparable wit in his own. The peroration of this pamphlet, devoted to a wholesale condemnation of the coffee-house, indulges in too frank and unsavoury metaphors for modern re-publication.

Of course there was an answer. Pamphleteering was one of the principal diversions of the age. "Coffee-Houses Vindicated" was the title of the reply. The second pamphlet was not the equal of the first in terseness or wit, but it had the advantage in argument. The writer did not find it difficult to make out a good case for the coffee-house. It was economical, conduced to sobriety, and provided innocent diversion. When one had to meet a friend, a tavern was an expensive place; "in an ale-house you must gorge yourself with pot after pot, sit dully alone, or be drawn in to club for others' reckonings." Not so at the coffee-house: "Here, for a penny or two, you may spend two or three hours, have the shelter of a house, the warmth of a fire, the diversion of company; and conveniency, if you please, of taking a pipe of tobacco; and all this without any grumbling or repining." On the score of sobriety the writer was equally cogent. It was stupid custom which insisted that any and every transaction should be carried out at a tavern, where continual sipping made men unfit for business. Coffee, on the contrary, was a " wakeful " drink. And the company of the coffee-house enabled its frequenter to follow the proper study of man, mankind. The triumphant conclusion was that a well-regulated coffee-house was " the sanctuary of health, the nursery of temperance, the delight of frugality, an academy of civility, and free-school of ingenuity."

But a still more serious-minded person took part in the assault upon the coffee-house. He was one of those amateur statesmen, who usually, as in this case, abrogate to themselves the title of " Lover of his Country," who have a remedy for every disease of the body politic. In a series of proposals offered for the consideration of Parliament, this patriot pleaded for the suppression of coffee-houses on the ground that if less coffee were drunk there would be a larger demand for beer, and a larger demand for beer meant the growing of more English grain. Apart from economics, however, there were adequate reasons for suppression. These coffee-houses have " done great mischiefs to the nation, and undone many of the King's subjects: for they, being great enemies to diligence and industry, have been the ruin of many serious and hopeful young gentlemen and tradesmen, who, before frequenting these places, were diligent students or shopkeepers, extraordinary husbands of their time as well as money; but since these houses have been set up, under pretence of good husbandry, to avoid spending above one penny or twopence at a time, have gone to these coffeehouses; where, meeting friends, they have sat talking three or four hours; after which, a fresh acquaintance appearing, and so one after another all day long, hath begotten fresh discourse, so that frequently they have staid five or six hours together," to the neglect of shops and studies, etc., etc.

Even yet, however, the worst had not been said. The wives of England had to be heard from. Hence the " Women's Petition against Coffee," which enlivens the annals of the year of grace 1674. The pernicious drink was indicted on three counts: " It made men as unfruitful as the deserts whence that unhappy berry is said to be brought; " its use would cause the offspring of their " mighty ancestors " to " dwindle into a succession of apes and pigmies; " and when a husband went out

on a domestic errand he " would stop by the
way to drink a couple of cups of coffee.''

These assaults — or, what is more probable,
the abuse of the coffee-house for political purposes — had an effect, for a time. The king,
although enjoying the excise from that " outlandish " drink, did issue a proclamation for
the suppression of the coffee-houses, only to
cancel it almost ere the ink was dry. But later,
to put a stop to that public discussion of state
affairs which was deemed sacrilege in the seventeenth century, an order was issued forbid-
ding coffee-houses to keep any written or other
news save such as appeared in the Gazette.

But the coffee-house as an institution was
not to be put down. Neither pamphlets nor
poems, nor petitions nor proclamations, had any
effect. It met a " felt want " apparently, or
made so effective an appeal to the social spirit
of seventeenth century Londoners that its success was assured from the start. Consequently
Pasqua Rosee soon had opposition in his own
immediate neighbourhood. It may be that the
Rainbow of Fleet Street was the second coffee-
house to be opened in London, or that the honour belonged elsewhere; what is to be noted
is that the establishments multiplied fast and
nowhere more than in the vicinity of the Royal

Exchange.   Several were to be found in Change
Alley, while in the Royal Exchange of to-day,
the third building of that name, are the headquarters of Lloyd's, which perpetuates in name
at least one of the most remarkable coffee-
houses of the seventeenth century.

Evidence is abundant that the early coffee-
houses took their colour from the district in
which they were established.   Thus it would be
idle in the main to expect a literary atmosphere
among the houses which flourished in the heart
of the city.   They became the resorts of men
of business, and gradually acquired a specific
character from the type of business man most
frequenting them.   In a way Batson's coffee-
house was an exception to the rule, inasmuch
as doctors and not merchants were most in
evidence here.   But the fact that it was tacitly
accepted as the physicians' resort shows how
the principle acted in a general way.   One of
the most constant visitors at Batson's was Sir
Richard Blackmore, that scribbling doctor who
was physician to William III and then to
Queen Anne.   Although his countless books
were received either with ridicule or absolute
silence, he still persisted in authorship, and
finally produced an "Heroick Poem" in
twelve books entitled, "Prince Alfred."   Lest

any should wonder how a doctor could court
the muse to that extent without neglecting his
proper work, he explained in his preface that
he had written the poem " by such catches and
starts, and in such occasional uncertain hours
as his profession afforded, and for the greater
part in coffee-houses, or in passing up and
down the streets,'' an apology which led to his
being accused of writing " to the rumbling of
his chariot wheels.'' But in the main the real
literary folk of the day would have none of
him. He belonged to the city, and what had
a mere city man to do with poetry? Even Dr.
Johnson, in taking note of a reply Blackmore
made to his critics, chided him with writing
" in language such as Cheapside easily furnished.''

Other physicians, however, resorted to Batson's coffee-house in a professional and not a
poetic way. The character of its frequenters
was described in a lively manner in the first
number of the Connoisseur, published in January, 1754. Having devoted a few sentences
to a neighbouring establishment, the writer
noted that it is " but a short step to a gloomy
class of mortals, not less intent on gain than
the stock-jobbers: I mean the dispensers of
life and death, who flock together like birds of

prey watching for carcasses at Batson's. I
never enter this place, but it serves as a *me-
mento mori* to me. What a formidable assemblage of sable suits, and tremendous perukes!
I have often met here a most intimate acquaintance, whom I have scarce known again; a
sprightly young fellow, with whom I have spent
many a jolly hour; but being just dubbed a
graduate in physic, he has gained such an entire conquest over the risible muscles, that he
hardly vouchsafes at any time to smile. I have
heard him harangue, with all the oracular importance of a veteran, on the possibility of
Canning's subsisting for a whole month on a
few bits of bread; and he is now preparing a
treatise, in which he will set forth a new and
infallible method to prevent the spreading of
the plague from France to England. Batson's
has been reckoned the seat of solemn stupidity:
yet it is not totally devoid of taste and common
sense. They have among them physicians, who
can cope with the most eminent lawyers or
divines; and critics, who can relish the *sal vol-
atile* of a witty composition, or determine how
much fire is requisite to sublimate a tragedy
*secundum artem.*" The house served a useful
purpose at a time when physicians were not
in the habit of increasing their knowledge by

visiting the wards of the hospitals. Batson's was a consulting-house instead, not alone for patients but for the doctors themselves. In this respect, then, it differed from the generally commercial character of the coffee-houses under the shadow of the Exchange.

But there was no mistaking the commercial character of a place like Garraway's in Change Alley. The essayist just quoted is responsible for a story to the effect that when a celebrated actor was cast for the part of Shylock he made daily visits to the coffee-houses near the Exchange that "by a frequent intercourse and conversation with 'the unforeskin'd race,' he might habituate himself to their air and deportment." And the same chronicler goes on to say that personally he was never more diverted than by a visit to Garraway's a few days before the drawing of a lottery. "I not only could read hope, fear, and all the various passions excited by a love of gain, strongly pictured in the faces of those who came to buy; but I remarked with no less delight, the many little artifices made use of to allure adventurers, as well as the visible alterations in the looks of the sellers, according as the demand for tickets gave occasion to raise or lower their price. So deeply were the countenances of

GARRAWAY'S COFFEE-HOUSE.

these bubble-brokers impressed with attention to the main chance, and their minds seemed so dead to all other sensations, that one might almost doubt, where money is out of the case, whether a Jew ' has eyes, hands, organs, dimensions, affections, passions.' '' But lottery tickets were not the only things offered for sale at Garraway's. Wine was a common article of sale there in the early days, and in the latter career of the house it became famous as an auction-room for land and house property.

Thomas Garraway was the founder of the house, the same who is credited with having been the first to retail tea in England. On the success of Pasqua Rosee he was not long, apparently, in adding coffee to his stock, and then turning his place of business into a coffee-house. The house survived till 1866, and even to its latest years kept an old-time character. A frequenter of the place says the ground-floor was furnished with cosy mahogany boxes and seats, and that the ancient practice of covering the floor with sand was maintained to the last.

Two other houses, Jonathan's and Sam's, were notorious for their connection with stock-jobbing. The latter, indeed, figured prom-

inently in the gigantic South Sea Bubble fraud.
And even when that was exposed Sam's continued to be the headquarters of all the get-
rich-quick schemes of the day. Thus in one
issue of a newspaper of 1720 there were two
announcements specially designed to catch the
unwary. One notice told that a book would be
opened for entering into a joint-partnership
" on a thing that will turn to the advantage
of the concerned," and the other was a modest proposal to raise two million pounds for
buying and improving the Fens of Lincolnshire.

Jonathan's is incidentally described by Addison as " the general mart of stock-jobbers,"
and in that amusing account of himself to which
he devoted the first number of the Spectator
he explained that he had been taken for a merchant on the exchange, " and sometimes passed
for a Jew in the assembly of stock-jobbers at
Jonathan's." Half a century later than these
allusions the Annual Register recorded a case
tried at the Guildhall arising out of an assault
at this coffee-house. It seems that the master,
Mr. Ferres, pushed the plaintiff, one Isaac
Renoux, out of his house, for which he was
fined one shilling damages on it being proved
at the trial that " the house had been a market,

MAD DOG IN A COFFEE-HOUSE.
(*From a Rowlandson Caricature.*)

time out of mind, for buying and selling government securities.''

Such houses as John's in Birchin Lane and the Jerusalem coffee-house, which was situated in a court off Cornhill, were typical places of resort for merchants trading to distant parts of the world. One of Rowlandson's lively caricatures, that of a '' Mad Dog in a Coffee-House,'' is a faithful representation of the interior of one of those houses. A bill on the wall shows how they were used for the publication of shipping intelligence, that particular placard giving details of the sailing of '' The Cerebus '' for the Brazils. In a private letter of July 30th, 1715, is an account of an exciting incident which had its origin in the Jerusalem coffee-house. At that time England was in a state of commotion over the Jacobite insurrection and the excitement seems to have turned the head of a Captain Montague, who was reputed to be '' a civil sober man,'' of good principles and in good circumstances. He had entered the Jerusalem coffee-house on the previous day, as the letter relates, and, without any provocation, '' of a sudden struck a gentleman who knew him a severe blow on the eye; immediately after, drawing his sword, ran out through the alley cross Cornhill still with it drawn; and at the South entrance of the Exchange uttered words to this effect, that he was come in the face of the Sun to proclaim James the third King of England, and that only he was heir.'' Whereupon he knocked down another gentleman, who, however, had sense enough to see that the captain was out of his mind and called for assistance to secure him. It took half a dozen men to hold him in the coach which carried him to a magistrate, who promptly committed him to a madhouse.

Tom's coffee-house was situated in the same thoroughfare as John's. This was the resort affected by Garrick on his occasional visits to the city, and is also thought to have been the house frequented by Chatterton. In a letter to his sister that ill-fated poet excused the haphazard nature of his epistle he was writing her from Tom's on the plea that there was '' such a noise of business and politics in the room.'' He explained that his present business — the concocting of squibs, tales and songs on the events of the day — obliged him to frequent places of the best resort.

In view of its subsequent career no coffee-house of the city proper was of so much importance as that founded by Edward Lloyd.

TOM'S COFFEE-HOUSE.

He first appears in the history of old London
as the keeper of a coffee-house in Tower Street
in 1688, but about four years later he removed
to Lombard Street in close proximity to the
Exchange, and his house gradually became the
recognized centre of shipbroking and marine
insurance business, for which the corporation
still bearing the name of Lloyd's is renowned
all over the world.

Two pictures of Lloyd's as it was in the first
decade of the eighteenth century are to be
found in the gallery of English literature, one
from the pen of Steele, the other from that of
Addison.    The first is in the form of a petition
to Isaac Bickerstaff, Esq., from the customers
of the house, and begged that he would use his
influence to get other coffee-houses to adopt a
custom which prevailed at Lloyd's.    Great
scandal, it seems, had been caused by coffee-
house orators of the irresponsible order.    Such
nuisances were not tolerated at Lloyd's.    The
petitioners explained — and by inference the
explanation preserves a record of the internal
economy of the house — that at Lloyd's a servant was deputed to ascend the pulpit in the
room and read the news on its arrival, '' while
the whole audience are sipping their respective
liquors.''    The application of the petition lay

in the suggestion that this method should be adopted in all coffee-houses, and that if any one wished to orate at large on any item of the news of the day he should be obliged to ascend the pulpit and make his comments in a formal manner.

Evidently the pulpit at Lloyd's was a settled institution. It played a conspicuous part in that ludicrous incident which Addison describes at his own expense. It was his habit, he explained, to jot down from time to time brief hints such as could be expanded into Spectator papers, and a sheetful of such hints would naturally look like a " rhapsody of nonsense " to any one save the writer himself. Such a sheet he accidentally dropped in Lloyd's one day, and before he missed it the boy of the house had it in his hand and was carrying it around in search of its owner. But Addison did not know that until it was too late. Many of the customers had glanced at its contents, which had caused them so much merriment that the boy was ordered to ascend the pulpit and read the paper for the amusement of the company at large. " The reading of this paper," continues Addison, " made the whole coffee-house very merry; some of them concluded that it was written by a madman, and others by some-

LLOYD'S COFFEE-HOUSE.

body that had been taking notes out of the Spectator. One who had the appearance of a very substantial citizen told us, with several political winks and nods, that he wished there was no more in the paper than what was expressed in it: that for his part, he looked upon the dromedary, the gridiron, and the barber's pole, to signify something more than what was usually meant by those words: and that he thought the coffee-man could not do better than to carry the paper to one of the secretaries of state.'' In the midst of the numerous other comments, wise and otherwise, Addison reached for the paper, pretended to look it over, shook his head twice or thrice, and then twisted it into a match and lit his pipe with it. The ruse diverted suspicion, especially as Addison applied himself to his pipe and the paper he was reading with seeming unconcern. And he consoled the readers of the Spectator with the reflection that he had already used more than half the hints on that unfortunate sheet of notes.

Since those almost idyllic days, Lloyd's has played a notable part in the life of the nation. At its headquarters in the Royal Exchange building are preserved many interesting relics of the history of the institution. From a simple coffee-house open to all and sundry, it has developed into the shipping-exchange of the world, employing 1,500 agents in all parts of the globe.

# CHAPTER II

IF there was a certain incongruity in the physicians having their special coffee-house in the heart of the city, there was none in clerics affecting the St. Paul's coffee-house under the shadow of the cathedral of that name. This being the chief church of the metropolis, notwithstanding the greater historic importance of Westminster Abbey, it naturally became the religious centre of London so far as clergymen were concerned. But the frequenters of this house were of a mixed type. That historian of Batson's who was quoted in the previous chapter, related that after leaving its dismal vicinity he was glad to " breathe the pure air in St. Paul's coffee-house," but he was obliged to add that as he entertained the highest veneration for the clergy he could not " contemplate the magnificence of the cathedral without reflecting on the abject condition of those ' tatter'd crapes,' who are said to ply here for an occasional burial or sermon, with the same reg-

ularity as the happier drudges who salute us
with the cry of ' coach, sir,' or ' chair, your
honour.' '' Somewhat late in the eighteenth
century St. Paul's coffee-house had a distinguished visitor in the person of Benjamin
Franklin, who here made the acquaintance of
Richard Price, that philosophical dissenting
divine whose pamphlet on American affairs is
said to have had no inconsiderable part in de-
termining Americans to declare their independence. The fact that Dr. Price frequented the
St. Paul's coffee-house is sufficient proof that
its clients were not restricted to clergymen of
the established church.

More miscellaneous was the patronage of
Child's, another resort in St. Paul's Churchyard. It is sometimes described as having been
a clerical house like the St. Paul's, and one
reference in the Spectator gives some support
to that view. The writer told how a friend of
his from the country had expressed astonishment at seeing London so crowded with doctors
of divinity, necessitating the explanation that
not all the persons in scarfs were of that dignity, for, this authority on London life continued, '' a young divine, after his first degree
in the university, usually comes hither only to
show himself; and on that occasion, is apt to

think he is but half equipped with a gown and cassock for his public appearance, if he hath not the additional ornament of a scarf of the first magnitude to entitle him to the appellation of Doctor from his landlady and the boy at Child's." There is another allusion to the house in the Spectator. "Sometimes I " — the writer is Addison — " smoke a pipe at Child's, and while I seem attentive to nothing but the Postman, overhear the conversation of every table in the room." Apart from such decided lay patrons as Addison, Child's could also claim a large constituency among the medical and learned men of the day.

Notwithstanding its ecclesiastical name, the Chapter coffee-house in Paul's Alley was not a clerical resort. By the middle of the eighteenth century it had come to be recognized as the rendezvous of publishers and booksellers. " The conversation here," to appeal to the Connoisseur once more, " naturally turns upon the newest publications; but their criticisms are somewhat singular. When they say a good book, they do not mean to praise the style or sentiment, but the quick and extensive sale of it. That book in the phrase of the Conger is best, which sells most; and if the demand for Quarles should be greater than for Pope, he would have the highest place on the rubric-post. There are also many parts of every work liable to their remarks, which fall not within the notice of less accurate observers. A few nights ago I saw one of these gentlemen take up a sermon, and after seeming to peruse it for some time with great attention, he declared that ' it was very good English.' The reader will judge whether I was most surprised or diverted, when I discovered that he was not commending the purity and elegance of the diction, but the beauty of the type; which, it seems, is known among printers by that appellation. We must not, however, think the members of the Conger strangers to the deeper parts of literature; for as carpenters, smiths, masons, and all mechanics, smell of the trade they labour at, booksellers take a peculiar turn from their connexions with books and authors.''

Could the writer of that gentle satire have looked forward about a quarter of a century he would have had knowledge on which to have based a greater eulogy of the Congers. It should be explained perhaps that Conger was the name of a club of booksellers founded in 1715 for co-operation in the issuing of expensive works. Booklovers of the present genera-

tion may often wonder at the portly folios of
bygone generations, and marvel especially that
they could have been produced at a profit when
readers were so comparatively few. Many of
those folios owed their existence to the scheme
adopted by the members of the Conger, a
scheme whereby several publishers shared in
the production of a costly work.

Such a sharing of expense and profit was
entered into at that meeting at the Chapter
coffee-house which led to Dr. Johnson's
" Lives of the English Poets." The London
booksellers of that time were alarmed at the
invasion of what they called their literary
property by a Scottish publisher who had pre-
sumed to bring out an edition of the English
poets. To counteract this move from Edin-
burgh the decision was reached to print " an
elegant and accurate edition of all the English
poets of reputation, from Chaucer down to the
present time." The details were thoroughly
debated at the Chapter coffee-house, and a dep-
utation was appointed to wait upon Dr. Johnson, to secure his services in editing the series.
Johnson accepted the task, " seemed exceedingly pleased " that it had been offered him,
and agreed to carry it through for a fee of two
hundred pounds. His moderation astonished

Malone; " had he asked one thousand, or even fifteen hundred guineas, the booksellers, who knew the value of his name, would doubtless have readily given it."

But writers of books as well as makers and sellers of books could be found on occasion within the portals of the Chapter coffee-house. Two memories of Goldsmith, neither of them pleasant, are associated with the house. One is concerned with his acceptance of an invitation to dinner here with Charles Lloyd, who, at the end of the meal, walked off and left his guest to pay the bill. The other incident introduces the vicious William Kenrick, that hack-writer who slandered Goldsmith without cause on so many occasions. Shortly after the publication of one of his libels in the press, Kenrick was met by Goldsmith accidentally in the Chapter and made to admit that he had lied. But no sooner had the poet left the house than the cowardly retractor began his abuse again to the company at large.

Chatterton, too, frequented the house in his brief days of London life. " I am quite familiar at the Chapter Coffee-House," he wrote his mother, " and know all the geniuses there." And five years later there is this picture of the democratic character of the resort from the shocked pen of one who had been attracted thither by the report of its large library and select company: " Here I saw a specimen of English freedom. A whitesmith in his apron and some of his saws under his arm came in, sat down, and called for his glass of punch and the paper, both which he used with as much ease as a lord. Such a man in Ireland and, I suppose, in France too, and almost any other country, would not have shown himself with his hat on, nor any way, unless sent for by some gentleman.''

Perhaps the most interesting association of the Chapter coffee-house was that destined to come to it when its race was nearly run. On a July evening in 1848 the waiter was somewhat startled at the appearance of two simply-dressed, slight and timid-looking ladies seeking accommodation. Women guests were not common at the Chapter. But these two were strangers to London; they had never before visited the great city; and the only hostelry they knew was the Chapter they had heard their father speak about. So it was to the Chapter that Charlotte and Anne Brontë went when they visited London to clear up a difficulty with their publishers, Smith and Elder. Mrs. Gaskell describes the house as it was in those

July days. '' It had the appearance of a dwell-
ing-house two hundred years old or so, such as
one sometimes sees in ancient country towns;
the ceilings of the small rooms were low, and
had heavy beams running across them; the
walls were wainscoted breast-high; the stairs
were shallow, broad, and dark, taking up much
space in the centre of the house. The gray-
haired elderly man who officiated as waiter
seems to have been touched from the very first
by the quiet simplicity of the two ladies, and
·he tried to make them feel comfortable and at
home in the long, low, dingy room upstairs.
The high, narrow windows looked into the
gloomy Row; the sisters, clinging together in
the most remote window-seat (as Mr. Smith
tells me he found them when he came that Saturday evening), could see nothing of motion
or of change in the grim, dark houses opposite, so near and close, although the whole
breadth of the Row was between.'' If it were
only for the sake of those startled sisters from
the desolate Yorkshire moors one could wish
that the Chapter coffee-house were still standing. But it is not. Nor are there any vestiges
remaining of the St. Paul's or Child's.

Nor will the pilgrim fare better in the adjacent thoroughfare of Ludgate Hill. Not far

down that highway could once be found the London coffee-house, which Benjamin Franklin frequented, and where that informal club for philosophical discussions of which Dr. Priestly was the chairman held its social meetings. The London continued in repute among American visitors for many years. When Charles Robert Leslie, the artist, reached London in 1811 intent on prosecuting his art studies, he tells how he stopped for a few days " at the London Coffee-house on Ludgate Hill, with Mr. Inskeep and other Americans."

Further west, in the yard of that Belle Sauvage inn described in an earlier chapter, there existed in 1730 a coffee-house known as Wills', but of which nothing save one somewhat pathetic incident is on record. The memory of this incident is preserved among the manuscripts of the Duke of Portland in the form of two letters to the Earl of Oxford. The first letter is anonymous. It was written to the earl on February 8th, 1730, in the interests of William Oldisworth, that unfortunate miscellaneous writer whose adherence to the Stuart cause helped, along with a liking for tavern-life, to mar his career. This anonymous correspondent had learnt that Oldisworth was in a starving condition, out of clothes likewise, and labouring under many infirmities. '' Though no man has deserved better of his country, yet is none more forgot.'' The letter also hinted at the fact that Oldisworth would not complain, nor suffer any one to do that office for him. But the writer was wise enough to enclose the address of the man in whose behalf he made so adroit an appeal, that address being Wills' coffee-house in the Belle Sauvage yard.

Edward Harley, that Earl of Oxford who preferred above all things to surround himself with poets and men of letters, and whose generosity helped to bring about his financial ruin, was not the man to ignore a letter of that kind. Some assistance was speedily on its way to Will's coffee-house, for on February 21st Oldisworth was penning an epistle which was to '' wait in all humility on your Lordship to return you my best thanks for the late kind and generous favour you conferred on me.'' He sent the earl an ancient manuscript as token of his gratitude, explained that he was ignorant of the one who had written in his behalf, and for the rest was determined to keep his present station, low as it was, with content and resignation. The inference is that Will's coffee-house was but a lowly and inexpensive abode and hence it is not surprising that it makes so small a showing in the annals of old London.

At the western end of Fleet Street the passer-by cannot fail to be attracted by the picturesque, timbered house which faces Chancery Lane. This unique survival of the past, which has been carefully restored within recent years, has often been described as " Formerly the Palace of Henry VIII and Cardinal Wolsey.'' Another legend is that the room on the first floor was the council-chamber of the Duchy of Cornwall under Henry, the eldest son of James I. More credible is the statement that Nando's coffee-house was once kept under this roof. In the days when he was a briefless barrister, Thurlow was a frequent visitor here, attracted, it is said, as were so many more of the legal fraternity, by the dual merits of the punch and the physical charms of the landlady's daughter. Miss Humphries was, as a punster put it, " always admired at the bar by the bar.'' The future Lord Chancellor had no cause to regret his patronage of Nando's. So convincingly did he one day prove his skill in argument that a stranger present bestirred himself, and successfully, to have the young advocate retained in a famous law case of the time, an apppointment which led to Thurlow's

becoming acquainted with the Duchess of
Queensbury, with after important results.

During those stirring days when the
" Wilkes and Liberty " riots caused such in-
tense excitement in London, one worthy merchant of the city found Nando's a valuable
place of refuge. Arrangements had been made
for a body of merchants and tradesmen of the
city to wait on George III at St. James's with
a loyal address and as token of their sympathy
with the position assumed by that obstinate
monarch. But on the night before handbills
had been scattered broadcast desiring all true
and loyal subjects to meet on the following day
and form a procession towards the city, taking
particular care " not to interfere with the Merchants going to St. James's." The handbill
had the desired effect. The cavalcade of merchants was scattered in confusion long before
it reached Temple-bar, and isolated members of
the party, few in number, did their best to
reach the royal palace by roundabout ways.
Even so they were a sorry spectacle. For the
other loyal subjects of the king had liberally
bespattered them with mud. Nor was this the
most disconcerting feature of their situation.
Having reached the presence of their sover-

eign it was certainly annoying that they could
not present the address which had brought
them into all this trouble. But the fact was the
address was missing. It had been committed
to the care of a Mr. Boehm, and he was not
present. As a matter of fact Mr. Boehm had
fled for refuge to Nando's coffee-house, leaving
the precious address under the seat of his
coach. The rioters were not aware of that
fact, and it seems that the document was eventually recovered, after his Majesty had been
" kept waiting till past five."

There is a fitness in the fact that as Thurlow's name is linked with Nando's coffee-house
so Cowper's memory is associated with the
adjacent establishment known as Dick's. The
poet and the lawyer had been fellow clerks in
a solicitor's office, had spent their time in " gig-
gling and making giggle " with the daughters
of Cowper's uncle, and been boon friends in
many ways. The future poet foretold the fame
of his friend, and extorted a playful promise
that when he was Lord Chancellor he would
provide for his fellow clerk. The prophecy
came true, but the promise was forgotten.
Thurlow did not even deign to notice the poetical address of his old companion, nor did he

acknowledge the receipt of his first volume of
verse. " Be great," the indignant poet
wrote —

> " Be great, be fear'd, be envied, be admired;
> To fame as lasting as the earth pretend,
> But not hereafter to the name of friend! "

For Thurlow the ungrateful, Nando's was associated with his first step up the ladder of
success; for Cowper, Dick's was the scene of
an agony that he remembered to his dying day.
For it was while he was at breakfast in this
coffee-house that he was seized with one of his
painful delusions. A letter he read in a paper
he interpreted as a satire on himself, and he
threw the paper down and rushed from the
room with a resolve either to find some house
in which to die or some ditch where he could
poison himself unseen.

Reference has already been made to the
Rainbow as one of the famous taverns of Fleet
Street, and also to the fact that it was a coffee-
house ere it became a tavern. But somehow
it was as a coffee-house that it was usually
regarded. It is so described in 1679, in 1708,
in 1710, and in 1736. Under the earliest date
it appears as playing a part in the astounding
story of Titus Oates. One of the victims of

that unrivalled perjurer was Sir Philip Lloyd, whom Oates declared had " in a sort of bravery presented himself in the Rainbow coffee-house, and declared he did not believe any kind of plot against the King's person, notwithstanding what any had said to the contrary." This was sufficient to arouse the enmity of the wily Oates, who had the knight haled before the council and closely examined. Sir Philip explained that he had only said he knew of no other than a fantastic plot, but, as a contemporary letter puts it, " Oates had got ready four shrewd coffee-drinkers, then present, who swore the matter point blank." So the perjurer won again, and Sir Philip was suspended during the king's pleasure as the outcome of his Rainbow coffee-house speech.

But there is a pleasanter memory with which to bid this famous resort farewell. It is enshrined in a letter of the early eighteenth century, wishing that the recipient might, if he could find a leisure evening, drop into the Rainbow, where he would meet several friends of the writer in the habit of frequenting that house, gentlemen of great worth and whom it would be a pleasure to know.

# CHAPTER III

How markedly the coffee-houses of London were differentiated from each other by the opening of the eighteenth century is nowhere more clearly demonstrated than in Steele's first issue of the Tatler. After hoodwinking his readers into thinking he had a correspondent " in all parts of the known and knowing world," he informed them that it was his intention to print his news under " such dates of places " as would provide a key to the matter they were to expect. Thus, " all accounts of gallantry, pleasure, and entertainment, shall be under the article of White's Chocolate-house; poetry, under that of Will's Coffee-house; learning, under the title of the Grecian; foreign and domestic news, you shall have from Saint James's Coffee-house, and what else I have to offer on any other subject shall be dated from my own apartment."

Several days elapsed ere there was anything to report from the Grecian coffee-house, which

was situated in Devereux Court, Strand, and
derived its name from the fact that it was kept
by a Greek named Constantine. When it does
make its appearance, however, the information
given under its name is strictly in keeping with
the character Steele gave the house. '' While
other parts of the town are amused with the
present actions, we generally spend the evening
at this table in inquiries into antiquity, and
think anything news which gives us new knowledge.'' And then follow particulars of how
the learned Grecians had been amusing themselves by trying to arrange the actions of the
Iliad in chronological order. This task seems
to have been accomplished in a friendly manner, but there was an occasion when a point of
scholarship had a less placid ending. Two gentlemen, so the story goes, who were constant
companions, drifted into a dispute at the Grecian one evening over the accent of a Greek
word. The argument was protracted and at
length grew angry. As neither could convince
the other by mere words, the resolve was taken
to decide the matter by swords. So the erst-
while friends stepped out into the court, and,
after a few passes, one of them was run through
the body, and died on the spot.

That the Grecian maintained its character

as the resort of learned disputants may be inferred from the heated discussions which took place within its walls when Burke confused the public with his imitation of the style and language of Bolinbroke in his "Vindication of Natural Society." All the critics were completely deceived. And Charles Macklin in particular distinguished himself by rushing into the Grecian one evening, flourishing a copy of the pamphlet, and declaring, "Sir, this must be Harry Bolinbroke; I know him by his cloven foot!"

Even if it were not for that fatal duel between the two Greek scholars, there are anecdotes to show that some frequenters of the house were of an aggressive nature. There is the story, for example, of the bully who insisted upon a particular seat, but came in one evening and found it occupied by another.

"Who is that in my seat?"

"I don't know, sir," replied the waiter.

"Where is the hat I left on it?"

"He put it in the fire."

"Did he? damnation! but a fellow who would do *that* would not mind flinging *me* after it!" and with that he disappeared.

Men of science as well as scholars gave liberal patronage to the Grecian. It was a com-

GRECIAN COFFEE-HOUSE.

mon thing for meetings of the Royal Society
to be continued in a social way at this coffee-
house, the president, Sir Isaac Newton, being
frequently of the parties. Hither, too, came
Professor Halley, the great astronomer, to
meet his friends on his weekly visit to London
from Oxford, and Sir Hans Sloane, that zealous collector of curiosities, was often to be met
at the Grecian. Nor did the house wholly lack
patrons of the pen, for Goldsmith, among others, used the resort quite frequently.

Goldsmith was also a faithful customer of
George's coffee-house which was situated close
to the Grecian. This was one of the places to
which he had his letters addressed, and the
house figures in one of his essays as the resort
of a certain young fellow who, whenever he had
occasion to " ask his friend for a guinea, used
to prelude his request as if he wanted two hundred, and talked so familiarly of large sums "
that no one would have imagined him ever to
be in need of small ones. It was the same
young fellow at George's who, whenever he
wanted credit for a new suit from his tailor,
used to dress himself in laced clothes in which
to give the order, for he had found that to appear shabby on such occasions defeated the
purpose he had in view.

204 Inns and Taverns of Old London

Most likely Goldsmith sketched his certain young fellow from life. There was another frequenter of the place who would have provided an original for another character study. This was that Sir James Lowther, afterwards Earl of Lonsdale, of whom the story is told that having one day changed a piece of silver in the coffee-house, and paid twopence for his cup of coffee, he was helped into his carriage and driven home, only to return a little later to call attention to the fact that he had been given a bad halfpenny in his change and demand another in exchange. All this was in keeping with the character of the man, for despite the fact that he had an income of forty thousand pounds a year, he was notorious for his miserly conduct, and would not pay even his just debts.

There was another legend connected with George's which Horace Walpole ought not to have destroyed. In telling a correspondent of the amusement with which he had been reading Shenstone's letters, he took ocasion to characterize as vulgar and devoid of truth an anecdote told of his father, Lord Orford. This was the story that his father, " sitting in George's, was asked to contribute to a figure of himself that was to be beheaded by the mob. I do re-

member something like it,'' Walpole continued,
'' but it happened to myself. I met a mob, just
after my father was put out, in Hanover-
square, and drove up to it to know what was
the matter. They were carrying about a figure
of my sister.'' Walpole traded so largely in
traditional stories himself that it was ungrateful of him to spoil so good a one.

On the way to Bedford Street, where Wildman's coffee-house was situated, the pilgrim
will pass the site of the Somerset coffee-house,
which was notable in its day from the fact that
some of the letters of Junius were left here,
the waiters being paid tips for taking them in.
Wildman's was notorious as being the favourite headquarters of the supporters of John
Wilkes, and hence the lines of Churchill:

" Each dish at Wildman's of sedition smacks;
    Blasphemy may be Gospel at Almacks.
        Peace, good Discretion, peace, — thy fears are vain;
    Ne'er will I herd with Wildman's factious train."

Among the notable coffee-houses of Covent
Garden were the Bedford, King's, Rawthmell's
and Tom's. The first was situated under the
Piazza, and could count among its patrons
Fielding, Pope, Sheridan, Churchill, Garrick,
Foote, Quinn, Collins, Horace Walpole and

others.  Its characters, according to the Connoisseur, afforded a greater variety of nearly
the same type as those to be found at George's.
It was, this authority asserts, crowded every
night with men of parts.  Almost every one to
be met there was a polite scholar and a wit.
" Jokes and *bon mots* are echoed from box to
box; every branch of literature is critically
examined, and the merit of every production
of the press, or performance at the theatres,
weighed and determined.  This school (to
which I am myself indebted for a great part
of my education, and in which, though un-
worthy, I am now arrived at the honour of being a public lecturer) has bred up many authors, to the amazing entertainment and instruction of their readers."

But the Bedford coffee-house has a more sen-
sational association.  It was here, according
to Horace Walpole, that James Hackman spent
his last few hours of freedom ere he murdered
Martha Ray as she was leaving Covent Garden
theatre on the night of April 17th, 1779.  No
tragedy of that period caused so great a sen-
sation.  Miss Ray had for some years been the
mistress of the Earl of Sandwich, at whose
house Hackman first met and fell in love with
her.  There are good reasons for believing that

his love was returned for a time, but that afterwards Miss Ray determined to continue in her irregular relation with the nobleman. On learning that his suit was wholly hopeless, Hackman conceived the plan which had so fatal an ending. The question as to whether the fact that he provided himself with two pistols was proof that he intended to take his own life as well as that of Miss Ray was the theme of a warm discussion between Dr. Johnson and his friend Beauclerk, the latter arguing that it was not, and the former maintaining with equal confidence that it was.

King's coffee-house was nothing more than a humble shed, an early representative of the peripatetic coffee-stall which is still a common sight of London streets in the early morning. Kept by a Thomas King who absconded from Eton because he feared that his fellowship would be denied him, it was the resort of every rake according to Fielding, and, in the phrase of another, was " well known to all gentlemen to whom beds are unknown." On the other hand Rawthmell's was an exceedingly fashionable house, and witnessed the founding of the Society of Arts in 1754. It had another claim to slight distinction as being the resort of Dr. John Armstrong, the poet of the " Art of Pre-

serving Health," and a man so generally un-
sociable that one acquaintance described him
as having a rooted aversion against the whole
human race, except a few friends, and they
were dead!

Judging from a poetical allusion of 1703,
Tom's coffee-house was at that time a political
resort. A little later it was distinguished for
its fashionable gatherings after the theatre. A
traveller through England in 1722 records that
at Tom's there was " playing at Picket, and
the best of conversation till midnight. Here
you will see blue and green ribbons and Stars
sitting familiarly, and talking with the same
freedom as if they had left their quality and
degrees of distance at home." But the most
interesting picture of this house is given by
William Till. He writes: " The house in
which I reside was the famous Tom's Coffee-
House, memorable in the reign of Queen Anne;
and for more than half a century afterwards:
the room in which I conduct my business as a
coin dealer is that which, in 1764, by a guinea
subscription among nearly seven hundred of
the nobility, foreign ministers, gentry, and
geniuses of the age — was made the card-room,
and place of meeting for many of the now illustrious dead, and remained so till 1768, when a

voluntary subscription among its members induced Mr. Haines, the then proprietor, to take in the next door westward, as a coffee-room; and the whole floor *en suite* was constructed into card and conversation rooms.'' It seems that the house took its name originally from the first landlord, a Captain Thomas West, who, driven distracted by the agony of gout, committed suicide by throwing himself from his own windows.

Interesting, as has been seen, as are the associations which cluster round the coffee-houses of this district already mentioned, their fame is slight compared with the glory of the houses known as Will's and Button's.

Macaulay has given us a glowing picture of the wits' room on the first floor at Will's. Through the haze of tobacco smoke with which he filled the apartment we can see earls, and clergymen, and Templars, and university lads, and hack-workers. We can hear, too, the animated tones in which discussions are being carried on, discussions as to whether '' Paradise Lost '' should have been written in rhyme, and many another literary question of little interest in these modern days. But, after all, the eye does not seek out earls, or clergy, or the rest; nor does the ear wish to fill itself with the sound of their voices. There is but one face, but one voice at Will's in which the interest of this time is as keen as the interest of the seventeenth century. That face and voice were the face and voice of John Dryden.

Exactly in what year Dryden first chose this coffee-house as his favourite resort is unknown. He graduated at Cambridge in 1654, and is next found in London lodging with a bookseller for whom he worked as a hack-writer. By 1662 he had become a figure of some consequence in London life, and a year later his first play was acted at the King's theatre. Then, in the pages of Pepys, he is seen as the centre of that group of the wits which he was to dominate for a generation. "In Covent Garden to-night," wrote Pepys under the date February 3rd, 1664, "going to fetch home my wife, I stopped at the great Coffee-house there, where I never was before; where Dryden, the poet, I knew at Cambridge, and all the wits of the town, and Harris the player, and Mr. Hoole, of our college. And, had I had time then, or could at other times, it will be good coming hither, for there, I perceive, is very witty and pleasant discourse."

With what persistence this tradition survived, the tradition of Dryden as the arbiter

JOHN DRYDEN.

of literary criticism at Will's is illustrated by
the story told by Dr. Johnson. When he was
a young man he had a desire to write the life
of Dryden, and as a first step in the gathering
of his materials he applied to the only two
persons then alive who had known him, Swin-
ney and Cibber. But all the assistance the
former could give him was to the effect that
at Will's Coffee-house Dryden had a particular
chair for himself, which was set by the fire in
winter, and removed to the balcony in summer;
and the extent of Cibber's information was
that he remembered the poet as a decent old
man, judge of critical disputes at Will's. But
happily a more detailed picture of Dryden as
the centre of the wits at Will's has survived.
On his first trip to London as a youth of seventeen, Francis Lockier, the future dean of Peter-
borough, although an odd-looking boy of awkward manners, thrust himself into the coffee-
house that he might gaze on the celebrated men
of the day. '' The second time that ever I was
there,'' Lockier said, '' Mr. Dryden was speaking of his own things, as he frequently did,
especially of such as had been lately published.
' If anything of mine is good,' says he, ' 'tis
Mac Flecknoe; and I value myself the more
upon it, because it is the first piece of ridicule

written in Heroics.' On hearing this, I plucked up my spirit to say, in a voice just loud enough to be heard, that ' Mac Flecknoe was a very fine poem; but that I had not imagined it to be the first that ever was writ that way.' On this, Dryden turned short upon me, as surprised at my interposing; asked how long I had been a dabbler in poetry; and added, with a smile, ' Pray, sir, what is it that you did imagine to have been writ so before? ' I named Boileau's *Lutrin,* and Tassoni's *Secchia Rapita,* which I had read, and knew Dryden had borrowed some strokes from each. ' 'Tis true,' said Dryden, ' I had forgot them.' A little after Dryden went out, and in going spoke to me again, and desired me to come and see him next day. I was highly delighted with the invitation; went to see him accordingly, and was well acquainted with him after, as long as he lived.''

As a companion to this picture in prose there is the poetic vignette which Prior and Montague inserted in their '' Country Mouse and the City Mouse,'' written in burlesque of Dryden's '' Hind and Panther.''

'' Then on they jogg'd; and since an hour of talk
Might cut a banter on the tedious walk,

As I remember, said the sober mouse,
I've heard much talk of the Wits' Coffee-house;
Thither, says Brindle, thou shalt go and see
Priests supping coffee, sparks and poets tea;
Here rugged frieze, there quality well drest,
These baffling the grand Senior, those the Test,
And there shrewd guesses made, and reasons given,
That human laws were never made in heaven;
But, above all, what shall oblige thy sight,
And fill thy eyeballs with a vast delight,
Is the poetic judge of sacred wit,
Who does i' th' darkness of his glory sit;
And as the moon who first receives the light,
With which she makes these nether regions bright,
So does he shine, reflecting from afar
The rays he borrowed from a better star;
For rules, which from Corneille and Rapin flow,
Admired by all the scribbling herd below,
From French tradition while he does dispense
Unerring truths, 'tis schism, a damned offence,
To question his, or trust your private sense."

Dryden appears to have visited Will's every
day. His rule of life was to devote his morn-
ings to writing at home, where he also dined,
and then to spend the remainder of the day at
the coffee-house, which he did not leave till late.
There came a night for the poet when this reg-
ularity of habit had unpleasant consequences.
A Newsletter of December 23rd, 1679, tells the
story: " On Thursday night last Mr. Dryden,

the poet, comeing from the coffee-house in
Covent Garden, was set upon by three or four
fellows, and very soarly beaten, but likewise
very much cutt and wounded with a sword. It
is imagined that this has happened to him because of a late satyr that is laid at his door,
though he positively disowned it.'' The com-
piler of that paragraph was correct in his sur-
mise. The hired ruffians who assaulted the
solitary poet on that December night were in
the pay of Lord Rochester, who had taken um-
brage at a publication which, although not written by Dryden, had been printed with such a
title-page as suggested that it was his work.
A reward of fifty pounds was offered for the
discovery of the perpetrators of this outrage,
but to no effect. Still it is some consolation to
know that the cowardly Rochester immediately
fell under suspicion as the author of the attack.
Less reprehensible is the story told of a Mr.
Finch, '' an ingenious young gentleman,'' who,
nearly a decade later, '' meeting with Mr. Dryden in a coffee-house in London, publickly before all the company wished him joy of his *new*
religion. ' Sir,' said Dryden, ' you are very
much mistaken; my religion is the *old* religion.' ' Nay,' replied the other, ' whatever it
be in itself I am sure "tis new to you, for within

JOSEPH ADDISON.

these three days you had no religion at
all.' ''

Dryden died in 1700 and for a time Will's
maintained its position as the resort of the
poets.  Did not Steele say that all his accounts
of poetry in the Tatler would appear under the
name of that house?  But the supremacy of
Will's was slowly undermined, so that even in
the Tatler the confession had soon to be made
that the place was very much altered since
Dryden's time.  The change had been for the
worse.  '' Where you used to see songs, epi-
grams, and satires in the hands of every man
you met, you now have only a pack of cards;
and instead of the cavils about the turn of the
expression, the elegance of the style, and the
like, the learned now dispute only about the
truth of the game.''  This is all confirmed by
that traveller who took notes in London in
1722, and found there was playing at Picket
at Will's after the theatre.

Addison was the chief cause of this transformation.  And Steele helped him.  The fact
is that about 1713 Addison set up coffee-house
keeper himself.  That is to say, he was the
means of getting one Daniel Button, once servant with the Countess of Warwick, to open such
an establishment in close proximity to Will's.

For Addison to remove his patronage from Will's to Button's meant the transference of the allegiance of the wits of the town also, consequently it soon became known that the wits were gone from the haunt of Dryden to the new resort affected by Addison. And a close scrutiny of the pages of the Guardian will reveal how adroitly Steele aided Addison's plan. Thus, the issue of the Guardian for June 17th, 1713, was devoted to the habits of coffee-house orators, and especially to the objectionable practice so many had of seizing a button on a listener's coat and twisting it off in the course of argument. This habit, however, was more common in the city than in the West-end coffee-houses; indeed, Steele added, the company at Will's was so refined that one might argue and be argued with and not be a button the poorer. All that delightful nonsense paved the way for a letter in the next number of the Guardian, a letter purporting to come from Daniel Button of Button's coffee-house.

"I have observed," so ran the epistle, "that this day you made mention of Will's Coffee-house, as a place where people are too polite to hold a man in discourse by the button. Everybody knows your honour frequents this house; therefore they will taken an advantage

SIR RICHARD STEELE.

against me, and say, if my company was as
civil as that at Will's, you would say so: therefore pray your honour do not be afraid of
doing me justice, because people would think
it may be a conceit below you on this occasion
to name the name of Your humble servant,
Daniel Button.'' And then there is this naïve
postscript: '' The young poets are in the back
room, and take their places as you directed.''

Nor did that end the plot. A few days later
Steele found another occasion to mention Button's. His plan this time was to concoct a letter from one Hercules Crabtree, who offered
his services as lion-catcher to the Guardian,
and incidentally mentioned that he already possessed a few trophies which he wished to present to Button's coffee-house. This lion business paved the way for Addison's interference
in the clever scheme to divert the wits from
Will's. Hence that paper of the Guardian
which he wound up by announcing that it was
his intention to erect, as a letter-box for the
receipt of contributions, a lion's head in imitation of those he had described in Venice,
through which all the private intelligence of
that commonwealth was said to pass.

'' This head,'' he explained, '' is to open a
most wide and voracious mouth, which shall

take in such letters and papers as are conveyed to me by my correspondents, it being my resolution to have a particular regard to all such matters as come to my hands through the mouth of the lion. There will be under it a box, of which the key will be kept in my own custody, to receive such papers as are dropped into it. Whatever the lion swallows I shall digest for the use of the public. This head requires some time to finish, the workman being resolved to give it several masterly touches, and to represent it as ravenous as possible. It will be set up in Button's coffee-house in Covent-garden, who is directed to shew the way to the lion's head, and to instruct young authors how to convey his works into the mouth of it with safety and secrecy.''

That lion's head was no myth. A fortnight later the leonine letter-box was actually placed in position at Button's, and, after doing service there for some years, was used by Dr. Hill when editing the Inspector. It was sold in 1804, the notice of the sale in the Annual Register stating that '' The admirable gilt lion's head letter-box, which was formerly at Button's coffee-house, and in which the valuable original copy of the Guardian was received, was yesterday knocked down at the Shake-

LION'S HEAD AT BUTTON'S COFFEE-HOUSE.

.

speare-tavern, Covent-garden, to Mr. Richardson, for seventeen pounds ten shillings.'' It
changed hands again in more recent times, and
is now the property of the Duke of Bedford,
who preserves it at Woburn.

For some months after the installation of the
lion's head at Button's, constant references are
made in the Guardian to that unique letter-box,
Addison being mainly responsible for the
quaint conceits which helped to keep attention
on the house where it was placed. In the final
number of the Guardian there is a lively letter
in response to an attack on masquerading
which had reached the public via the lion's
head. '' My present business,'' the epistle ran,
'' is with the lion; and since this savage has
behaved himself so rudely, I do by these presents challenge him to meet me at the next masquerade, and desire you will give orders to Mr.
Button to bring him thither, in all his terrors,
where, in defence of the innocence of these midnight amusements, I intend to appear against
him, in the habit of Signior Nicolimi, to try the
merits of this cause by single combat.''

But Addison and his lion's head and Steele
were not the only notable figures to be seen at
Button's. Pope was a constant visitor there,
as he was reminded by Cibber in his famous

letter. Those were the days when, in Cibber's phrase, the author of the " Dunciad " was remarkable for his satirical itch of provocation, when there were few upon whom he did not fall in some biting epigram. He so fell upon Ambrose Philips, who forthwith hung a rod up in Button's, and let Pope know that he would use it on him should he ever catch him under that roof. The poet took a more than ample revenge in many a stinging line of satire afterwards.

Pope was cut adrift from Button's through the controversy as to which was the better version of the Iliad, his or Tickell's. As the latter belonged to the Addisonian circle, the opinion at Button's turned in favour of his version, especially as Addison himself thought Tickell had more of Homer than Pope. This ended Pope's patronage of Button's, and, indeed, it was not long ere the glory it had known began to wane. Various causes combined to take away one and another of its leading spirits, and when the much-talked-of Daniel Button passed away in 1730 it was to a pauper's grave. Yet farewell of so famous a house should not be made with so melancholy a story  There is a brighter page in its history, which dates three years earlier. Aaron Hill had been so moved

by the misfortunes of his brother poet, Richard
Savage, that he had penned an appeal on his
behalf and arranged for subscriptions for a
volume of his poems. The subscriptions were
to be left at Button's, and when Savage called
there a few days later he found a sum of seventy guineas awaiting him. Hill may, as has
been asserted, have been a bore of the first
water, but that kindly deed may stand him in
stead of genius.

# CHAPTER IV

SEVERAL favourite coffee-houses might once have been found in the neighbourhood of Charing Cross. One of these bore the name of the Cannon and was much frequented by John Philpot Curran, of whom it was said " there never was so honest an Irishman," and Sir Jonas Barrington, that other Irish judge who was at first intended for the army, but who, on learning that the regiment to which he might be appointed was likely to be sent to America for active service, declined the commission, and requested that it might be bestowed on " some hardier soldier." Evidently Sir Jonas desired no further acquaintance with cannon than was involved in visiting the coffee-house of that name. The legend is that he and Curran affected one particular box at the end of the room, where they might be seen almost any day.

In the same vicinity, but close to the Thamesside, was the coffee-house kept by Alexander Man, and known as Man's. The proprietor had

BRITISH COFFEE-HOUSE.

the distinction of being appointed " coffee, tea, and chocolate-maker " to William III, which gave him a place in the vast army of " By Appointment " tradesmen, and resulted further in his establishment being sometimes described as the Royal Coffee-house. This resort had a third title, Old Man's Coffee-house, to distinguish it from the Young Man's, which was situated on the other side of the street.

Of greater note than any of these was the British coffee-house which stood in Cockspur Street. There is a record of its existence in 1722, and in 1759 it was presided over by the sister of Bishop Douglas, who was described as " a person of excellent manners and abilities." She was succeeded by a Mrs. Anderson, on whom the encomium was passed that she was " a woman of uncommon talents and the most agreeable conversation." As the names of these ladies suggest, they were of Scottish birth, and hence it is not surprising to learn that their house was greatly in favour among visitors from north of the Tweed. That the Scottish peers were sometimes to be found here in great numbers is the only conclusion to be drawn from an incident recorded by Horace Walpole. There was a motion before the House of Lords for which the support of the

Scots was required, and the Duke of Bedford wrote to sixteen of their number to solicit their votes, enclosing all the letters under one cover directed to the British coffee-house. It was under this roof, too, that the Scottish club called The Beeswing used to meet, one of whose members was Lord Campbell, that legal biographer who shared with most of his countrymen the ability of '' getting on.'' The club in question consisted of about ten members, and the agreement was to meet once a month at the British coffee-house to dine and drink port wine. The other members included Spankie, Dr. Haslam, author of several works on insanity, Andrew Grant, a merchant of considerable literary acquirements, and George Gordon, known about town as '' the man of wit.'' The conversation is described as being as good as any to be enjoyed anywhere in the London of that day, and the drinking was voted '' tremendous.'' The last-named fact is one illustration out of many that during the latter years of their existence the coffee-houses of London did not by any means confine their liquors to the harmless beverage from which they took their name.

Among the earliest coffee-houses to be established in the West-end of London was that

SLAUGHTER'S COFFEE-HOUSE.

opened by Thomas Slaughter in St. Martin's
Lane in 1692 and known as Slaughter's. It
remained under the oversight of Mr. Slaughter
until his death in 1740, and continued to enjoy
a prosperous career for nearly a century
longer, when the house was torn down. The
bulk of its customers were artists, and the
famous men numbered among them included
Wilkie, Wilson, and Roubiliac. But the most
pathetic figure associated with its history is
that of Abraham De Moivre, that French
mathematician who became the friend of Newton and Leibnitz. Notwithstanding his wonderful abilities he was driven to support himself
by the meagre pittances earned by teaching
and by solving problems in chess at Slaughter's. In his last days sight and hearing both
failed, and he finally died of somnolence,
twenty hours' sleep becoming habitual with
him. By the time of De Moivre's death, or
shortly after, the character of the frequenters
of Slaughter's underwent a change, for when
Goldsmith alluded to the house in 1758 it was
to make the remark that if a man were passion-
ate '' he may vent his rage among the old orators at Slaughter's Coffee-house, and damn the
nation, because it keeps him from starving.''

Politics and literature were the topics most

under discussion at the Smyrna coffee-house which had its location on the north side of Pall Mall. It makes its appearance in an early number of the Tatler, where reference is made to "that cluster of wise heads" that might be found "sitting every evening from the left hand side of the fire, at the Smyrna, to the door." Five months later Steele entered into fuller particulars.

"This is to give notice," he wrote, "to all ingenious gentlemen in and about the cities of London and Westminster, who have a mind to be instructed in the noble sciences of music, poetry, and politics, that they repair to the Smyrna coffee-house in Pall-mall, betwixt the hours of eight and ten at night, where they may be instructed gratis, with elaborate essays, by word of mouth on all or any of the above-mentioned arts. The disciples are to prepare their bodies with three dishes of bohea, and purge their brains with two pinches of snuff. If any young student gives indication of parts, by listening attentively, or asking a pertinent question, one of the professors shall distinguish him, by taking snuff out of his box in the presence of the whole audience." And the further direction is given that "the seat of learning is now removed from the corner of the chimney on the left towards the window, to the round table in the middle of the floor over against the fire; a revolution much lamented by the porters and chairmen, who were much edified through a pane of glass that remained broken all last summer.''

That Steele and Addison knew their Smyrna well may be inferred from their familiar references to the house, and there are equal proofs that Swift and Prior were often within its doors. The Journal to Stella has many references to visits from the poet and the satirist, such as, '' The evening was fair, and I walked a little in the Park till Prior made me go with him to the Smyrna Coffee-house, where I sat a while, and saw four or five Irish persons, who are very handsome, genteel fellows, but I know not their names.'' From Prior's pen there is an allusion to be found in the manuscripts of the Marquis of Bath in a letter the poet addressed to Lord Harley from London in the winter of 1719. Prior was lying low on that visit to town, for the main purpose of his presence was medicinal. '' I have only seen Brown, the surgeon,'' he writes, '' to whom I have made an *auricular confession,* and from him have received *extreme unction,* and applied it, which may soften the obduracy of my ear, and

make it capable of receiving the impression of
ten thousand lies which will be poured into it
as soon as I shall take my seat at the Smyrna.''

Two other figures not unknown to fame
haunt the shades of the Smyrna, Beau Nash
and Thomson of the '' Seasons.'' It is Goldsmith who tells of the first that he used to idle
for a day at a time in the window of the Smyrna
to receive a bow from the Prince of Wales or
the Duchess of Marlborough as they drove by;
and of the second is it not on record that he
in person took subscriptions at the Smyrna for
the '' Four Seasons? ''

In the Cocoa-Tree Club of to-day may be
found the direct representative of the most
famous Tory chocolate-house of the reign of
Queen Anne. It had its headquarters first in
Pall Mall, but removed not long after to St.
James's Street, the Mecca of clubland at the
present time. Perhaps the best picture of the
house and its ways is that given by Gibbon, who
in his journal for November 24th, 1762, wrote:
'' I dined at the Cocoa-Tree with ——, who,
under a great appearance of oddity, conceals
more real humour, good sense, and even knowledge, than half those who laugh at him. We
went thence to the play, the ' Spanish Friar,'
and when it was over, retired to the Cocoa-

Tree. That respectable body, of which I have
the honour of being a member, affords every
evening a sight truly English; twenty, or perhaps thirty, of the first men in the kingdom in
point of fashion and fortune, supping at little
tables covered with a napkin in the middle of
a coffee room, upon a bit of cold meat or a sandwich, and drinking a glass of punch. At present we are full of King's Councillors and Lords
of the Bedchamber, who, having jumped into
the ministry, make a very singular medley of
their old principles and language with their
modern one.'' It is easy to infer from Gibbon's account, what was a fact, that by his time
the house had been turned into a club, the use
of which was restricted to members, as at the
present time. The change was made before
1746, when the Cocoa-Tree was the rendezvous
of the Jacobites. One of the most curious features of the present premises is a carved palm-
tree which is thrust up through the centre of
the front rooms on the first and second floors.
What its age is no one knows, nor who was
responsible for the freak of botanical knowledge implied by utilizing a palm-tree as sym-
bolical of cocoa.

Soon after the transformation of the house
into a club it became notorious for the high

play which went on under the shadow of the palm-tree. Walpole, for example, tells the story of a gamble between an Irish gamester named O'Birne and a young midshipman named Harvey who had just fallen heir to a large estate by his brother's death. The stake was for one hundred thousand pounds, and when O'Birne won he said, " You can never pay me." But the youth replied, " I can, my estate will sell for the debt." O'Birne, however, had some scruples left, so said he would be content with ten thousand pounds, and suggested another throw for the balance. This time Harvey won, and it would be interesting to know that the lesson had not been lost. But Walpole does not throw any light on that matter.

Another lively scene took place under the palm-tree of the Cocoa-Tree late in the eighteenth century. The principal figure on that occasion was Henry Bate, that militant editor of the Morning Post whose duel at the Adelphi has already been recorded. It seems that Mr. Bate, who, by the way, held holy orders, and eventually became a baronet under the name of Dudley, was at Vauxhall one evening with a party of ladies, when Fighting Fitzgerald and several companions met them and indulged in insults. An exchange of cards followed, and a meeting was arranged for the following morning at the Cocoa-Tree to settle details of the inevitable duel. Fitzgerald, however, was late, and by the time he arrived apologies had been tendered and accepted by Mr. Bate. When Fitzgerald arrived on the scene with a Captain Miles he insisted on a boxing-match with the supposed captain, who, he affirmed, had been among the assailants of the previous night. Mr. Bate objected, inasmuch as he did not recognize Mr. Miles, and moreover scouted the indignity of settling such a matter with fists. He was willing to decide the dispute with sword or pistol. Fitzgerald, however, roused Bate's ire by dubbing him a coward. After that it did not take many minutes to form a ring under the shade of the palm-tree, and in less than a quarter of an hour the " coward " had pulverized Captain Miles in an eminently satisfactory manner.

Earlier and more sedate references to the Cocoa-Tree are in existence. There is, for example, a letter from General William Stewart, of October 27th, 1716, addressed to the father of William Pitt, placing this incident on record: " The other night, at the Cocoa-Tree, I saw Colonel Pitt and your brother-in-law Chomeley. The former made me a grave bow without speaking, which example I followed. I suppose he is directed to take no notice of me." Nor should the lively episode placed to the credit of a spark of the town in 1726 be overlooked. " The last masquerade," says a letter of that period, " was fruitful of quarrels. Young Webb had quarrelled at the Cocoa-Tree with Oglethorp, and struck him with his cane; they say the quarrel was made up." But " Young Webb " was evidently spoiling that night for more adventures, for while still in his cups he went to the masquerade and, meeting a German who had a mask with a great nose, he asked him what he did with such an ornament, pulled it off and slapped his face. " He was carried out by six grenadiers," is the terse climax of the story.

Florio was, of course, a frequenter of the Cocoa-Tree. And that his manners there as elsewhere must have been familiar is illustrated by the fact that one of the waiters addressed an epistle to him in the following terms: " Sam, the waiter at the Cocoa-Tree, presents his compliaments to the Prince of Wales." The rebuke was characteristic: " You see, Sam, this may be very well between you and me, but it would never do with the Norfolks and Arundels! "

Of course the house has its George Selwyn story. An American captain began it by asserting that in his country hot and cold springs were often found side by side, which was convenient, for fish could be caught in the one and boiled in the other in a few minutes. The story was received as belonging to the " tall " order, until Selwyn gravely accepted it as true, because at Auvergne he had met a similar experience, with the addition that there was a third spring which supplied parsley and butter for the sauce.

Just as the Tories were faithful to the Cocoa-Tree, so the Whigs were stout in their loyalty to the St. James's coffee-house nearby. This was the resort named by Steele as the origin of the political news served up in the Tatler, and it was favoured with many references in the Spectator of Addison. The latter gives an amusing account of a general shift-round of the servants of the house owing to the resignation of one of their number, and in a later paper, devoted to coffee-house speculations on the death of the King of France, he gives the place of honour to the Whig resort as providing the most reliable information. " That I might be as near the fountain-head as possible, I first of all called at St. James's, where I found the whole outward room in a buzz of politics. The speculations were but very indifferent towards the door, but grew finer as you advanced to the upper end of the room, and were so very much improved by a knot of theorists, who sat in the inner room, within the steams of the coffee-pot, that I there heard the whole Spanish monarchy disposed of, and all the line of Bourbon provided for in less than a quarter of an hour.''

Politics, however, did not claim all the interest of the frequenters of the St. James's. Verdicts were passed upon the literary products of the day in much the same manner as at Button's, and it should not be forgotten that Goldsmith's '' Retaliation '' had its origin at a meeting at this house.

To judge from their present-day dignified appearance, no one would imagine that the Old Palace and the New Palace Yards at Westminster ever tolerated such mundane things as coffee-houses and taverns within their precincts. The evidence of history, however, shows that at one time there were numerous establishments of both kinds situated under the shadow of Westminster Hall and the Abbey. A drawing not more than a century old shows several such buildings, and the records of the

OLD PALACE YARD, WESTMINSTER.

city enumerate public houses of the sign of the
Coach and Horses, and the Royal Oak, and the
White Rose as being situated in the Old Palace
Yard, while the coffee-houses there included
Waghorne's and Oliver's. Nor was it different
with New Palace Yard. In the latter were to
be found Miles's coffee-house and the Turk's
Head, both associated with James Harrington,
that early republican whose '' Oceana '' got
him into so much trouble. One story credits
Cromwell with having seized the manuscript
of that work, and with its restoration having
been effected by Elizabeth Claypole, the favourite daughter of the Protector, whom Harrington is said to have playfully threatened
with the theft of her child if her father did not
restore his. The author of '' Oceana '' seems
to have thought the occasion of Cromwell's
death a favourable one for the discussion of
his political theories, and hence the Rota club
he founded, which used to meet at Miles's. Au-
brey gives a vivid account of the room at the
coffee-house where the club met, with its
'' large oval-table, with a passage in the middle
for Miles to deliver his coffee. About it sat
his disciples and the virtuosi. Here we had
(very formally) a ballotting box, and ballotted
how things should be carried by way of Ten-

tamens. The room was every evening full as it could be crammed.'' But when it became obvious that the Restoration would soon be an accomplished fact the meetings at Miles's came to a sudden end. And shortly after, Harrington was committed to the Tower to meditate upon ideal commonwealths amid less congenial surroundings.

Westminster Hall itself had a coffee-house at the beginning of the last century. It was named Alice's, presumably after the proprietor, and was on one occasion the scene of a neat version of the confidence trick. The coffee-house was used almost entirely by barristers engaged in the different courts of law then held in Westminster Hall, and they availed themselves of the house for robing before going to the courts, and as the storeroom of their wigs and gowns when the business of the day was ended. Armed with this knowledge, a needy individual by the name of William Lill applied to the waiter at Alice's, and made a request for a Mr. Clarke's gown and wig, saying that he had been sent by a well-known lawyers' wigmaker and dresser. It happened, however, that Mr. Clarke's clerk had a little before fetched away the wig and gown Mr. Lill was so anxious to receive. But when the waiter imparted that information he did not lose his self-possession. He also wanted, he said, Mr. Ellison's wig and gown. Taken with the man's knowledge of the barrister's names, the waiter not only handed over the wig and gown, but also informed the obliging Mr. Lill that when Mr. Ellison was last in court he had left his professional coat and waistcoat at the coffee-house; perhaps Mr. Lill would take those too? Mr. Lill readily obliged, and disappeared. Later in the day the waiter's wits began to work. Being, too, in the neighbourhood of the wig-maker's shop, it occurred to him to drop in. There he learnt that no Mr. Lill had been sent for any wigs or gowns. The alarmed waiter next proceeded to Mr. Ellison's office, to learn there that no messenger had been sent to Alice's. At this stage the waiter, as he subsequently confessed, had no doubt but that Mr. Lill was '' an impostor.'' Mr. Lill was more. He was courageous. Having secured his prey so simply on the one day, he came back on another, trusting, no doubt, that his waiter friend would be as obliging as before. But it was not to be; a few questions confirmed the waiter's suspicions that Mr. Lill really was '' an impostor; '' and a police-officer finished the story. One feels rather sorry for Mr. Lill. Of course it was wrong of him to annex those wigs and gowns, and sell them for theatrical " properties," but it is impossible not to admire the pluck of a man who stole from a lawyer in the precincts of a law-court. Alice's deserves immortality if only for having been the scene of that unique exploit.

By far the most curious of the coffee-houses of old London was that known as Don Saltero's at Chelsea. There was nothing of the don really about the proprietor, whose unadorned name was James Salter. The prefix and the affix were bestowed by one of his customers, Vice-Admiral Munden, who, having cruised much upon the coast of Spain, acquired a weakness for Spanish titles, and bestowed a variant of one on the Chelsea coffee-house keeper.

That same Mr. Salter was an odd character. Not content with serving dishes of coffee, nor with drawing people's teeth and cutting their hair, he indulged in attempts at fiddle-playing and set up a museum in his house.

Steele's description of a visit to this many-sided resort is by far the best picture of its owner and its contents. " When I came into the coffee-house," he wrote, " I had not time to salute the company, before my eye was diverted by ten thousand gimcracks round the

DON SALTERO'S COFFEE-HOUSE.

room, and on the ceiling. When my first astonishment was over, comes to me a sage of thin and meagre countenance; which aspect made me doubt, whether reading or fretting had made it so philosophic: but I very soon perceived him to be of that sect which the ancients call Gingivistæ; in our language, tooth-drawers. I immediately had a respect for the man; for these practical philosophers go upon a very rational hypothesis, not to cure, but to take away the part affected." And then follows that delightful dissertation which linked Mr. Salter in the line of succession with the barber of Don Quixote. But Steele could not forgive the Chelsea barber and coffee-house keeper one thing. "I cannot allow the liberty he takes of imposing several names (without my license) on the collections he has made, to the abuse of the good people of England; one of which is particularly calculated to deceive religious persons, to the great scandal of the well-disposed, and may introduce heterodox opinions. He shews you a straw hat, which I know to be made by Madge Peskad, within three miles of Bedford; and tells you, 'It is Pontius Pilate's wife's chambermaid's sister's hat.' To my knowledge of this very hat it may be added, that the covering of straw was never

used among the Jews, since it was demanded
of them to make bricks without it.''

Don Saltero had a poetic catalogue of his
curiosities, of which one verse ran:

> " Monsters of all sorts here are seen,
>     Strange things in nature as they grew so;
> Some relics of the Sheba Queen,
>     And fragments of the famed Bob Crusoe."

These treasures, however, could not avert the
fate which was due to befall the house on January 8th, 1799, when the lease of the building
and all within were disposed of by public sale.
A philosophic journalist, not possessing Steele's
sense of humour, gravely remarked of the
Don's gimcracks that they, with kindred collections, helped to cherish the infancy of science,
and deserved to be appreciated as the play-
things of a boy after he is arrived at maturity.
Happily the Don himself did not survive to see
his precious treasures fetch less than ten shillings a-piece.

# III

# THE CLUBS OF OLD LONDON

# CHAPTER I

PENDING the advent of a philosophical historian who will explain the psychological reason why the eighteenth century was distinguished above all others in the matter of clubs, the fact is to be noted in all its baldness that the majority of those institutions which are famous in the annals of old London had their origin during that hundred years. One or two were of earlier date, but those which made a noise in the world and which for the most part survive to the present time were founded at the opening of the eighteenth century or later in its course.

Although the exact date of the establishment of the Kit-Cat club has never been decided, the consensus of opinion fixes the year somewhere about 1700. More debatable, however, is the question of its peculiar title. The most recent efforts to solve that riddle leave it where the contemporary epigram left it:

" Whence deathless Kit-Cat took his name,
　　Few critics can unriddle;
　Some say from pastry-cook it came,
　　And some from Cat and Fiddle.
　From no trim beaus its name it boasts,
　　Gray statesmen or green wits;
　But from this pell-mell pack of toasts
　　Of old Cats and young Kits."

Equally undecided is the cause of its origin. Ned Ward, however, had no doubts on that score. That exceedingly frank and coarse historian of the clubs of London attributed the origin of the club to the astuteness of Jacob Tonson the publisher. That " amphibious mortal," according to Ward, having a sharp eye to his own interests, " wriggled himself into the company of a parcel of poetical young sprigs, who had just weaned themselves of their mother university" and, having more wit than experience, " put but a slender value, as yet, upon their maiden performances." Faced with this golden opportunity to attach a company of authors to his establishment, the alert Tonson baited his trap with mutton pies. In other words, according to Ward, he invited the poetical young sprigs to a " collation of oven-trumpery " at the establishment of one named Christopher, for brevity called Kit, who was an expert in pastry delicacies. The ruse succeeded; the poetical young sprigs came in a band; they enjoyed their pies; and when Tonson proposed a weekly meeting of a similar kind, on the understanding that the poetical young sprigs "would do him the honour to let him have the refusal of all their juvenile products," there was no dissentient voice. And thus the Kit-Cat club came into life.

Some grains of truth may be embedded in this fanciful narrative. Perhaps the inception of the club may have been due to Tonson's astuteness from a business point of view; but at an early stage of the history of the club it became a more formidable institution. Its membership quickly comprised nearly fifty nobles and gentlemen and authors, all of whom found a bond of interest in their profession of Whig principles and devotion to the House of Hanover, shortly to be established on the throne of England in the person of George I. Indeed, one poetical epigram on the institution specifically entitles it the "Hanover Club."

It seems that the earliest meetings of the club were held at an obscure tavern in Shire Lane, which no longer exists, but ran parallel with Chancery Lane near Temple-bar. This was the tavern kept by Christopher Cat, and when he removed to the Fountain tavern in the Strand the club accompanied. Its principle place of meeting, however, was at the mansion of Tonson at Barn Elms, where a room was specially built for its accommodation. The dimensions of this room were responsible for the application of the term Kit-Cat to portraits of a definite size. Thus, on the suggestion of Tonson the portraits of the members were painted by Sir Godfrey Kneller for the bookseller, but as the walls of the room at Barn Elms were not lofty enough to accommodate full-lengths, the painter reverted to a canvas measuring thirty-six by twenty-eight inches, a size of portrait which preserves the name of Kit-Cat to this day.

Apart from its influence on the nomenclature of art, the club is memorable for the additions it caused to be made to the poetic literature of England. One of the customs of the club was to toast the reigning beauties of the day regularly after dinner, and the various poets among its members were called upon to cast those toasts in the form of verse, which were afterwards engraved on the toasting-glasses of the club. Addison was responsible for one of those tributes, his theme being the Lady Manchester:

" While haughty Gallia's dames, that spread
O'er their pale cheeks an artful red,
Beheld this beauteous stranger there,
In native charms divinely fair;
Confusion in their looks they show'd;
And with unborrow'd blushes glow'd."

But the Earl of Halifax and Sir Samuel Garth
were the most prolific contributors to Kit-Cat
literature, the former being responsible for six
and the latter for seven poetical toasts. For
the Duchess of St. Albans, Halifax wrote this
tribute:

" The line of Vere, so long renown'd in arms,
Concludes with lustre in St. Albans charms.
Her conquering eyes have made their race complete;
They rose in valour, and in beauty set."

To the Duchess of Beaufort these lines were
addressed:

" Offspring of a tuneful sire,
Blest with more than mortal fire;
Likeness of a mother's face,
Blest with more than mortal grace;
You with double charms surprise,
With his wit, and with her eyes."

Next came the turn of Lady Mary Churchill:

" Fairest and latest of the beauteous race,
Blest with your parent's wit, and her first blooming
    face;
Born with our liberties in William's reign,
Your eyes alone that liberty restrain."

Other ladies celebrated by Halifax included the Duchess of Richmond, Lady Sutherland, and Mademoiselle Spanheime. To Garth fell the task of singing the attractions of Lady Carlisle, Lady Essex, Lady Hyde, and Lady Wharton, the first three have two toasts each. Perhaps the most successful of his efforts was the toast to Lady Hyde.

" The god of wine grows jealous of his art,
  He only fires the head, but Hyde the heart.
  The queen of love looks on, and smiles to see
  A nymph more mighty than a deity."

Whether the businesslike Tonson derived much profit from his contract with the poetical young sprigs does not transpire; it is of moment, however, to recall that the members of the club did something to encourage literature. They raised a sum of four hundred guineas to be offered as prizes for the best comedies. It may be surmised that Thomas D'Urfey stood no chance of winning any of those prizes, for he was too much of a Tory to please the Kit-

Cat members. Hence the story which tells how
the members requested Mr. Cat to bake some
of his pies with D'Urfey's works under them.
And when they complained that the pies were
not baked enough, the pastrycook made the retort that D'Urfey's works were so cold that
the dough could not bake for them.

For all their devotion to literature, the Kit-
Cats did not forget to eat, drink, and be merry.
That their gatherings were convivial enough is
illustrated by the anecdote of Sir Samuel
Garth, physician to George I as well as poet.
He protested at one meeting that he would have
to leave early to visit his patients. But the
evening wore on and still he stayed, until at
length Steele reminded him of his engagements.
Whereupon Garth pulled out a list of fifteen
patients, and remarked, " It matters little
whether I see them or not to-night. Nine or
ten are so bad that all the doctors in the world
could not save them, and the remainder have
such tough constitutions that no doctors are
needed by them." It is to be hoped that the
bottle had not circulated so freely on that evening when the little girl who afterwards became Lady Mary Wortley Montagu was ush-
ered into the presence of the members. Her
proud father, Lord Kingston, nominated her

as a toast, but as the members protested that
they did not know her, the child was sent for
on the spot. On her arrival the little beauty
was elected by acclamation. That triumph, she
afterwards declared, was the happiest hour of
her life.

Despite the fact that it had no formal constitution, and that membership therein depended upon a lady's favour, the Blue-Stocking
Club was too important a factor in the literary
life of old London to be overlooked. It owed
its existence to Elizabeth Robinson, who as the
wife of Edward Montagu found herself in the
possession of the worldly means essential to
the establishment of a literary salon. It had its
origin in a series of afflictions. Mrs. Montagu
first lost her only child, and shortly after her
mother and favourite brother. These bereave-
ments put her on the track of distractions, and
a visit to Bath, where she made the acquaintance of the poet Young, appears to have suggested that she would find relief from her sor-
rows in making her house in London a meeting-
place for the intellectual spirits of the capital.
At first she confined her enterprise to the giving of literary breakfasts, but these were soon
followed by evening assemblies of a more pre-
tentious nature, known as " conversation par-

ties.'' The lady was particular to whom she
sent her invitations. In a letter to Garrick,
inviting him to give a recital, she wrote: '' You
will find here some friends, and all you meet
must be your admirers, for I never invite Idiots
to my house.'' Unless when Garrick or some
famous French actor was invited to give a
recital, no diversion of any kind was allowed
at these gatherings; card-playing was not tolerated, and the guests were supposed to find
ample enjoyment in the discussion of bookish
topics.

Why Mrs. Montagu's assemblies were
dubbed the Blue-Stocking Club has never been
definitely decided. On the one hand the term
is supposed to have originated from the fact
that Benjamin Stillingfleet, taking advantage
of the rule which stipulated that full dress was
optional, always attended in blue worsted instead of black silk stockings. But the other
theory derives the name from the fact that the
ladies who frequented the gatherings wore
'' blue stockings as a distinction '' in imitation of a fashionable French visitor of the time.

Plenty of ridicule was bestowed upon Mrs.
Montagu and her '' conversation parties,'' but
there seems some truth in the contention of
Hannah More that those '' blue-stocking ''

meetings did much to rescue fashionable life from the tyranny of whist and quadrille. Whether Mrs. Montagu really possessed any literary ability is a matter which does not call for discussion at this late hour, but it is something to her credit that she was able to attract under her roof such men as Horace Walpole, Dr. Johnson, Burke, Garrick, Reynolds, and many other conspicuous figures of the late eighteenth century. The hostess may have wished her guests to credit her with greater knowledge than she really had; Johnson said she did not know Greek, and had but a slight knowledge of Latin, though she was willing her friends should imagine she was acquainted with both; but the same authority was willing to admit that she was a very extraordinary woman, and that her conversation always had meaning. But, as usual, we must turn to a member of her own sex for the last word in the matter. Fanny Burney met her frequently, and made several recording entries in her diary. Here is the first vignette: '' She is middle-sized, very thin, and looks infirm; she has a sensible and penetrating countenance, and the air and manner of a woman accustomed to being distinguished, and of great parts. Dr. Johnson, who agrees in this, told us that a Mrs.

Hervey, of his acquaintance, says she can remember Mrs. Montagu *trying* for this same air and manner. Mr. Crisp has said the same: however, nobody can now impartially see her, and not confess that she has extremely well succeeded.'' And later there is this entry: '' We went to dinner, my father and I, and met Mrs. Montagu, in good spirits, and very unaffectedly agreeable. No one was there to awaken ostentation, no new acquaintance to require any surprise from her powers; she was therefore natural and easy, as well as informing and entertaining.''

Almost to the end of her long life Mrs. Montagu maintained her Blue-Stocking Club. So late as 1791, when she had reached her seventy-first year, she gave a breakfast of which Fanny Burney wrote: '' The crowd of company was such that we could only slowly make our way in any part. There could not be fewer than four or five hundred people. It was like a full Ranelagh by daylight.'' That other breakfast-giver, Samuel Rogers, who only knew Mrs. Montagu towards the close of her life, described her as '' a composition of art '' and as one '' long attached to the trick and show of life.'' But the most diverting picture of the Queen of the Blue-Stockings was given by

Richard Cumberland in a paper of the Observer. In answer to one of her invitation cards he arrived at her salon before the rest of the company, and had opportunity to observe that several new publications, stitched in blue paper, were lying on the table, with scraps of paper stuck between the leaves, as if to mark where the hostess had left off reading. Vanessa, for under that title did Cumberland present Mrs. Montagu, entered the room shortly afterwards, dressed in a petticoat embroidered with the ruins of Palmyra. The lady is made to mistake the author for the inventor of a diving-bell, and to address him accordingly, with delightful results. The various visitors are described in the same humourous manner, and then comes the climax. '' Vanessa now came up, and desiring leave to introduce a young muse to Melpomene, presented a girl in a white frock with a fillet of flowers twined round her hair, which hung down her back in flowing curls; the young muse made a low obeisance in the style of an oriental salaam, and with the most unembarrassed voice and countenance, while the poor actress was covered with blushes, and suffering torture from the eyes of all the room, broke forth as follows.'' But the recorder of that particular meeting of the

Blue-Stocking Club could endure no more. He fled the house as hastily as though he had just learnt it was infected with the plague.

Although several lists are printed which profess to give the names of '' the principal clubs of London,'' they may be searched in vain for that one which can rightly claim to be The Club. Nevertheless, ignorance of its existence can hardly be reckoned a reproach in view of the confession of Tennyson. When asked by a member, the Duke of Argyll, to allow him to place his name in nomination, Tennyson rejoined, '' Before answering definitely, I should like to know something about expenses. ' The Club? ' It is either my fault or my misfortune that I have never heard of it.'' When the poet made that confession he was in his fifty-sixth year, and up to that time, apparently, had not read his Boswell. Or if he had, he was not aware that the club Reynolds had founded in 1764 under the name of The Club, of which the title had subsequently been changed to the Literary Club, still existed under its original designation.

Another fact is likely to confuse the historian of this club unless he is careful. Owing to the fact that Dr. Johnson was one of the original members, and dominated its policy after his usual autocratic manner, it is sometimes known as Dr. Johnson's Club. However, there is no disputing the fact that the credit of its origin belongs to the " dear knight of Plympton," as the great painter was called by one of his friends. The idea of its establishment at once won the approval of Johnson, and it started on its illustrious career having as its members those two and Edmund Burke, Dr. Nugent, Topham Beauclerk, Bennet Langton, Oliver Goldsmith, Anthony Chamier and Sir John Hawkins. Soon after its foundation, the number of members was increased to twelve, then it was enlarged to twenty, and subsequently to twenty-six, then to thirty, and finally to thirty-five with a proviso that the total should never exceed forty.

To set forth a list of the members of The Club from 1764 to the present year would be to write down the names of many of the men most eminent in English history. In Boswell's time those who had been admitted to its select circle included David Garrick, Adam Smith, Edward Gibbon, Sir William Jones, Sir William Hamilton, Charles James Fox, Bishop Percy, Dr. Joseph Warton, and Richard Brinsley Sheridan. In more modern days the members have included Tennyson, Macaulay, Huxley, Gladstone, Lord Acton, Lord Dufferin, W. H. E. Lecky and Lord Salisbury. The limit of membership is still maintained; it is yet the rule that one black ball will exclude; and the election of a member is still announced in the stilted form which Gibbon drafted by way of a joke: " Sir, I have the pleasure to inform you that you had last night the honour to be elected as a member of The Club."

As The Club had no formal constitution it was an easy matter to regulate its gatherings by the convenience of the members. Thus, at first the meetings were held at seven on Monday evenings, then the day was changed to Friday, and afterwards it was resolved to come together once a fortnight during the sitting of Parliament. Although admission was so strictly guarded that its membership was accounted a rare honour, The Club does not appear to have been in a flourishing condition in its second decade. Otherwise Beauclerk would hardly have written, " Our club has dwindled away to nothing; nobody attends but Mr. Chamier, and he is going to the East Indies. Sir Joshua and Goldsmith have got into such a round of pleasures that they have no time." Two or three years later Edmund Malone, the literary critic and Shakesperian scholar, was moving

heaven and earth to secure his own election.
'' I have lately,'' he wrote to a member, '' made
two or three attempts to get into your club, but
have not yet been able to succeed — though I
have some friends there — Johnson, Burke,
Steevens, Sir J. Reynolds and Marlay — which
in so small a society is a good number. At
first they said, I think, they thought it a respect
to Garrick's memory not to elect one for some
time in his room — which (in any one's case
but my own I should say) was a strange kind
of motive — for the more agreeable he was,
the more need there is of supplying the want,
by some substitute or other. But as I have no
pretensions to ground even a hope upon, of
being a succedaneum to such a man — the argument was decisive and I could say nothing
to it. ' Anticipation ' Tickell and J. Townshend are candidates as well as myself — and
they have some thoughts of enlarging their
numbers; so perhaps we may be all elected
together. I am not quite so anxious as Ag-
mondisham Vesey was, who, I am told, had
couriers stationed to bring him the quickest
intelligence of his success.''

Malone appears to have thought that it was
a mere subterfuge to instance the death of Garrick as a reason for not electing him. But it

was nothing of the kind. The Club did actually impose upon itself a year's widowhood, so to speak, when Garrick died. And yet his election had not been an easy matter. That was largely his own fault. When Reynolds first mentioned The Club to him, he ejaculated in his airy manner, '' I like it much; I think I shall be of you.'' Of course Reynolds reported the remark to Johnson, with a result that might have been anticipated. *'' He'll be of us,''* Johnson repeated, and then added, '' How does he know we will *permit* him? The first duke in England has no right to hold such language.'' Other recorders of Johnson's conversation credit him with threatening to black-ball the actor, and with the expression of the wish that he might have one place of resort where he would be free of the company of the player. Whatever Johnson's attitude was, the fact remains that Garrick's election was opposed for a considerable time, though when he was made a member he approved himself a welcome addition to the circle.

Unconsciously amusing is the account Boswell gives of his own election. The Club had been in existence some nine years when the fatal night of the balloting arrived. Beauclerk had a dinner party at his house before the club-meeting, and when he and the other members left for the ceremony the anxious Boswell was committed to the hospitality of Lady Di, whose "charming conversation" was not entirely adequate to keep up his spirits. In a short time, however, the glad tidings of his election came, and the fussy little Scotsman hurried off to the place of meeting to be formally received. It is impossible to read without a smile the swelling sentences with which he closes his narrative. He was introduced "to such a society as can seldom be found. Mr. Edmund Burke, whom I then saw for the first time, and whose splendid talents had long made me ardently wish for his acquaintance; Dr. Nugent, Mr. Garrick, Dr. Goldsmith, Mr. (afterwards Sir William) Jones, and the company with whom I had dined. Upon my entrance, Johnson placed himself behind a chair, on which he leaned as on a desk or pulpit, and with humourous formality gave me a charge, pointing out the conduct expected from me as a good member of this club." There was probably more than "humourous formality" at the back of Johnson's mind that night. He was responsible for Boswell's election, and may well have had a doubt or two as to how that inconsequential person would behave in such a circle.

As Johnson had had his way in the case of Boswell, he could not very well object when some were proposed as members with whom, from the political and religious point of view, he had little sympathy. But he had the grace to regard the matter with philosophy. When its numbers were increased to thirty, he declared he was glad of it, for as there were several with whom he did not like to consort, something would be gained by making it " a mere miscellaneous collection of conspicuous men, without any determinate character." The political difficulty was felt by other members. That fact is oppressively illustrated by an account of a meeting recorded by Dr. Burney, the father of the talented Fanny, in a letter to his daughter, dated January 31st, 1793, at a time, consequently, when excitement still ran high at the execution of Louis XVI of France: " At the Club on Tuesday, the fullest I ever knew, consisting of fifteen members, fourteen all seemed of one mind, and full of reflections on the late transaction in France; but, when about half the company was assembled, who should come in but Charles Fox! There were already three or four bishops arrived, hardly one of whom could look at him, I believe, without horror. After the first bow and cold salutation, the conversation stood still for several minutes. During dinner Mr. Windham, and Burke, jun., came in, who were obliged to sit at a side table. All were *boutonnés,* and not a word of the martyred king or politics of any kind was mentioned; and though the company was chiefly composed of the most eloquent and loquacious men in the kingdom, the conversation was the dullest and most uninteresting I ever remember at this or any such large meeting.'' There were evidently serious disadvantages then in the mixed nature of the club, as there have been since. For example, how did Gladstone meet Huxley after his Gadarene swine had been so unmercifully treated by the man of science?

When Johnson reached his seventy-fourth year, and found himself the victim of infirmities which prompted him to seek his social intercourse near at hand, he conceived the idea of founding what was known as his Essex Street Club. One of his first invitations was sent to Reynolds, but the painter did not see his way to join. The members included the inevitable Boswell, the Hon. Daines Barring-

ton, famous for his association with Gilbert
White, and others whom Boswell noted as men
of distinction, but whose names are no more
than names at this distance. Johnson drew up
the rules of the club, which restricted its membership to two dozen, appointed the meetings
on Monday, Thursday and Saturday of each
week, allowed a member to introduce a friend
once a week, insisted that each member should
spend at least sixpence at each gathering, en-
forced a fine of threepence for absence, and
laid down the regulation that every individual
should defray his own expense. And a final
rule stipulated a penny tip for the waiter. The
meeting-place was a tavern in Essex Street,
known as the Essex Head, of which the host
was an old servant of Mr. Thrale's. Boswell,
as in duty bound, seeing he was a member, declared there were few societies where there
was better conversation or more decorum. And
he added that eight years after the loss of its
" great founder " the members were still holding happily together. But it was founded too
late in the day to gather around it many notable Johnsonian associations, and after his
death it was, on Boswell's showing, too happy
to have any history.

Among the informal clubs of old London, a

distinguished place belongs to that assemblage
of variously-talented men, who, under the title
of the Wittenagemot abrogated to themselves
the exclusive use of a box in the north-east
corner of the Chapter coffee-house. It found
a capable if terse historian in one of its members, who explains that the club had two sections. The one took possession of the box at
the earliest hour of the morning, and from their
habit of taking the papers fresh from the news-
men were called the Wet Paper Club. In the
afternoon the other section took possession,
and were as keen to scan the wet evening papers as their colleagues to peruse those of the
forenoon. Among the members of the Wittenagemot were Dr. Buchan, the author of a
standard treatise on medicine, who although a
Tory was so tolerant of all views that he was
elected moderator of the meetings; a Mr. Ham-
mond, a manufacturer, who had not been absent
for nearly forty-five years; a Mr. Murray, a
Scottish Episcopal minister, who every day accomplished the feat of reading through at least
once all the London papers; a '' growling person of the name of Dobson, who, when his
asthma permitted, vented his spleen '' upon
both sides of politics; and Mr. Robison the

publisher, and Richard, afterwards Sir Richard, Phillips, so keenly alert in recruiting for his Monthly Magazine that he used to attend with a waistcoat pocket full of guineas as an earnest of his good intentions and financial solvency.

Perhaps, however, the most original member of the Wittenagemot was a young man of the name of Wilson, to whom the epithet of '' Long-Bow '' was soon applied on account of the extraordinary stories he retailed concerning the secrets of the upper ten. Just as he appeared to be established in the unique circle at the Chapter he disappeared, the cause being that he had run up a bill of between thirty and forty pounds. The strange thing was, however, that the keeper of the coffee-house, a Miss Brun, begged that if any one met Mr. Wilson they would express to him her willingness to give a full discharge for the past and future credit to any amount, for, she said, '' if he never paid us, he was one of the best customers we ever had, contriving, by his stories and conversation, to keep a couple of boxes crowded the whole night, by which we made more punch, and brandy and water, than from any other single customer.'' But the useful Long-Bow

Wilson was never seen again, and several years later the Wittenagemot itself died of disintegration. It was more fortunate, however, than scores of similar clubs in old London, of which the history is entirely wanting.

# CHAPTER II

## SOCIAL AND GAMING

NEITHER of the literary societies described in the previous chapter could claim to be a club in the present accepted meaning of that term. Even Dr. Johnson's famous definition, " An assembly of good fellows, meeting under certain conditions," needs amplification. Perhaps the most satisfactory exposition is that given in " The Original " which was applied in the first instance to the Athenæum. " The building," said Walker, " is a sort of palace, and is kept with the same exactness and comfort as a private dwelling. Every member is a master without any of the trouble of a master. He can come when he pleases, and stay away as long as he pleases, without anything going wrong. He has the command of regular servants without having to pay or to manage them. He can have whatever meal or refreshment he wants, at all hours, and served up with the cleanliness and comfort of his own house. He orders just what he pleases, having no interest

267

to think of but his own. In short, it is impossible to suppose a greater degree of liberty in living.'' This is somewhat copious for a definition, but it would be difficult to put into smaller compass the various traits which marked the social and gaming clubs of old London.

All those qualities, however, were not in evidence from the first. They were a matter of growth, of adaptation to needs as those needs were realized. The evolution of the club in that sense is nowhere better illustrated than in the case of White's, which can claim the proud honour of being the oldest among London clubs. It was established as a Chocolate-house about 1698, and as such was a resort open to all. Even in those days it was notorious for the high play which went on within its walls. Swift has recorded that the Earl of Oxford never passed the building in St. James's Street without bestowing a curse upon it as the bane of half the English nobility. And a little later it was frankly described as " a Den of Thieves.''

Fire destroyed the first White's a little more than a generation after it was opened. Its owner at that time was one named Arthur, and the account of the conflagration tells how his

ST. JAMES'S STREET.

*(Showing White's on the left and Brooks's on the right.)*

wife leaped out of a window two stories high
onto a feather bed and thus escaped without
injury. George II went to see the fire, accompanied by the Prince of Wales, both of whom
encouraged the firemen with liberal offers of
money. But royal exhortations did not avail
to save the building; it was utterly consumed,
with a valuable collection of paintings.

Two or three years after the opening of the
new building White's ceased to be a public resort as a Chocolate-house and became a club
in the strict meaning of the word. It remained
under the direction of Mr. Arthur till his death
in 1761, and then passed into the control of
Robert Mackreth, who had begun his career
as a billiard-marker in the establishment.
Mackreth married Arthur's only daughter a
few months after her father's death, and thus
gained an assured hold on the property, which
he seems to have retained till his death, although managing the club through an agent.
This agent was known as '' the Cherubim,''
and figures in the note Mackreth addressed to
George Selwyn when he retired from the active
oversight of the club. '' Sir,'' he wrote,
'' Having quitted business entirely and let my
house to the Cherubim, who is my near relation, I humbly beg leave, after returning you

my most grateful thanks for all favours, to recommend him to your patronage, not doubting by the long experience I have had of his fidelity but that he will strenuously endeavour to oblige.'' Before this change took place the club had removed to its present premises, which, however, have been considerably altered both inside and out. The freehold of the house realized forty-six thousand pounds when offered for sale a generation ago.

From a study of the club records, which extend back to 1736, it is possible to trace its evolution to the close corporation it has become. Rules of a more and more stringent nature were gradually adopted, but at the same time its reputation for gambling was on the increase. There was hardly any probability upon which the members did not stake large sums of money. The marriage of a young lady of rank led to a bet of one hundred guineas that she would give birth to a child before a certain countess who had been married several months earlier; another wager was laid that a member of infamous character would be the first baronet hung; and when a man dropped dead at the door of the club and was carried into the building, the members promptly began betting whether he was dead or not, and protested against the bleeding of the body on the plea that it would affect the fairness of the wagers. Well might Young write in one of his epistles to Pope:

" Clodio dress'd, danc'd, drank, visited, (the whole
    And great concern of an immortal soul!)
    Oft have I said, ' Awake! exist! and strive
    For birth! nor think to loiter is to live!'
    As oft I overheard the demon say,
    Who daily met the loiterer in his way,
  ' I'll meet thee, youth, at White's:' the youth replies,
  ' I'll meet thee there,' and falls his sacrifice;
    His fortune squander'd, leaves his virtue bare
    To every bribe, and blind to every snare."

Another witness to the prevalent spirit of White's at this time is supplied by Lord Lyttelton in a private letter, wherein he wrote that he had fears, should his son become a member of that club, the rattling of a dice-box would shake down all the fine oaks of his estate.

Mackreth manifested great worldly wisdom in addressing himself to George Selwyn when he retired from the active management of the club, for he knew that no other member had so much influence in the smart set of the day. Selwyn was a member of Brooks's as well, and for a time divided his favours pretty equally between the two houses, but in his latter years seems to have felt a preference for White's. The incidental history of the club for many years finds more lively chronicle in his letters than anywhere else, for he was constant in his attendance and was the best-known of its members. Through those letters we catch many glimpses of Charles James Fox at all stages of his strange career. We see him, for example, loitering at the club drinking hard till three o'clock in the morning, and find him there sitting up the entire night preceding his mother's death, planning a kind of " itinerant trade, which was of going from horse-race to horse-race, and so, by knowing the value and speed of all the horses in England, to acquire a certain fortune.'' Later, we see the brilliant statesman flitting about the club rooms, " as much the minister in all his deportment, as if he had been in office forty years.''

Among the countless vignettes of club life at White's as they crop up in Selwyn's letters it is difficult to pick and choose, but a few taken almost at random will revive scenes of a long-past time. Here is one of a supper-party in 1781 : " We had a pretty group of Papists — Lord Petres at the head of them — some Papists reformed, and one Jew. A club that used to be quite intolerable is now becoming tolerating and agreeable, and Scotchmen are naturalized and received with great good humour. The people are civil, not one word of party, no personal reflections.'' A few days later Selwyn tells this story against himself. '' On my return home I called in at White's, and in a minute or two afterwards Lord Loughborough came with the Duke of Dorset, I believe the first time since his admittance. I would be extraordinarily civil, and so immediately told him that I hoped Lady Loughborough was well. I do really hope so, now that I know that she is dead. But the devil a word did I hear of her since he was at your house in St. James's Street. He stared at me, as a child would have done at an Iroquois, and the Duke of Dorset seemed *tout confus*. I felt as if I looked like an oaf, but how I appeared God knows. I turned the discourse, as you may suppose.'' And here is a peep of a gambling party at faro. '' I went last night to White's, and stayed there till two. The Pharo party was amusing. Five such beggars could not have met; four lean crows feeding on a dead horse. Poor Parsons held the bank. The punters were Lord Carmarthen, Lord Essex, and one of the Fauquiers; and Denbigh sat at the table, with what hopes I know not, for he did not punt.

Essex's supply is from his son, which is more than he deserves, but Malden, I suppose, gives him a little of his milk, like the Roman lady to her father.''

Other glimpses might be taken such as would give point to Rowlandson's caricature of a later day in which he depicted a scene in '' The Brilliants '' club-room. The rules to be observed in this convivial society set forth that each member should fill a bumper to the first toast, that after twenty-four bumper toasts every member might fill as he pleased, and that any member refusing to comply with the foregoing was to be fined by being compelled to swallow a copious draught of salt and water. Rowlandson did not overlook the gambling propensities of such clubs, as may be seen by his picture of '' E O, or the Fashionable Vowels.'' By 1781 there were swarms of these E O tables in different parts of London, where any one with a shilling might try his luck. They had survived numerous attempts at their suppression, some of which dated as far back as 1731.

All the characteristic features of White's were to be found at Brooks's club on the opposite side of St. James's Street, the chief difference between the two being that the former was

THE BRILLIANTS.

(A Rowlandson Caricature of London Club Life in the 18th Century.)

the recognized haunt of the Tories and the latter of the Whigs. This political distinction is underlined in Gillray's amusing caricature of 1796, in which he depicted the "Promised Horrors of the French Invasion." The drawing was an ironical treatment of the evil effects Burke foretold of the "Regicide Peace," and takes for granted the landing of the French, the burning of St. James's Palace and other disasters. According to the artist, the invaders have reached the vicinity of the great clubs, and are wreaking vengeance on that special Tory club — White's — while Brooks's over the way is a scene of rejoicing. The figures hanging from the lamp-post are those of Canning and Jackson, while Pitt, firmly lashed to the Tree of Liberty, is being vigorously flogged by Fox.

During the earlier years of its history Brooks's was known as Almack's, its founder having been that William Almack who also established the famous assembly-rooms known by his name. The club was opened in Pall Mall as a gaming-salon in 1763, and it speedily acquired a reputation which even White's would have been proud to claim. Walpole relates that in 1770 the young men of that time lost five, ten, fifteen thousand pounds in an

evening's play. The two sons of Lord Holland
lost thirty-two thousand pounds in two nights,
greatly, no doubt, to the satisfaction of the
Hebrew money-lenders who awaited gamblers
in the outer room, which Charles Fox accordingly christened the Jerusalem Chamber.
While it still retained its original name, Gibbon became a member of the club, and Reynolds
wished to be. " Would you imagine," wrote
Topham Beauclerk, " that Sir J. Reynolds is
extremely anxious to be a member of Almack's?
You see what noble ambition will make men
attempt." Gibbon found the place to his liking. " Town grows empty," he wrote in June,
1776, " and this house, where I have passed
very agreeable hours, is the only place which
still invites the flower of English youth. The
style of living, though somewhat expensive, is
exceedingly pleasant; and, notwithstanding
the rage of play, I have found more entertainment and even rational society here than in
any other club to which I belong."

Two years later Almack's became Brooks's.
Why the original proprietor parted with so
valuable a property is not clear, but the fact
is indisputable that in 1778 the club passed into
the possession of a wine merchant and money-
lender of the name of Brooks, whose fame was

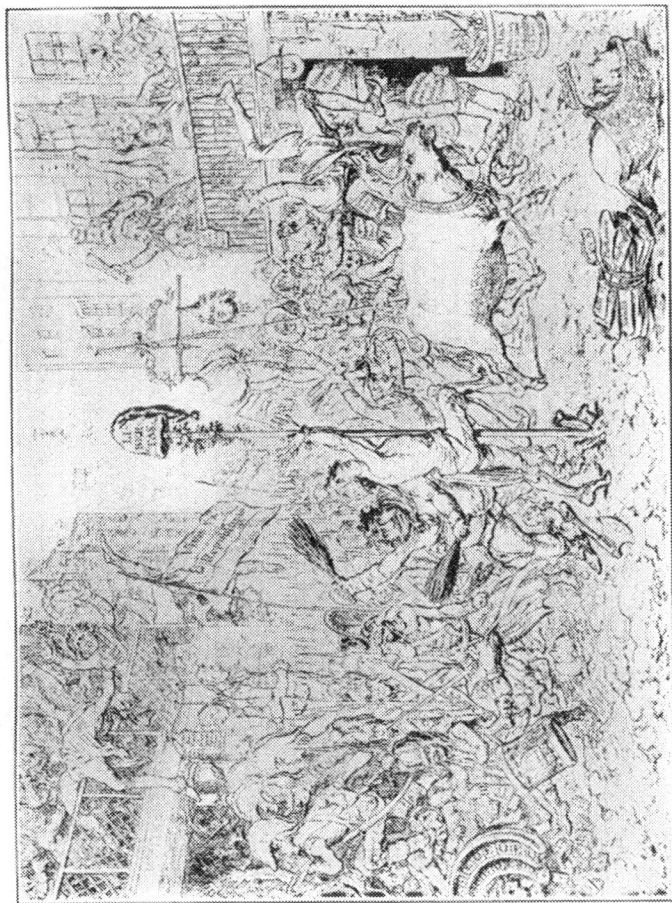

"PROMISED HORRORS OF THE FRENCH INVASION."
(From a Caricature by Gillray.)

celebrated a few years later by the poet Tickell.

> " Liberal Brooks, whose speculative skill
> Is hasty credit, and a distant bill;
> Who, nursed in clubs, disdains a vulgar trade,
> Exults to trust, and blushes to be paid."

It was the new owner who built the premises
in which the club still meets, but that particular speculation does not appear to have prospered, for the story is that he died in poverty.

Under the new régime the house kept up its
reputation for high play. But there was a time
soon after the change when its future did not
look promising. Thus in 1781 Selwyn wrote:
" No event at Brooks's, but the general opinion is that it is *en decadence*. Blue has been
obliged to give a bond with interest for what
he has eat there for some time. This satisfies
both him and Brooks; he was then, by provision, to sup or dine there no more without paying. Jack Townshend told me that the other
night the room next to the supper room was
full of the insolvents or freebooters, and no
supper served up; at last the Duke of Bolton
walked in, ordered supper; a hot one was
served up, and then the others all rushed in
through the gap, after him, and eat and drank
in spite of Brooks's teeth." A state of affairs

which goes far to explain why the club was in a precarious condition.

Charles Fox was of course as much at home at Brooks's as White's. It was, naturally, more of a political home for him than the Tory resort. This receives many illustrations in the letters of Selwyn, especially at the time when he formed his coalition with Lord North. Even then he managed to mingle playing and politics. " I own," wrote Selwyn, " that to see Charles closeted every instant at Brooks's by one or other, that he can neither punt or deal for a quarter of an hour but he is obliged to give an audience, while Hare is whispering and standing behind him, like Jack Robinson, with a pencil and paper for mems., is to me a scene *la plus parfaitement que l'on puisse imaginer,* and to nobody it seems more risible than to Charles himself." The farce was being continued a few days later. " I stayed at Brooks's this morning till between two and three, and then Charles was giving audiences in every corner of the room, and that idiot Lord D. telling aloud whom he should turn out, how civil he intended to be to the Prince, and how rude to the King."

Notwithstanding his preference for White's, Selwyn exercised his voting power at Brooks's

GAMBLING SALOON AT BROOKS'S CLUB.

in a rigid manner. For some reason, probably
because he could not boast a long descent,
Sheridan's nomination as a member provoked
his opposition. Fox, who had been enamoured
of Sheridan's witty society, proposed him on
numerous occasions and all the members were
earnestly canvassed for their votes, but the
result of the poll always showed one black ball.
When this had gone on for several months, it
was resolved to unearth the black-baller, and
the marking of the balls discovered Selwyn to
be the culprit. Armed with this knowledge,
Sheridan requested his friends to put his name
up again and leave the rest to him. On the
night of the voting, and some ten minutes before the urn was produced, Sheridan arrived
at the club in the company of the Prince of
Wales, and on the two being shown into the
candidates' waiting-room a message was sent
upstairs to Selwyn to the effect that the Prince
wished to speak to him below. The unsuspect-
ing Selwyn hurried downstairs, and in a few
minutes Sheridan had him absorbed in a diverting political story, which he spun out for
a full halfhour. Ere the narrative was at an
end, a waiter entered the room and by a pre-
arranged signal conveyed the news that Sheridan had been elected. Excusing himself for a

few minutes, Sheridan remarked as he left to
go upstairs that the Prince would finish the
story. But of course the Prince was not equal
to the occasion, and when he got hopelessly
stuck he proposed an adjournment upstairs
where Sheridan would be able to complete his
own yarn. It was then Selwyn realized that
he had been fooled, for the first to greet him
upstairs was Sheridan himself, now a full member of the club, with profuse bows and thanks
for Selwyn's "friendly suffrage." Happily
Selwyn had too keen a sense of humour not to
make the best of the situation, and ere the
evening was over he shook hands with the new
member and bade him heartily welcome.

Far less hilarious was that evening when the
notorious George Robert Fitzgerald forced his
way into the club. As this bravo had survived
numerous duels — owing to the fact, as was
stated after his death, that he wore a steel
cuirass under his coat — and was of a generally quarrelsome disposition, he was not regarded as a desirable member by any of the
London clubs. But he had a special desire to
belong to Brooks's, and requested Admiral
Keith Stewart to propose him as a candidate.
As the only alternative would have been to
fight a duel, the admiral complied with the

request, and on the night of the voting Fitzgerald waited downstairs till the result was
declared. When the votes were examined it
was discovered that every member had cast in
a black ball. But who was to beard the lion in
his den below? The members agreed that the
admiral should discharge that unpleasant duty,
and on his protesting that he had fulfilled his
promise by proposing him, it was pointed out,
that as there was no white ball in the box,
Fitzgerald would know that even he had not
voted for his admission. Posed for a moment
the admiral at length suggested that one of
the waiters should be sent to say that there
was one black ball, and that the election would
have to be postponed for another month. But
Fitzgerald would not credit that message, nor
a second which told him a recount had shown
two black balls, nor a third which said that
he had been black balled all over. He was sure
the first message implied a single mistake, that
the second had been the result of two mistakes
instead of one, and the third convinced him
that he had better go upstairs and investigate
on his own account. This he did in spite of
all remonstrance, and when he had gained the
room where the members were assembled he
reduced the whole company to perplexity by

asking each in turn whether he had cast a black ball. Of course the answer was in the negative in every case, and the triumphant bully naturally claimed that he had consequently been elected unanimously. Proceeding to make himself at home, and to order numerous bottles of champagne, which the waiters were too frightened to refuse, he soon found himself sent to Coventry and eventually retired. As a precaution against a repetition of that night it was resolved to have half a dozen sturdy constables in waiting on the following evening. But their services were not required. Fighting Fitzgerald never showed himself at the club again, though he boasted everywhere that he had been elected unanimously.

Perhaps it is hardly surprising that the national dish of England was laid under contribution for the name of a club, but it is somewhat confusing to find that in addition to the Beef Steak Club founded in the reign of Queen Anne there was a Beef Steak Society of which the origin is somewhat hazy. The former society is described with great gusto by Ned Ward, who had for it many more pleasant adjectives than he could find for the Kit-Cat Club. The other society appears to have owed its existence to John Rich, of Covent Garden theatre, and the scene-painter, George Lambert. For some unexplained reason, but probably because of its bohemian character, the club quickly gained many distinguished adherents, and could number royal scions as well as plebeians in its circle. According to Henry B. Wheatley, the '' room the society dined in, a little Escurial in itself, was most appropriately fitted up: the doors, wainscoting, and roof of good old English oak, ornamented with gridirons as thick as Henry VII's Chapel with the portcullis of the founder. The society's badge was a gridiron, which was engraved upon the rings, glass, and the forks and spoons. At the end of the dining-room was an enormous grating in the form of a gridiron, through which the fire was seen and the steaks handed from the kitchen. Over this were the appropriate lines: —

" ' If it were done when 'tis done, then 'twere well
It were done quickly.'

Saturday was from time immemorial the day of dining, and of late years the season commenced in November and ended in June.'' The last elected member of the fraternity was known as Boots, and, no matter how high his social rank, there were certain lowly duties he had to discharge until set free by another newcomer. There was another officer known as the Bishop, whose duty it was to sing the grace, and to read to each new member, who was brought in blindfolded, the following oath of allegiance: '' You shall attend duly, vote impartially, and conform to our laws and orders obediently. You shall support our dignity, promote our welfare, and at all times behave as a worthy member of this sublime society. So Beef and Liberty be your reward.'' Although there is a Beef Steak Club in existence to-day, it must not be identified with either of the two described above.

Another St. James's Street club which can date back to the middle of the eighteenth century is that known as Boodle's. The building was erected somewhere about 1765, but has been materially improved in more recent years. Presumably it takes its singular and not euphonious name from its founder, but on that point no definite information is forthcoming. Practically its only claim to distinction resides in the fact that Gibbon, who was almost as fond of clubs as Pepys was of taverns, was a member, as readers of his correspondence will recollect. In 1773 and the following year the great historian appears to have used the club as his writing-room, for many of his letters of those years are on Boodle's note-paper. One of the epistles recalls the fact that the clubs of London were wont to hold their great functions, such as balls or masquerades, at the Pantheon in Oxford Street, erected as a kind of in-town rival to Ranelagh. It was opened in 1772, and on the fourth of May two years later Gibbon wrote: '' Last night was the triumph of Boodle's. Our masquerade cost two thousand guineas; a sum that might have fertilized a province, vanished in a few hours, but not without leaving behind it the fame of the most splendid and elegant *fête* that was perhaps ever given in a seat of the arts and opulence. It would be as difficult to describe the magnificence of the scene, as it would be easy to record the humour of the night. The one was above, the other below, all relation. I left the Pantheon about five this morning.'' Gibbon does not note that two '' gentlemen,'' coming from that masquerade dressed in their costumes, '' used a woman very indecently,'' and were so mauled by some spectators that they had difficulty in escaping with their lives. It is to be hoped they were not members of Boodle's, who, on the whole, appear to have been somewhat

inoffensive persons. At any rate they allowed
Gibbon ample quietude for his letter-wri-
ting.

Two other clubs of some note in their day are
now nothing but a memory. The first of these,
the Dover House, was formed by George IV
when Prince of Wales in opposition to Brooks's,
where two of his friends had been black-balled.
He placed it in the care of one Weltzie, who
had been his house steward, and for a time it
threatened to become a serious rival to the
other establishments in St. James's Street.
There is Selwyn's confession that the club began to alarm the devotees of Brooks's, for it
lived well, increased in numbers, and was chary
in the choice of members. That, surely, was
the club of which Selwyn tells this vivid story.
"The Duke of Cumberland holds a Pharaoh
Bank, deals standing the whole night; and last
week, when the Duke of Devonshire sat down
to play, he told him there were two rules; one
was, 'not to let you punt more than ten
guineas;' and the other, 'no tick.' Did you
ever hear a more princely declaration? Derby
lost the gold in his pocket, and the Prince of
Wales lent him fifty guineas; on which the
Duke of Cumberland expressed some surprise,
and said he had never lent fifty pounds in his

whole life. ' Then,' says the Prince of Wales,
' it is high time for you to begin.' "

Notwithstanding the promise it gave, Weltzie's club does not seem to have had a protracted history. Nor did the Alfred Club survive a half century. It was one of the earliest
clubs to cater for a distinct class, and may have
failed because it was born out of due time.
This resort for men of letters, and members of
kindred taste, does not appear to have been a
lively place in its first years, for at that time
Lord Dudley described it as the dullest place in
the world, full of bores, an " asylum of doting
Tories and drivelling quidnuncs." Nor was
Byron, another member, much more compli-
mentary. His most favourable verdict pro-
nounced the place a little too sober and literary,
while later he thought it the most tiresome of
London clubs. Then there is the testimony of
another member who said he stood it as long as
he could, but gave in when the seventeenth
bishop was proposed, for it was impossible to
enter the place without being reminded of the
catechism.

Because Arthur's Club is described as having been founded in 1811 that is no reason for
overlooking the fact that its age is much more
venerable than that date would imply. The

word " founded " is indeed misleading; a more suitable term would be " reconstructed." For that is what happened in 1811. The club can really trace an ancestry back to 1756, when it was the " Young Club " at Arthur's, the freedom of which Selwyn desired to present in a dice box to William Pitt. That the club has maintained the old-time spirit to a remarkable degree may be inferred from the fact that no foreigners are admitted as members, and from the further regulation which does not allow a member to entertain a friend at the club. There is a " Strangers' room " in which visitors may wait for members, and where they may be served with light refreshments as a matter of courtesy, but none save members are allowed in the public rooms of the building. This rigid exclusiveness has not militated against the prosperity of the club. Despite a high entrance fee and a considerable annual subscription, candidates have to wait an average of three years for election to its limited circle of six hundred. Which goes to show that the old type of London club is in no danger of extinction just yet.

# IV

## PLEASURE GARDENS OF OLD LONDON

# CHAPTER I

NUMEROUS and diversified as were the out-door resorts of old London, no one of them ever enjoyed the patronage of the gardens at Vauxhall. Nor can any pleasure resort of the English capital boast so long a history. For nearly two centuries, that is, from about 1661 to 1859, it ministered to the amusement of the citizens.

At the outset of its career it was known as New Spring Gardens, and it continued to be described as Spring Gardens in the official an-nouncements till 1786, although for many years previously the popular designation was Vaux-hall. The origin of that name is involved in obscurity, but it is supposed to have been de-rived from a family of the name of Faux who once held the manor.

For the earliest pictures of the resort we must turn to the pages of Pepys, whose first visit to the gardens was paid in May, 1662. On this occasion he was accompanied by his wife, the two maids, and the boy, the latter distinguishing himself by creeping through the hedges and gathering roses. Three years later Pepys went to the gardens on several occasions within a few weeks of each other, the first visit being made in the company of several Admiralty friends, who, with himself, were ill at ease as to what had been the result of the meeting between the English and Dutch fleets. Still, on this, the " hottest day that ever I felt in my life," Pepys did not fail to find enjoyment in walking about the garden, and stayed there till nine o'clock for a moderate expenditure of sixpence. Not many days later he was back again, this time alone and in a philosophic mood. The English fleet had been victorious, and the day was one of thanksgiving. So the diarist strolled an hour in the garden observing the behaviour of the citizens, " pulling of cherries, and God knows what." Quite a different scene met his gaze on his third visit that year; the place was almost deserted, for the dreaded plague had broken out and London was empty.

Then came the year of the Great Fire, and Pepys was in too serious a mood to wend his way to Vauxhall. But he had recovered his spirits by the May of 1667, and gives us this record of a visit of that month: " A great deal

of company, and the weather and garden pleasant: and it is very pleasant and cheap going
thither, for a man may go to spend what he
will, or nothing, all as one. But to hear the
nightingale and other birds, and hear fiddles,
and there a harp, and here a Jew's trump, and
here laughing, and there fine people walking,
is mighty divertising. Among others, there
were two pretty women alone, that walked a
great while, which being discovered by some
idle gentlemen, they would needs take them up;
but to see the poor ladies how they were put to
it to run from them, and they after them, and
sometimes the ladies put themselves along with
other company, then the other drew back; at
last, the last did get off out of the house, and
took boat and away. I was troubled to see
them abused so; and could have found in my
heart, as little desire of fighting as I have, to
have protected the ladies.'' But a time was
to come, on a later visit, when Pepys found
himself in the company of a couple who were
just as rude as the gentlemen he had a mind
to fight. For on a May evening the next year
he fell in with Harry Killigrew and young Newport, as '' very rogues as any in the town,''
who were '' ready to take hold of every woman
that comes by them.'' Yet Pepys did not shake

their company; instead he went with the
rogues to supper in an arbour, though it made
his heart " ake " to listen to their mad talk.
When sitting down to his diary that night he
reflected on the loose company he had been in,
but came to the conclusion that it was not
wholly unprofitable to have such experience of
the lives of others. Perhaps he really enjoyed
the experience; at any rate, he was back again
the following evening, and saw the young Newport at his tricks again. Nor was that rogue
singular in his behaviour. Pepys had other
illustrations on subsequent visits of the rude-
ness which had become a habit with the gallants
of the town.

By the numerous references which may be
found in the comedies of the Restoration period
it is too obvious that Vauxhall fully sustained
its reputation as a resort for the " rogues "
of the town. But, happily, there are not lack-
ing many proofs that the resort was also
largely affected by more serious-minded and
respectable members of the community. It is
true they were never free from the danger of
coming in contact with the seamy side of London life, but that fact did not deter them from
seeking relaxation in so desirable a spot. There
is a characteristic illustration of this blending

of amusement and annoyance in that classical number of the Spectator wherein Addison described his visit to the garden with his famous friend Sir Roger de Coverley. As was usual in the early days of the eighteenth century, and for some years later, the two approached the garden by water. They took boat on the Thames at Temple-stairs, and soon arrived at the landing-place. It was in the awakening month of May, when the garden was in the first blush of its springtime beauty. '' When I considered,'' Addison wrote, '' the fragrancy of the walks and bowers, with the choirs of birds that sung upon the trees, and the loose tribe of people that walked under their shades, I could not but look upon the place as a kind of Mahometan paradise. Sir Roger told me it put him in mind of a little coppice by his house in the country, which his chaplain used to call an aviary of nightingales. ' You must understand,' said the knight, ' there is nothing in the world that pleases a man in love so much as your nightingale. Ah, Mr. Spectator, the many moon-light nights that I have walked by myself, and thought on the widow by the music of the nightingale! ' He here fetched a deep sigh.'' But the worthy old man's fit of musing was abruptly broken by too tangible a reminder that this was indeed a kind of Mahometan paradise.

Up to 1732 Vauxhall appears to have been conducted in a haphazard way. That is, no settled policy had been followed in its management or the provision of set attractions. The owner seems to have depended too much on the nightingales, and the natural beauties of the place. From the date mentioned, however, a new régime began. At that time the garden passed into the control of Jonathan Tyers, who introduced many alterations and improvements. A regular charge was now made for admission, and season tickets in the shape of silver medals were instituted. Several of these were designed by Hogarth, in recognition of whose services in that and other ways Mr. Tyers presented him with a gold ticket entitling him to admission for ever. Among the improvements dating from this new ownership was adequate provision of music. An orchestra was erected, and in addition to instrumental music many of the most famous singers of the day were engaged. The innovations of Mr. Tyers have left their impress on the literature of the place in prose and verse. A somewhat cloying example of the latter is found in an

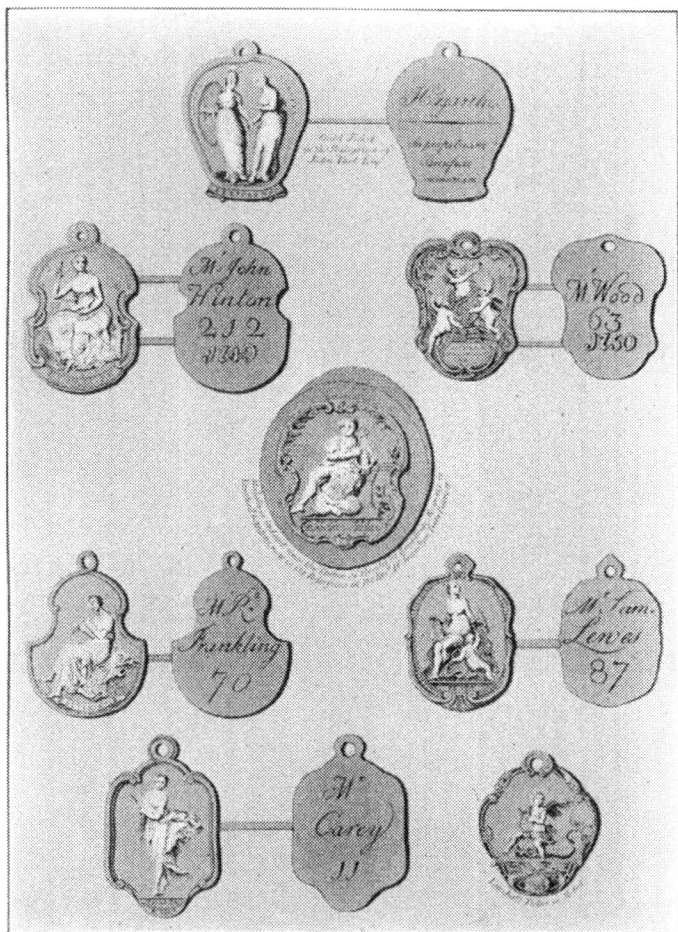

TICKETS FOR VAUXHALL.

effusion describing the visit of Farmer Colin
in 1741:

    " Oh, Mary! soft in feature,
        I've been at dear Vauxhall;
    No paradise is sweeter,
        Not that they Eden call.

    " Methought, when first I entered,
        Such splendours round me shone,
    Into a world I ventured,
        Where rose another sun:

    " While music, never cloying,
        As skylarks sweet, I hear:
    The sounds I'm still enjoying,
        They'll always soothe my ear."

Ten years later Mr. Tyers was paid a more
eloquent tribute by the pen of Fielding. Perhaps he took his beloved Amelia to Vauxhall
for the purpose of heightening his readers'
impression of her beauty, for it will be remembered that she was greatly distressed by the
admiration of some of the " rogues " of the
place; but incidentally he has a word of high
praise for the owner of the garden. " To de-
lineate the particular beauties of these gardens
would, indeed," the novelist writes, " require

as much pains, and as much paper too, as to
rehearse all the good actions of their master,
whose life proves the truth of an observation
which I have read in some ethic writer, that a
truly elegant taste is generally accompanied
with an excellency of heart." But Fielding
does not quite dodge his responsibility to say
something of the place itself, only he is adroit
enough to accentuate his words by placing them
in the mouth of the fair Amelia. " The delicious sweetness of the place," was her verdict,
" the enchanting charms of the music, and the
satisfaction which appears on every one's
countenance, carried my soul almost to heaven
in its ideas." That her rapture should have
been spoilt by the impertinents who forced
themselves on the little party later, is a proof
that the evils which Pepys lamented were still
in evidence at the middle of the eighteenth century.

And another proof may be cited to show that
Vauxhall was at the time in high favour with
the smart set. It occurs in a letter to Lord
Carlisle of July, 1745. The correspondent of
the peer thinks he will be interested in a piece
of news from Vauxhall. One of the boxes in
the garden was, he said, painted with a scene
depicting a gentleman far gone in his cups, in

the company of two ladies of pleasure, and his hat lying on the ground beside him. This appealed so strongly to a certain marquis as typical of his own tastes that he appropriated the box for his own use, stipulating, however, that a marquis's coronet be painted over the hat. Notwithstanding the high character attributed to him by Fielding, Mr. Tyers agreed to the proposal, and the waiters were given authority to instruct any company that might enter that box that it belonged to the marquis in question, and must be vacated if he came on the scene.

Although changes were made from time to time, the general arrangement of Vauxhall remained as it existed at the height of Mr. Tyers' tenancy. The place extended to about twelve acres, laid out in formal walks but richly wooded. The principal entrance led into what was known as the Grand Walk, a tree-lined promenade some three hundred yards in length, and having the South Walk parallel. The latter, however, was distinguished by its three triumphal arches and its terminal painting of the ruins of Palmyra. Intersecting these avenues was the Grand Cross Walk, which traversed the garden from north to south. In addition there were those numerous " Dark

Walks '' which make so frequent an appearance in the literature of the place. Other parts of the garden were known as the Rural Downs, the Musical Bushes, and the Wilderness. In the farthest removed of these the nightingales and other birds for which Vauxhall was famous contributed their quota to the attractions of the place.

In addition to the supper-boxes and pavilions, which were arranged in long rows or in curving fashion, the buildings consisted of the orchestra and the Rotunda, the latter being a circular building seventy feet in diameter. It was fitted up in a style thought attractive in those days, was provided with an orchestra where the band played on wet evenings, and was connected with a long gallery known as the Picture Room. The amusements provided by the management varied considerably. Even at their best, however, they would be voted tame by amusement-seekers of the twentieth century. Fireworks took their place on the programme in 1798, and nearly twenty years later what was deemed a phenomenal attraction was introduced in the person of Mme. Saqui of Paris, who used to climb a long rope leading to the firework platform, whence she descended to the accompaniment of a " tempest

ENTRANCE TO VAUXHALL.

of fireworks.'' One of the earliest and most
popular attractions was that known as the Cas-
cade, which was disclosed to view about nine
o'clock in the evening. It was a landscape
scene illuminated by hidden lights, the central
feature of which was a miller's house and
waterfall having the '' exact appearance of
water.'' More daring efforts were to come
later, such as the allegorical transparency of
the Prince of Wales leaning against a horse
held by Britannia, a Submarine Cavern, a
Hermit's Cottage, and balloon ascents. The
most glorious of these attractions presented
a sordid sight by daylight, but in the dim light
of the countless lamps hung in the trees at
night passed muster with the most critical.

Enough evidence has been produced to show
how the '' rogues '' amused themselves at
Vauxhall, but the milder pleasures of sober
citizens have not been so fully illustrated. Yet
there is no lack of information on that score.
There is, for example, that lively paper in the
Connoisseur which gives an eavesdropping report of the behaviour and conversation of a
London merchant and his wife and two daughters. The Connoisseur took notes from the adjoining box.

'' After some talk, ' Come, come,' said the

old don, ' it is high time, I think, to go to supper.'

" To this the ladies readily assented; and
one of the misses said, ' Do let us have a chick,
papa.'

" ' Zounds! ' said the father, ' they are half-
a-crown a-piece, and no bigger than a sparrow.'

" Here the old lady took him up, ' You are so
stingy, Mr. Rose, there is no bearing with you.
When one is out upon pleasure, I love to appear
like somebody: and what signifies a few shillings once and away, when a body is about it? '

" This reproof so effectually silenced the old
gentleman, that the youngest miss had the courage to put in a word for some ham likewise:
accordingly the waiter was called, and dis-
patched by the old lady with an order for a
chicken and a plate of ham. When it was
brought, our honest cit twirled the dish about
three or four times, and surveyed it with a very
settled countenance; then taking up the slice
of ham, and dangling it to and fro on the end
of his fork, asked the waiter how much there
was of it.

" ' A shilling's worth, Sir,' said the fellow.

" ' Prithee,' said the don, ' how much dost
think it weighs? An ounce? A shilling an
ounce! that is sixteen shillings per pound!

CONNOISSEUR

THE CITIZEN AT VAUXHALL.

A reasonable profit truly! Let me see, suppose now the whole ham weighs thirty pounds; at a shilling per ounce, that is, sixteen shillings per pound, why! your master makes exactly twenty-four pounds of every ham; and if he buys them at the best hand, and salts and cures them himself, they don't stand him in ten shillings a-piece.'

'' The old lady bade him hold his nonsense, declared herself ashamed for him, and asked him if people must not live: then taking a coloured handkerchief from her own neck, she tucked it into his shirt-collar (whence it hung like a bib), and helped him to a leg of the chicken. The old gentleman, at every bit he put into his mouth, amused himself with saying, ' There goes two-pence, there goes three-pence, there goes a groat. Zounds, a man at these places should not have a swallow as wide as a tom-tit.' ''

But having been launched on a career of temporary extravagance, the honest citizen grew reckless. So he called for a bottle of port, and enjoyed it so much as to call for a second. But the bill brought him to his senses again, and he left Vauxhall with the conviction that one visit was enough for a lifetime.

So long as Vauxhall existed the thinness and

dearness of its plates of ham were proverbial.
There is a legend to the effect that a man secured the position of carver on the understanding that he was able to cut a ham so thin that
the slices would cover the entire garden.
Writer after writer taxed his ingenuity to find
metaphors applicable to those shadowy slices.
One scribe in 1762 declared that a newspaper
could be read through them; Pierce Egan decided that they were not cut with a knife but
shaved off with a plane; and a third averred
that they tasted more of the knife than anything else.

Of course Goldsmith made his philosophical
Chinaman visit Vauxhall, the other members
of the party consisting of the man in black, a
pawnbroker's widow, and Mr. Tibbs, the sec-
ond-rate beau, and his wife.  The Chinaman
was delighted, and, by a strange coincidence,
Addison's metaphor crops up once more in
his rapturous description.  '' The illuminations
began before we arrived, and I must confess
that, upon entering the gardens, I found every
sense overpaid with more than expected pleasure; the lights everywhere glimmering through
the scarcely moving trees; the full-bodied concert bursting on the stillness of the night; the
natural concert of the birds, in the more retired

part of the grove, vying with that which was
formed by art; the company gaily-dressed
looking satisfaction, and the tables spread with
various delicacies, all conspired to fill my imagination with the visionary happiness of the
Arabian lawgiver, and lifted me into an ecstasy
of admiration. ' Head of Confucius,' cried I
to my friend, ' this is fine! this unites rural
beauty with courtly magnificence: if we except
the virgins of immortality that hang on every
tree, and may be plucked at every desire, I do
not see how this falls short of Mahomet's paradise!' ''

But the Celestial rhapsody was interrupted
by Mr. Tibbs, who wanted to know the plan of
campaign for the evening. This was a matter
on which Mrs. Tibbs and the widow could not
agree, but an adjournment to a box in the mean-
time was accepted as a compromise. Even
there, however, the feminine warfare was continued, to the final triumph of Mrs. Tibbs, who,
being prevailed upon to sing, not only distracted the nerves of her listeners, but pro-
longed her melody to such an extent that the
widow was robbed of a sight of the water-
works.

No account of Vauxhall however brief should
overlook the attractions the place had to the

sentimental young lady of the late eighteenth century. From the character of the songs which the vocalists affected it might be inferred that love-lorn misses were expected to form the bulk of their audience. Perhaps that was so; for the Dark Walks were ideal places in which to indulge the tender sentiment. The elder daughter of the Connoisseur's citizen confessed a preference for those walks because "they were so solentary," and Tom Brown noted that the ladies who had an inclination to be private took delight in those retired and shady avenues, and in the windings and turnings of the little Wilderness, where both sexes met and were of mutual assistance in losing their way.

Smollett, however, made his impressionable Lydia Melford sum up the attractions of Vauxhall for the young lady of the period. It is a tender picture she draws, with the wherry in which she made her journey, "so light and slender that we looked like so many fairies sailing in a nutshell." There was a rude awakening at the landing-place, where the rough and ready hangers-on of the place rushed into the water to drag the boat ashore; but that momentary disturbance was forgotten when Miss Lydia entered the resort.

"Imagine to yourself, my dear Letty," she

wrote, " a spacious garden, part laid out in delightful walks, bounded with high hedges and trees, and paved with gravel; part exhibiting a wonderful assemblage of the most picturesque and striking objects, pavilions, lodges, groves, grottos, lawns, temples, and cascades; porticos, colonnades, and rotundas; adorned with pillars, statues, and paintings; the whole illuminated with an infinite number of lamps, disposed in different figures of suns, stars, and constellations; the place crowded with the gayest company, ranging through those blissful shades, or supping in different lodges, on cold collations, enlivened with mirth, freedom, and good humour." Lydia has a word, too, for the musical charms of the place, and seems pleased to have heard a celebrated vocalist despite the fact that her singing made her head ache through excess of pleasure. All this was enhanced, no doubt, by the presence of that Mr. Barton, the country gentleman of good fortune, who was so " particular " in his attentions.

Perhaps the best proof of the place Vauxhall occupied in popular esteem is afforded by the number of occasions on which the garden was chosen as the scene of a national event. This was notably the case in 1813, when a preten-

tious festival took place in the grounds in celebration of the victory achieved at Vittoria by
the Allies under Wellington. An elaborate
scheme of decoration, both interior and exterior, was a striking feature of the occasion,
while to accommodate the numerous dinner
guests a large temporary saloon became necessary. This was constructed among the trees,
the trunks of which were adorned with the flags
of the Allies and other trophies. The Duke of
York presided over the banquet, and the company included, in addition to Wellington, most
of the royal and other notables of the day.
Dinner, whereat the inevitable ham appeared
but probably not so finely cut, lasted from five
to nearly nine o'clock, at which hour the ladies
and general guests of the evening began to
arrive. Vauxhall outdid itself in illuminations
that night. And the extra attractions included
a transparency of the King, a mammoth picture of Wellington, a supply of rockets that
rose to a " superior height," and innumerable
bands, some of which discoursed music from
the forest part of the garden, presenting some
idea of " soldiers in a campaign regaling and
reposing themselves under the shade." In fact,
the whole occasion was so unusual that the
electrified reporter of the Annual Register was

SCENE AT VAUXHALL.

at his wit's end to know what to praise most.
For a moment he was overpowered by the exalted rank of the leading personages, and then
fascinated by the charms and costumes of the
ladies, only to find fresh subjects for further
adjectives in the fineness of the weather, the
blaze of lights that seemed to create an arti-
ficial day, and the unity of sentiment and disposition that pervaded all alike.

At this date, of course, the Tyers of Fielding's eulogy had been dead some years. He
was succeeded by his two sons, one of whom,
Tom, was a favourite with Dr. Johnson. At
the Vittoria fête the resort was still controlled
by the Tyers family, but it passed out of their
possession in 1821, and had many owners before the end came in 1859.

Another Amelia, however, was to visit Vauxhall before its gates were closed for the last
time, — the Amelia beloved of all readers of
"Vanity Fair." Naturally, she does not go
alone. Thackeray had too much affection for
that gentle creature to make her face such an
ordeal. No, there was the careless, high-
spirited George Osborne, and the ever-faithful
Dobbin, and the slow-witted Jos Sedley, and
the scheming Rebecca Sharp. That Vauxhall
episode was to play a pregnant part in the

destiny of Becky. Such an auspicious occasion would surely lead to a proposal from the nearly-captured Jos. For a time it seemed as though such might be the case. Becky and her corpulent knight lost themselves in one of those famous Dark Walks, and the situation began to develop in tenderness and sentiment. Jos was so elated that he told Becky his favourite Indian stories for the sixth time, giving an opening for the lady's '' How I should like to see India! '' But at that critical moment the bell rang for the fireworks, and at the same time tolled the knell of Becky's chances of becoming Mrs. Jos Sedley. For the fireworks somehow created a thirst, and the bowl of rack punch for which Jos called, and which he was left to consume, as the young ladies did not drink it and Osborne did not like it, speedily worked its disastrous effects. In short, as we all know, Jos made a fool of himself, and when he came to himself the following morning and saw himself as Osborne wished he should, all his tender passion for Becky evaporated once and for all.

Perhaps these visitors to Vauxhall who never had an existence are more real to us to-day than all the countless thousands of men and

women who really trod its gravel walks.  But
the real and the unreal alike are of the past,
a memory for the fancy to play with as is that
of Vauxhall itself.

# CHAPTER II

## RANELAGH

During the latter half of the eighteenth century Vauxhall had a serious rival in Ranelagh. No doubt the success of the former was the cause of the latter. It may have been, too, that as the gardens at Vauxhall became more and more a popular resort without distinction of class, the need was felt of a rendezvous which should be a little more select.

No doubt exists as to how Ranelagh came by its name. Toward the end of the seventeenth century the Earl of Ranelagh built himself a house at Chelsea, and surrounded it with gardens which were voted the best in England for their size. This peer, who was Paymaster-General of the Forces, seems to have taken keen pleasure in house-planning and the laying out of grounds. Among the manuscripts of the Marquis of Ormonde are many letters written by him to the bearer of that title in the early eighteenth century, which show that he assumed the oversight of building operations at

Ormonde's London house at that time. The minute attention he gave to all kinds of details proves that he had gained experience by the building of his own house not many years before.

But Ranelagh house and gardens had a short history as the residence and pleasance of a nobleman. The earl died in 1712, and in 1730 it became necessary to secure an act of Parliament to vest his property at Chelsea in trustees. Three years later a sale took place, and the house and larger portion of the grounds were purchased by persons named Swift and Timbrell. It was at this stage the project of establishing a rival to Vauxhall first took shape. The idea seems to have originated with James Lacy, that patriotic patentee of Drury Lane theatre who raised a band of two hundred men at the time of the Jacobite Rebellion of 1745. He it was, also, who afterwards became a partner with David Garrick. But, however successful he was to prove as an organizer of volunteers, Lacy was not to shine as the founder of a rival to Vauxhall. For some unexplained reason he abandoned his share in the Ranelagh project, and eventually the matter was taken in hand by Sir Thomas Robinson, who soon secured sufficient financial support to carry the plan to a successful issue. Sir Thomas provided a considerable share of the capital of sixteen thousand pounds himself, and took a leading part in the management of Ranelagh till his death in 1777. His gigantic figure and cheery manners earned for him the titles óf Ranelagh's Maypole and Gardand of Delights.

As the gardens were already laid out in a handsome manner, the chief matter requiring attention was the planning and erection of a suitable main building. Hence the erection of the famous Rotunda, the architectural credit of which is given to one William Jones. But that honour is disputed. It is claimed that no less a person than Henry VIII was responsible for the idea on which the Rotunda was based. That king, according to one historian, caused a great banqueting-house to be erected, eight hundred feet in compass, after the manner of a theatre. '' And in the midst of the same banqueting-house,'' continued the historian, '' was set up a great pillar of timber, made of eight great masts, bound together with iron bands for to hold them together: for it was a hundred and thirty-four feet in length, and cost six pounds thirteen shillings and fourpence to set it upright. The banqueting-house was covered

over with canvas, fastened with ropes and iron
as fast as might be devised; and within the
said house was painted the heavens, with stars,
sun, moon, and clouds, with divers other things
made above men's heads. And above the high
pillar of timber that stood upright in the midst,
was made stages of timber for organs and
other instruments to stand upon, and men to
play on them.'' Such, it is asserted, was the
model the architect of the Rotunda at Ranelagh
had in view.

And really there appears to be good ground
for laying this charge of constructive plagiar-
ism against the memory of William Jones. It
is true the building was on a scale somewhat
smaller than that erected at the order of Henry
VIII, for its circumference was limited to four
hundred and fifty feet, while its greatest diameter was but one hundred and eighty-five feet.
But the planning of the interior of the Rotunda
bore a suspicious likeness to the royal banqueting-house. The central portion of the building
was a square erection consisting of pillars and
arches, and seems to have been a direct copy
of those eight great masts. Nor did the parallel end there. In the Rotunda at Ranelagh
as in the king's banqueting-house, this central
construction was designed as the place for the

musicians. And even the ceiling was something of a copy, for that of the Rotunda was divided into panels, in each of which was painted a celestial figure on a sky-blue ground.

On the general idea of the banqueting-house, however, Mr. Jones made a number of improvements. The entrances to the Rotunda were four in number, corresponding with the points of the compass, each consisting of a portico designed after the manner of a triumphal arch. The interior of the building presented, save for its central erection, the aspect of a modern opera-house. Around the entire wall was a circle of boxes, divided by wainscoting, and each decorated with a " droll painting " and hung with a candle-lamp. Above these was another tier of boxes, similarly fitted, each of them, fifty-two in number, having accommodation for seven or eight persons. Higher up was a circle of sixty windows. Although the building itself was constructed of wood, it could boast of a plaster floor, which was covered with matting. Scattered over that floor were numerous tables covered with red baize whereon refreshments were served. Such was the general arrangement of the Rotunda, but one alteration had speedily to be made. It was quickly discovered that the central erection was ill adapted for the use of the orchestra, and consequently it was transformed into four fireplaces, which were desirable locations in the cold months of the year.

Perhaps no surprise need be felt that Ranelagh was not ready when it was opened. What public resort ever has been? The consequence was that there were at least two opening ceremonies. The first took the form of a public breakfast on April 5th, 1742, and was followed by other early repasts of a like nature. One of these, seventeen days later, provided Horace Walpole with the subject of the first of his many descriptions of the place. " I have been breakfasting this morning at Ranelagh Gardens; " he wrote, " they have built an immense amphitheatre, with balconies full of little ale houses; it is in rivalry to Vauxhall, and costs above twelve thousand pounds. The building is not finished, but they get great sums by people going to see it and breakfasting in the house: there were yesterday no less than three hundred and eighty persons, at eighteen pence a piece." About a month later another inaugural ceremony took place, which Walpole duly reported. " Two nights ago Ranelagh Gardens were opened at Chelsea; the prince, princess, duke, much nobility, and much mob besides were there. There is a vast amphitheatre, finely gilt, painted, and illuminated; into which everybody that loves eating, drinking, staring, or crowding is admitted for twelve pence. The building and disposition of the gardens cost sixteen thousand pounds. Twice a week there are to be ridottos at guinea tickets, for which you are to have a supper and music. I was there last night, but did not feel the joy of it. Vauxhall is a little better, for the garden is pleasanter, and one goes by water.'' In time, however, Walpole was converted to the superior attractions of the new resort. Two years later he confessed that he went every night to Ranelagh, that it had totally beaten Vauxhall, and that it had the patronage of everybody who was anybody. Lord Chesterfield had fallen so much in love with the place that he had ordered all his letters to be directed thither.

Many red-letter days are set down in the history of Ranelagh during the sixty years of its existence, but its historians are agreed that the most famous of the entertainments given there was the Venetian Masquerade in honour of the Peace of Aix-la-Chapelle on April 26th, 1749. For the most spirited narrative of that festival, recourse must be had to the letters of

VENETIAN MASQUERADE AT RANELAGH, 1749.

Walpole. Peace was proclaimed on the 25th,
and the next day, Walpole wrote, " was what
was called a Jubilee Masquerade in the Venetian manner, at Ranelagh; it had nothing Venetian in it, but was by far the best understood
and prettiest spectacle I ever saw; nothing in
a fairy tale even surpassed it. One of the proprietors, who is a German, and belongs to the
Court, had got my Lady Yarmouth to persuade
the King to order it. It began at three o'clock,
and about five people of fashion began to go.
When you entered you found the whole garden
filled with masks and spread with tents, which
remained all night very commodely. In one
quarter was a Maypole dressed with garlands
and people dancing round it to a tabor and
pipes and rustic music, all masqued, as were
all the various bands of music that were dis-
persed in different parts of the garden; some
like huntsmen with French horns, some like
peasants, and a troop of harlequins and scara-
mouches in the little open temple on the mount.
On the Canal was a sort of gondola adorned
with flags and streamers, and filled with music,
rowing about. All round the outside of the
amphitheatre were shops filled with Dresden
china, Japan, etc., and all the shopkeepers in
mask. The amphitheatre was illuminated, and

in the middle was a circular bower, composed
of all kinds of firs in tubs, from twenty to
thirty feet high: under them orange trees with
small lamps in each orange, and below them
all sorts of the finest auriculas in pots; and
festoons of natural flowers hanging from tree
to tree. Between the arches, too, were firs, and
smaller ones in the balconies above. There
were booths for tea and wine, gaming tables
and dancing, and about two thousand persons.
In short it pleased me more than anything I
ever saw.''

But there was another side to all this. Vauxhall evidently looked on with envious eyes, and
those who were interested in the welfare of that
resort managed to engineer opposition to the
Venetian fête in the form of satirical prints
and letterpress. Perhaps they did more. At
any rate it is a significant fact that shortly
afterwards the justices of Middlesex were
somehow put in motion, and made such representations to the authorities at Ranelagh that
they were obliged to give an undertaking not
to indulge in any more public masques. This,
however, did not prevent the subscription car-
nival in celebration of a royal birthday in May,
1750, when there was '' much good company
but more bad company,'' the members of which

were "dressed or undress'd" as they thought fit.

Ranelagh was evidently an acquired taste. It has been seen that Walpole did not take to the place at first, but afterwards became one of its most enthusiastic admirers. And there was a famous friend of Walpole who passed through the same experience. This was the poet Gray, who, three years after the resort was opened declared that he had no intention of following the crowd to Ranelagh.

"I have never been at Ranelagh Gardens since they were opened," is his confession to a friend. "They do not succeed: people see it once, or twice, and so they go to Vauxhall."

"Well, but is it not a very great design, very new, finely lighted?"

"Well, yes, aye, very fine truly, so they yawn and go to Vauxhall, and then it's too hot, and then it's too cold, and here's a wind and there's a damp."

Perhaps it is something of a surprise to find the author of the "Elegy" interested in public gardens at all, but given such an interest it would have been thought that Ranelagh was more to his taste than Vauxhall. And so it proved in the end. Like his Eton friend Walpole, he became a convert and so hearty an admirer of the Chelsea resort that he spent many evenings there in the August of 1746.

Other notable visitors to Ranelagh included Goldsmith and Sir Joshua Reynolds, and Dr. Johnson and Tobias Smollett. It seems more than likely that Ranelagh with the first couple figured largely in that round of pleasures which kept them from the meetings of The Club to the disgust of Beauclerk, but Goldsmith might have justified his visits on the plea that he was gathering " local colour " for that letter by Belinda which he introduced into the " Citizen of the World." No doubt he saw many a colonel there answering to that " irresistible fellow " who made such an impression on Belinda's heart. " So well-dressed, so neat, so sprightly, and plays about one so agreeably, that I vow he has as much spirits as the Marquis of Monkeyman's Italian greyhound. I first saw him at Ranelagh: he shines there: he is nothing without Ranelagh, and Ranelagh nothing without him." Perhaps Sir Joshua would have excused his idling at Ranelagh on the ground of looking for models, or the hints it afforded for future pictures.

With Dr. Johnson it was different. Ranelagh was to him a " place of innocent recreation " and nothing more. The " *coup d'œil*

was the finest thing he had ever seen," Boswell
reports, and then makes his own comparison
between that place and the Pantheon. " The
truth is, Ranelagh is of a more beautiful form;
more of it, or rather, indeed, the whole Rotunda, appears at once, and it is better lighted.
However, as Johnson observed, we saw the Pantheon in time of mourning, when there was a
dull uniformity; whereas we had seen Ranelagh, when the view was enlivened with a gay
profusion of colours." No small part of Johnson's pleasure during his visits to Ranelagh
was derived from uncomplimentary reflections
on the mental conditions of its frequenters.
Boswell had been talking one day in the vein
of his hero's poem on the " Vanity of Human
Wishes," and commented on the persistence
with which things were done upon the supposi-
tion of happiness, as witness the splendid
places of public amusement, crowded with company.

" Alas, Sir," said Johnson, in a kind of
appendix to his poem, " these are all only
struggles for happiness. When I first entered
Ranelagh, it gave an expansion and gay sensa-
tion to my mind, such as I never experienced
any where else. But, as Xerxes wept when he
viewed his immense army, and considered that

not one of that great multitude would be alive
a hundred years afterwards, so it went to my
heart to consider that there was not one in all
that brilliant circle, that was not afraid to go
home and think; but that the thoughts of each
individual there would be distressing when
alone.''

Smollett, like Goldsmith, made good use of
his visits to Ranelagh. With the enterprise of
the observant novelist, he turned his experi-
ences into '' copy.'' And with that ubiquity
of vision which is the privilege of the master
of fiction he was able to see the place from two
points of view. To Matt. Bramble, that devo-
tee of solitude and mountains, the Chelsea resort was one of the worst inflictions of London.

'' What are the amusements of Ranelagh? ''
he asked. '' One half of the company are following one another's tails, in an eternal circle;
like so many blind asses in an olive-mill, where
they can neither discourse, distinguish, nor be
distinguished; while the other half are drinking hot water, under the denomination of tea,
till nine or ten o'clock at night, to keep them
awake for the rest of the evening. As for the
orchestra, the vocal music especially, it is well
for the performers that they cannot be heard
distinctly.'' But Smollett does not leave Rane-

lagh at that. Lydia also visited the place and
was enraptured with everything. To her it
looked like an enchanted palace '' of a genio,
adorned with the most exquisite performances
of painting, carving, and gilding, enlighted
with a thousand golden lamps, that emulate
the noon-day sun; crowded with the great, the
rich, the gay, the happy, and the fair; glitter-
ing with cloth of gold and silver, lace, embroid-
ery, and precious stones. While these exulting
sons and daughters of felicity tread this round
of pleasure, or regale in different parties, and
separate lodges, with fine imperial tea and
other delicious refreshments, their ears are entertained with the most ravishing music, both
instrumental and vocal.'' If the management
of Ranelagh had been on the lookout for a press
agent, they would doubtless have preferred
Smollett in his Lydia mood.

Only occasionally was the even tenor of
Ranelagh amusement disturbed by an untoward
event. One such occasion was due to that notorious Dr. John Hill who figures so largely in
Isaac Disraeli's '' Calamities and Quarrels of
Authors.'' Few men have tried more ways of
getting a living than he. As a youth he was
apprenticed to an apothecary, but in early manhood he turned to botany and travelled all over

England in search of rare plants which he intended drying by a special process and publishing by subscription. When that scheme failed, he took to the stage, and shortly after wrote the words of an opera which was sent to Rich and rejected. This was the beginning of authorship with Hill, whose pen, however, brought more quarrels on his head than guineas into his pockets. And it was his authorship which connected him with the history of Ranelagh.

One of Hill's ventures was to provide the town with a daily paper called The Inspector, in the pages of which he made free with the character of an Irish gentleman named Brown. Usually the men Hill attacked were writers, who flayed him with their pens whenever they thought there was occasion. Hence the conclusive epigram with which Garrick rewarded an attack on himself:

" For physic and farces, his equal there *scarce* is,
His farces are physic, his physic a farce is."

But Mr. Brown was a man of action, not words. So he sought out his assailant at Ranelagh on the night of May 6th, 1752, and caned him in the Rotunda in the presence of a large company. Here was excitement indeed for Ranelagh, and the affair was the talk of the town for

THE ASSAULT ON DR. JOHN HILL AT RANELAGH.

many a day afterwards. Of course Hill did not retort in kind; on the contrary he showed himself to be an abject coward and took his thrashing without any bodily protest. That he made loud vocal protest seems likely enough. Hence the point of the pictorial satire which was quickly on sale at the London print-shops. This drawing depicted Hill being seized by the ear by the irate Mr. Brown, who is represented as exclaiming, " Draw your sword, libeller, if you have the spirit of a mouse."

The only reply of Hill was, " What? against an illiterate fellow that can't spell? I prefer a drubbing. Oh, Mr. P——, get me the constable, for here's a gentleman going to murder me! "

Mr. P——, who is seen hastening from behind a pillar of the Rotunda, replies: " Yes, sir, yes. Pray young gentleman don't hurt him, for he never has any meaning in what he writes."

Hill took to his bed, raised an action against Mr. Brown for assault, and proclaimed from the housetops that there was a conspiracy to murder him. This brought forth a second print, showing Hill in bed and attended by doctors, one of whom, in reply to the patient's plea that he had no money, responds, " Sell your sword, it is only an encumbrance."

Another lively episode disturbed the peace

of Ranelagh on the night of May 11th, 1764. Several years previously some daring spirits among the wealthier classes had started a movement for the abolition of vails, otherwise "tips," to servants, and the leaders of that movement were subjected to all kinds of annoyance from the class concerned. On the night in question the resentment of coachmen, footmen and other servants developed into a serious riot at Ranelagh, special attention being paid to those members of the nobility and gentry who would not suffer their employees to take vails from their guests. "They began," says a chronicle of the time, "by hissing their masters, they then broke all the lamps and outside windows with stones; and afterwards putting out their flambeaux, pelted the company, in a most audacious manner, with brickbats, etc., whereby several were greatly hurt." This attack was not received in the submissive spirit of Dr. Hill; the assaulted gentry drew their swords to beat back the rioters and severely wounded not a few. They probably enjoyed the diversion from the ordinary pleasures of Ranelagh.

How gladly the frequenters of the gardens welcomed the slightest departure from the normal proceedings of the place may be inferred from the importance which was attached to an incident which took place soon after 1770. Public mourning was in order for some one, and of course the regular patrons of Ranelagh expressed their obedience to the court edict by appropriate attire. One evening, however, it was observed that there were two gentlemen in the gardens dressed in coloured clothes. It was obvious they were strangers to the place and unknown to each other. Their inappropriate costume quickly attracted attention, and became the subject of general conversation, and, such a dearth was there of excitement, Lord Spencer Hamilton aroused feverish interest by laying a wager that before the night was out he would have the two strangers walking arm in arm. The wager taken, he set to work in an adroit manner. Watching one of the strangers until he sat down, he immediately placed himself by his side, and entered into conversation. A few minutes later Lord Spencer left his new friend in search of the other stranger, to whom he addressed some civil remark, and accompanied on a stroll round the gardens. Coming back eventually to the seat on which the first stranger was still resting, Lord Spencer had no difficulty in persuading his second new acquaintance to take a seat also. The conversation of the trio naturally became general, and a little later Lord Spencer suggested a promenade. On starting off he offered his arm to the first stranger, who paid the same compliment to stranger number two, with the result that Lord Spencer was able to direct the little procession to the vicinity of his friends, and so demonstrate that the wager was won. So simple an incident furnished Ranelagh with great amusement for an entire evening!

What the management provided by way of entertainment has been partially hinted at. Music appears to have been the chief stand-by from the first and was provided at breakfast time as well as at night. Many notable players and singers appeared in the Rotunda, including Mozart, who, as a boy of eight, played some of his own compositions on the harpsichord and organ, and Dibdin, the famous ballad singer. Fireworks were a later attraction, as also was the exhibition named Mount Etna, which called for a special building. Occasional variety was provided by regattas and shooting-matches, and balloon-ascents, and displays of diving.

No doubt Ranelagh was at its best and gay-est when the scene of a masquerade. But unfortunately those entertainments had their sinister side. Fielding impeaches them in " Amelia " by their results, and the novelist was not alone in his criticism. The Connoisseur devoted a paper to the evils of those gatherings, deriding them as foreign innovations, and recalling the example of the lady who had proposed to attend one in the undress garb of Iphigenia. " What the above-mentioned lady had the hardiness to attempt alone," the writer continued, " will (I am assured) be set on foot by our persons of fashion, as soon as the hot days come in. Ranelagh is the place pitched upon for their meeting; where it is proposed to have a masquerade *al fresco,* and the whole company are to display all their charms *in puris naturalibus.* The pantheon of the heathen gods, Ovid's Metamorphoses, and Titian's prints, will supply them with sufficient variety of undressed characters." A cynic might harbour the suspicion that this critic was in the pay of Vauxhall.

Even he, however, did not utter the worst about the amusements of Ranelagh. The truth was known to all but confessed by few. The outspoken Matt. Bramble in the indictment cited above gave emphatic utterance to the fact that the chief recreation at Ranelagh was worse

than none at all. " One may be easily tired "
of the place, was the verdict of a noble lord in
1746; " it is always the same." And to the
same effect is the conclusion reached by a
French visitor, who was delighted for five minutes, and then oppressed with satiety and in-
difference. When the visitor had made the
promenade of the Rotunda, there was practically nothing for him to do save make it
again. Hence the mill-round of monotony so
aptly expressed by the Suffolk village poet,
Robert Bloomfield, who was lured to Ranelagh
one night shortly before its doors were finally
closed.

" To Ranelagh, once in my life,
    By good-natur'd force I was driven;
The nations had ceas'd their long strife,
    And Peace beam'd her radiance from Heaven.
What wonders were there to be found,
    That a clown might enjoy or disdain?
First, we trac'd the gay ring all around;
    Aye — *and then we went round it again.*

" A thousand feet rustled on mats,
    A carpet that once had been green,
Men bow'd with their outlandish hats,
    With corners so fearfully keen!
Fair maids, who, at home in their haste,
    Had left all their clothes but a train,

Swept the floor clean, as slowly they pac'd,
    Then — *walked round and swept it again.*

" The music was truly enchanting,
    Right glad was I when I came near it;
But in fashion I found I was wanting —
    'Twas the fashion to walk, and not hear it.
A fine youth, as beauty beset him,
    Look'd smilingly round on the train,
' The King's nephew,' they cried, as they met him.
    Then — *we went round and met him again.*

" Huge paintings of heroes and peace
    Seem'd to smile at the sound of the fiddle,
Proud to fill up each tall shining space,
    Round the lantern that stood in the middle.
And George's head too; Heaven screen him;
    May he finish in peace his long reign:
And what did we when we had seen him?
    Why — *went round and saw him again."*

That poem ought to have killed Ranelagh
had the resort not been near its demise at the
time it was written. But there was to be one
final flare-up ere the end came. On a June
night in 1803 the Rotunda was the scene of its
last ball. The occasion was the Installation of
the Knights of the Bath, and produced, on the
authority of the Annual Register, " one of the
most splendid entertainments ever given in this
country." The cost was estimated at seven

thousand pounds, which may well have been
the case when the guests ate cherries at a
guinea a pound and peas at fourteen shillings
a quart. That fête was practically the last of
Ranelagh; about a month later the music
ceased and the lamps were extinguished for
ever. And the " struggles for happiness " of
sixty years were ended.

## CHAPTER III

PRIOR to the eighteenth century the Londoner was ill provided with outdoor pleasure resorts. It is true he had the Paris Garden at Bankside, which Donald Lupton declared might be better termed " a foul den than a fair garden. It's a pity," he added, " so good a piece of ground is no better employed; " but, apart from two or three places of that character, his *al fresco* amusements were exceedingly limited. It should not be forgotten, however, that the ale-houses of those days frequently had a plot of land attached to them, wherein a game of bowls might be enjoyed.

But the object-lesson of Vauxhall changed all that. From the date when that resort passed into the energetic management of Jonathan Tyers, smaller pleasure gardens sprang into existence all over London. By the middle of the eighteenth century they had grown so numerous that it would be a serious undertaking to attempt an exhaustive catalogue.

As, however, they had so many features in
common, and passed through such kindred
stages of development, the purpose of this survey will be sufficiently served by a brief history of four or five typical examples.

How general was the impression that Vauxhall had served as a model in most instances
may be seen from the remark of a historian of
1761 to the effect that the Marylebone Garden
was to be " considered as a kind of humble
imitation of Vauxhall." Had Pepys' Diary
been in print at that date, and known to the
proprietor, he would have been justified in re-
senting the comparison. For, as a matter of
fact, the diarist, under the date of May 7th,
1668, had actually set down this record: " Then
we abroad to Marrowbone, and there walked in
the garden, the first time I ever was there, and
a pretty place it is." At a first glance this
entry might be regarded as disposing of the
charge of imitation on the part of Marylebone
Gardens. Such, however, is not strictly the
case. It is true there were gardens here at the
middle of the seventeenth century, but they
were part of the grounds of the old manor-
house, and practically answered to those tavern
bowling-alleys to which reference has been
made. The principal of these was attached to

the tavern known as the Rose, which was a favourite haunt of the Duke of Buckingham, and the scene of his end-of-the-season dinner at which he always gave the toast: "May as many of us as remain unhanged next spring meet here again."

What needs to be specially noted in connection with the history of this resort is, that it was not until 1737 — five years after the opening of Vauxhall under Tyers — that the owner of Marylebone Gardens, Daniel Gough, sufficiently put the place in order to warrant a charge for admission. In the following year the place was formally advertised as a resort for evening amusement, that announcement marking a definite competition with Vauxhall. The buildings at this time comprised a spacious garden-orchestra fitted with an organ, and what was called the Great Room, an apartment specially adapted for balls and suppers.

Many singers, some famous and other notorious, entertained the patrons of Marylebone Gardens. From 1747 to 1752 the principal female vocalist was Mary Ann Falkner, who, after a respectable marriage, became the subject of an arrangement on the part of her idle husband whereby she passed under the protection of the Earl of Halifax. She bore two children to that peer, and so maintained her power over him that for her sake he broke off an engagement with a wealthy lady. Another songstress, fair and frail, was the celebrated Nan Catley, the daughter of a coachman, whose beauty of face and voice and freedom of manners quickly made her notorious. She had already been the subject of an exciting law suit when she appeared at Marylebone at the age of eighteen. Miss Catley had been engaged by Thomas Lowe, the favourite tenor, who in 1763 became the lessee of the gardens, and opened his season with a '' Musical Address to the Town,'' sung by himself, Miss Catley and Miss Smith. The address apologized for the lack of some of the attractions of Vauxhall and Ranelagh, but added —

" Yet nature some blessings has scatter'd around;
  And means to improve may hereafter be found."

Presuming that Lowe kept his promise, that did not prevent failure overtaking him as a caterer of public amusement. He lacked enterprise as a manager, and a wet summer in 1767 resulted in financial catastrophe.

More serious musical efforts than ballad concerts were attempted at Marylebone from time

to time. That this had been the case even before Dr. Samuel Arnold became proprietor of
the gardens is illustrated by an anecdote of
Dr. Fountayne and Handel, who often frequented the place. Being there together on one
occasion the great composer asked his friend's
opinion of a new composition being played by
the band. After listening a few minutes, Dr.
Fountayne proposed that they resume their
walk, for, said he, " it's not worth listening
to — it's very poor stuff." " You are right,
Mr. Fountayne," Handel replied, " it *is* very
poor stuff. I thought so myself when I had
finished it."

Fireworks were not added to the attractions
until 1751, and even then the displays were only
occasional features for some years. In 1772,
however, that part of the entertainment was
deputed to the well-known Torré, whose unique
fireworks were the talk of London. He had
one set piece called the Forge of Vulcan, which
was so popular that its repetition was frequently demanded. According to George Steevens, it was the fame of Torré's fireworks
which impelled Dr. Johnson to visit the gardens
one night in his company. " The evening had
proved showery," wrote Steevens in his account of the outing, " and soon after the few

people present were assembled, public notice was given that the conductors of the wheels, suns, stars, etc., were so thoroughly water-soaked that it was impossible any part of the exhibition should be made. ' That's a mere ex-cuse,' says the Doctor, ' to save their crackers for a more profitable company. Let us both hold up our sticks, and threaten to break these coloured lamps that surround the orchestra, and we shall soon have our wishes gratified. The core of the fireworks cannot be injured; let the different pieces be touched in their re-spective centres, and they will do their offices as well as ever.' Some young men who over-heard him immediately began the violence he had recommended, and an attempt was speedily made to fire some of the wheels which appeared to have received the smallest damage; but to little purpose were they lighted, for most of them completely failed.''

Apparently that was not the only occasion when the management failed to keep faith with the public. In July, 1774, the newspaper se-verely criticised the proprietors for having charged an admission fee of five shillings to a Fête Champétre, which consisted of nothing more than a few tawdry festoons and extra

MARYLEBONE GARDENS.

lamps, and another mentor of an earlier date
had dismissed the whole place as " nothing
more than two or three gravel roads, and a
few shapeless trees." Altogether, popular as
Torré's fireworks were when they went off, it
is not improbable that they had a considerable
share in terminating the existence of the gardens. Houses were increasing fast in the
neighbourhood, and the dwellers in those
houses objected to being bombarded with rockets. At any rate, six years after the renowned
Torré began his pyrotechnics, the site of the
gardens fell into the hands of builders and the
seeker of out-door amusement had to find his
enjoyment elsewhere.

Perhaps some of the frequenters of Marylebone Gardens transferred their patronage to
the White Conduit House, situated two or three
miles to the north-east. Here again is an example of a pleasure resort developing partially
from an ale-house, for the legend is that the
White Conduit House was at first a small tavern, the finishing touches to which were given,
to the accompaniment of much hard drinking,
on the day Charles I lost his head.

Unusual as is the name of this resort, it is
largely self-explanatory. There was a water-

conduit in an adjacent field, which was faced with white stone, and hence the name. The house itself, however, had its own grounds, which were attractively laid out when the whole property was reconstructed somewhere about 1745. At that time a Long Room was erected, and the gardens provided with a fish-pond and numerous arbours. The popularity of the place seems to date from the proprietorship of Robert Bartholomew, who acquired the property in 1754, and to have continued unabated till nearly the end of the century. Mr. Bartholomew did not overlook any of his attractions in the announcement he made on taking possession. "For the better accommodation of ladies and gentlemen," so the advertisement ran, "I have completed a long walk, with a handsome circular fish-pond, a number of shady pleasant arbours, inclosed with a fence seven feet high to prevent being the least incommoded from people in the fields; hot loaves and butter every day, milk directly from the cows, coffee, tea, and all manner of liquors in the greatest perfection; also a handsome long room, from whence is the most copious prospects and airy situation of any now in vogue. I humbly hope the continuance of my friends' favours, as I make it my chief study to have the

WHITE CONDUIT HOUSE.

best accommodations, and am, ladies and gentlemen, your obliged humble servant, Robert Bartholomew. Note. My cows eat no grains, neither any adulteration in milk or cream.'' It is obvious that Mr. Bartholomew's enthusiasm made him reckless of grammar, and that some of his ladies and gentlemen might have objected to have their butter hot; but it is equally plain that here was a man who knew his business.

And he did not fail of adequate reward. Six years after the publication of that seductive announcement the resort had become so popular, especially as the objective of a Sunday outing, that its praises were sung in poetry in so reputable a periodical as the Gentleman's Magazine. The verses describe the joy of the London 'prentice on the return of Sunday, and give a spirited picture of the scene at the gardens.

> " His meal meridian o'er,
> With switch in hand, he to White Conduit House
> Hies merry-hearted.  Human beings here
> In couples multitudinous assemble,
> Forming the drollest groups that ever trod
> Fair Islingtonian plains.  Male after male,
> Dog after dog succeeding — husbands, wives,
> Fathers and mothers, brothers, sisters, friends,
> And pretty little boys and girls.  Around,
> Across, along, the gardens' shrubby maze,

They walk, they sit, they stand.  What crowds press on,
Eager to mount the stairs, eager to catch
First vacant bench or chair in long room plac'd.
Here prig with prig holds conference polite,
And indiscriminate the gaudy beau
And sloven mix.  Here he, who all the week
Took bearded mortals by the nose, or sat
Weaving dead hairs, and whistling wretched strain,
And eke the sturdy youth, whose trade it is
Stout oxen to contund, with gold-bound hat
And silken stocking strut.  The red arm'd belle
Here shows her tasty gown, proud to be thought
The butterfly of fashion: and forsooth
Her haughty mistress deigns for once to tread
The same unhallow'd floor. — 'Tis hurry all
And rattling cups and saucers.  Waiter here,
And waiter there, and waiter here and there,
At once is call'd — Joe — Joe — Joe — Joe — Joe —
Joe on the right — and Joe upon the left,
For ev'ry vocal pipe re-echoes Joe.
Alas, poor Joe!  Like Francis in the play
He stands confounded, anxious how to please
The many-headed throng.  But shou'd I paint
The language, humours, custom of the place,
Together with all curts'ys, lowly bows,
And compliments extern, 'twould swell my page
Beyond its limits due.  Suffice it then
For my prophetic muse to say, ' So long
As fashion rides upon the wings of time,
While tea and cream, and butter'd rolls can please,
While rival beaux and jealous belles exist,
So long, White Conduit House, shall be thy fame.' "

More distinguished members of the community than the London 'prentice and the " red arm'd belle " frequented the gardens now and then. About 1762 the place was a favourite resort with Oliver Goldsmith, and was the scene of a typical episode in his life. While strolling in the gardens one afternoon he met the three daughters of a tradesman to whom he was under obligation, and of course must needs invite them to take tea as his guests. But when the time of reckoning came he found, characteristically enough, that his pocket was empty. Happily some friends were near to rescue him from his difficulty, but the crucial moment of the incident was to be perpetuated in all its ludicrous humour by an artist of a later generation, who, in the painting entitled " An Awkward Position," depicted the poet at the moment when he discovered his pockets were empty.

Later in its history the White Conduit House became known as the " Minor Vauxhall " and was the scene of balloon ascents, fireworks, and evening concerts. Gradually, however, it fell on evil days, and in 1849 it passed permanently into the history of old London.

No one traversing that sordid thoroughfare known as King's Cross Road in the London of to-day could imagine that that highway was the locality in the mid-eighteenth century of one of the most popular resorts of the English capital. Such, however, was the case. At that time the highway was known as Bagnigge Wells Road, and at its northern extremity was situated the resort known as Bagnigge Wells. The early history of the place is somewhat obscure. Tradition has it that the original house was a summer residence of Nell Gwynne, where she frequently entertained her royal lover. It has also been stated that there was a place of public entertainment here as early as 1738.

Whatever truth there may be in both those assertions, there is no gainsaying the fact that the prosperity of Bagnigge Wells dates from a discovery made by a Mr. Hughes, the tenant of the house, in 1757. This Mr. Hughes took a pride in his garden, and was consequently much distressed to find that the more he used his watering-can the less his flowers thrived. At this juncture a Dr. Bevis appeared on the scene, to whom the curious circumstance was mentioned. On tasting the water from the garden well he was surprised to find its " flavour so near that of the best chalybeates," and at once informed Mr. Hughes that it might be made of great benefit both to the public and himself. The next day a huge bottle of the water was delivered at Dr. Bevis's house, and analysis confirmed his first impression. Before he could proceed further in the matter, Dr. Bevis fell ill, and by the time he had recovered notable doings had been accomplished at Bagnigge Wells.

For Mr. Hughes was not wholly absorbed in the cultivation of flowers. Visions of wealth residing in that well evidently captured his imagination, and he at once set to work fitting up his gardens as a kind of spa, where the public could drink for his financial benefit. A second well was sunk and found to yield another variety of mineral water, and the two waters were connected with a double pump over which a circular edifice named the Temple was constructed. Other attractions were added as their necessity became apparent. They included a spacious banqueting hall known as the Long Room, provided with an organ, and the laying out of the gardens in approved style. No doubt the curative qualities of the waters speedily became a secondary consideration with the patrons of the place, but that probably troubled Mr. Hughes not at all so long as those patrons came in sufficient numbers.

That they did come in crowds is demonstrated by the literature which sprang up around the gardens, and by many other evidences. On its medicinal side the place was celebrated by one poet in these strains:

" Ye gouty old souls and rheumatics crawl on,
Here taste these blest springs, and your tortures are gone;
Ye wretches asthmatick, who pant for your breath,
Come drink your relief, and think not of death.
Obey the glad summons, to Bagnigge repair,
Drink deep of its waters, and forget all your care.

" The distemper'd shall drink and forget all his pain,
When his blood flows more briskly through every vein;
The headache shall vanish, the heartache shall cease,
And your lives be enjoyed in more pleasure and peace
Obey then the summons, to Bagnigge repair,
And drink an oblivion to pain and to care."

Twenty years later the muse of Bagnigge Wells was pitched in a different key. The character of the frequenters had changed for the worse. Instead of '' gouty old souls,'' and '' rheumatics,'' and '' asthmaticks,'' the most noted Cyprians of the day had made the place their rendezvous. So the poet sings of

" Thy arbours, Bagnigge, and the gay alcove,
Where the frail nymphs in am'rous dalliance rove."

BAGNIGGE WELLS.

Concurrently with this change the gentlemen of the road began to favour the gardens with their presence, chief among their number being that notorious highwayman John Rann, otherwise known as Sixteen-String Jack from his habit of wearing a bunch of eight ribbons on each knee. But he came to Bagnigge once too often, for, after insisting on paying unwelcome attentions to a lady in the ball-room, he was seized by some members of the company and thrown out of a window into the Fleet river below.

Notwithstanding this deterioration, the proprietor of the place in 1779 in announcing the opening for the season still dwelt upon the invaluable properties of the waters, not forgetting to add that '' ladies and gentlemen may depend on having the best of Tea, Coffee, etc., with hot loaves, every morning and evening.'' But nothing could ward off the pending catastrophe. '' Bagnigge Wells,'' wrote the historian of its decline, '' sported its fountains, with little wooden cupids spouting water day and night, but it fearfully realized the *facilis descensus Averni*. The gardens were curtailed of their fair proportions, and this once famous resort sank down to a threepenny concert-room.'' It struggled on in that lowly guise for a number of years, but the end came in 1841, and now even the name of the road in which it existed is wiped off the map of London.

More fortunate in that respect was the Bermondsey Spa, the name of which is perpetuated to this day in the Spa Road of that malodorous neighbourhood. This resort, which, like Bagnigge Wells, owed its creation to the discovery of a chalybeate spring, is bound up with the life-story of a somewhat remarkable man, Thomas Keyse by name. Born in 1722, he became a self-taught artist of such skill that several of his still-life paintings were deemed worthy of exhibition at the Royal Academy. He was also awarded a premium of thirty guineas by the Society of Arts for a new method of fixing crayon drawings.

But thirty guineas and the glory of being an exhibitor at the Royal Academy were hardly adequate for subsistence, and hence, somewhere about 1765, Keyse turned to the less distinguished but more profitable occupation of tavern-keeper. Having purchased the Waterman's Arms at Bermondsey, with some adjoining waste land, he transformed the place into a tea-garden. Shortly afterwards a chalybeate spring was discovered in the grounds, an event which obliterated the name of the Waterman's

Arms in favour of the Bermondsey Spa Gardens. The ground was duly laid out in pleasant walks, with the usual accompaniments of leafy arbours and other quiet nooks for tea-parties. The next step was to secure a music license, fit up an orchestra, adorn the trees with coloured lamps, organize occasional displays of fireworks, and challenge comparison with Vauxhall if only on a small scale. One of the attractions reserved for special occasion was a scenic representation of the Siege of Gibraltar, in which fireworks, transparencies, and bomb shells played a prominent part. Keyse himself was responsible for the device by which the idea was carried out, and the performance was so realistic that it was declared to give " a very strong idea of the real Siege."

Hearty as were the plaudits bestowed upon the Siege of Gibraltar, there is not much risk in hazarding the opinion that Keyse took more pride in the picture-gallery of his own paintings than in any other feature of his establishment. The canvases included representations of all kinds of still life, and, thanks to the recording pen of J. T. Smith, that enthusiastic lover of old London, it is still possible to make the round of the gallery in the company of the artist-proprietor. Mr. Smith visited the gardens when public patronage had declined to a low ebb, so that he had the gallery all to himself, as he imagined. '' Stepping back to study the picture of the ' Greenstall,' ' I ask your pardon,' said I, for I had trodden on some one's toes. ' Sir, it is granted,' replied a little, thick-set man with a round face, arch looks, and close-curled wig, surmounted by a small three-cornered hat put very knowingly on one side, not unlike Hogarth's head in his print of the ' Gates of Calais.' ' You are an artist, I presume; I noticed you from the end of the gallery, when you first stepped back to look at my best picture. I painted all the objects in this room from nature and still life.' ' Your Greengrocer's Shop,' said I, ' is inimitable; the drops of water on that savoy appear as if they had just fallen from the element. Van Huysun could not have pencilled them with greater delicacy.' ' What do you think,' said he, ' of my Butcher's Shop?' ' Your pluck is bleeding fresh, and your sweetbread is in a clean plate.' ' How do you like my bull's eye?' ' Why, it would be a most excellent one for Adams or Dolland to lecture upon. Your knuckle of veal is the finest I ever saw.' ' It's young meat,' replied he; ' any one who is a judge of meat can tell that from the blueness of its bone.'

' What a beautiful white you have used on the fat of that Southdown leg! or is it Bagshot? ' ' Yes,' said he, ' my solitary visitor, it is Bagshot: and as for my white, that is the best Nottingham, which you or any artist can procure at Stone and Puncheon's, Bishopsgate Street Within.' ' Sir Joshua Reynolds,' continued Mr. Keyse, ' paid me two visits. On the second, he asked me what white I had used; and when I told him, he observed, " It's very extraordinary, sir, that it keeps so bright. I use the same." " Not at all, sir," I rejoined: " the doors of this gallery are open day and night; and the admission of fresh air, together with the great expansion of light from the sashes above, will never suffer the white to turn yellow." ' "

And then the enthusiastic artist and his solitary patron walked out to the orchestra in the gardens, sole auditors of the singer who had to sing by contract whether few or many were present. It is a pathetic record, portending the final closing of Bermondsey Spa but a few years later.

On the return journey to Southwark, the Southwark of Chaucer's Tabard, the pilgrim among these memories of the past may tread the ground where Finch's Grotto Gardens once re-echoed to laughter and song. They were established in 1760 by one Thomas Finch, who was of the fraternity of Thomas Keyse, even though he was but a Herald Painter. Falling heir to a house and pleasant garden, encircled with lofty trees and umbrageous with evergreens and shrubs, he decided to convert the place into a resort for public amusement. The adornments consisted of a grotto, built over a mineral spring, and a fountain, and an orchestra, and an Octagon Room for balls and refuge from wet evenings. The vocalists included Sophia Snow, afterwards as Mrs. Baddeley to become notorious for her beauty and frailty, and Thomas Lowe, the one-time favourite of Vauxhall, whose financial failure at Marylebone made him thankful to accept an engagement at this more lowly resort. But Finch's Grotto Gardens were not destined to a long life. Perhaps they were too near Vauxhall to succeed; perhaps the policy of engaging had-been favourites was as little likely to bring prosperity in the eighteenth as in the twentieth century. Whatever the cause, the fact is on record that after a career of less than twenty years the gardens ceased to exist.

As has been seen in an earlier chapter, the great prototype of the pleasure gardens of old

FINCH'S GROTTO, SOUTHWARK.

London, Vauxhall, outlived all its competitors for half a century. But upon even that favourite resort the changing manners of a new time had fatal effect. As knowledge grew and taste became more diversified, it became less and less easy to cater for the amusement of the many. To the student of old-time manners, however, the history of the out-door resorts of old London is full of instruction and suggestion, if only for the light it throws on those " struggles for happiness " which help to distinguish man from the brute creation.

THE END.

# INDEX

" A Cup of Coffee, or Coffee in its Colours," 166.
Adam and Eve Tavern, 153, 154.
Adam, the brothers, 108.
Addison, Joseph, 74, 178, 181, 183, 187, 215, 216, 217, 219, 220, 227, 233, 246, 295, 304.
Adelphi hotel, 108, 109, 110.
Aix-la-Chapelle, Peace of, 318.
Alice's coffee-house, 236, 237, 238.
Alfred Club, 287.
Almack, William, 275.
Almack's, 275, 276.
" Amelia," 297, 298, 331.
Anderson, Mrs., 223.
Anderton's Hotel, 78.
Angel Inn, Fleet Street, 101.
Angel Inn, Islington, 157, 158.
Anne, Queen, 113, 143, 173, 228, 282.
Annual register, 178, 218, 308, 333.
Anstey's " Pleaders' Guide," 121.
Apollo room at the Devil tavern, 94, 95, 98, 99, 100.
Archer, Mrs. Mary, 127.
Argyll, Duke of, 255.
Aristophanes, 133.
Armstrong, Dr. John, 207.
Arnold, Dr. Samuel, 339.
Arthur's Club, 287, 288.
Arthur, Mr., 268, 269.
Athenæum Club, 267.

Bacon, Anthony, 48.
Baddeley, Mrs., 354.

Bagnigge Wells, 346–350.
Bailley, Christian, 6.
Bailley, Henry, 6, 10.
Barrington, Hon. Daines, 262.
Barrington, Sir Jonas, 222.
Bartholomew Fair, 156, 157.
Bartholomew, Robert, 342, 343.
Bate, Henry, 108, 109, 230, 231.
Bath, Installation of the Knights of, 333.
Batson's coffee-house, 173, 174, 175, 176, 185.
Bear inn, 14, 15, 16, 17, 18, 19, 20, 21.
Beauclerk, Lady Sydney, 137, 138.
Beauclerk, Topham, 137, 207, 256, 257, 259, 276, 322.
Beaufort, Duchess of, 247.
Beaumont, Francis, 55.
Becket, Thomas à, 4, 5, 14.
Bedford coffee-house, 205, 206.
Bedford, Duke of, 219, 224.
Bedford Head tavern, 117, 118, 119.
Beeswing Club, The, 224.
Beef Steak Club, 282, 283, 284.
Bell tavern, 141, 142, 143.
Belle Sauvage inn, 73, 74, 75, 76, 77.
Bermondsey Spa Gardens, 350–353.
Bevis, Dr., 346, 347.
Bickerstaff, Sir Isaac, 181.
Bishopsgate Street Within, inns of, 47.

Bishopsgate Street Without, inns of, 50, 51.
Blackmore, Sir Richard, 173, 174.
Bloomfield, Robert, 332.
Blount, Sir Henry, 164.
Blue Boar inn, 70, 71, 72.
Blue Posts tavern, 148, 149.
Blue-Stocking Club, 250, 251, 253, 255.
Boar's Head inn, Eastcheap, 30, 31, 33, 34, 35, 36, 37, 38.
Boar's Head inn, Southwark, 21, 22.
Bochm, Mr., 197.
Boileau's *Lutrin*, 212.
Bolinbroke, Viscount, 202.
Boodle's Club, 284, 285.
Bordeaux, merchants of, 39.
Boswell, James, 30, 33, 63, 81, 88, 89, 90, 91, 103, 104, 105, 117, 130, 255, 256, 259, 260, 262, 263, 323.
Bowen, William, 52, 53.
Bowman, Mrs., 164.
Bramble, Matt., 324, 331.
British coffee-house, 223, 224.
British Institution, 132, 133.
Broghill, Lord, 70.
Brontë, Anne, 191, 192.
Brontë, Charlotte, 191, 192.
Brooks's Club, 271, 274, 276, 277, 278, 280, 286.
Brown, Tom, 306.
Buchan, Dr., 264.
Buckingham, Duke of, 337.
Bull and Gate inn, 69, 70.
Bull Head tavern, 57.
Bull inn, 48.
Burke, Edmund, 202, 252, 256, 258, 260, 275.
Burney, Dr., 261.
Burney, Fanny, 252, 253.
Burton's, Thomas, " Parliamentary Diary," 141.
Button's coffee-house, 209, 216, 217, 218, 219, 220, 221.
Buttony, Daniel, 215, 217, 220.
Byron, Lord, 145, 146, 147.

Byron, Lord, the poet, 146, 287.
Cade, Jack, 24, 25, 26, 27, 29.
" Calamities and Quarrels of Authors," 325.
Calf's Head Club, 147.
Campbell, Lord, 150, 224.
Campbell, Thomas, 121.
Cannon coffee-house, 222.
Canterbury, 5, 10.
Canterbury Tales, 7, 8, 9, 13.
Cambridge carriers, 48, 49.
Carlisle, Lord, 298.
Carlyle, Thomas, 141.
Cat, Christopher, 244, 245, 249.
Catley, Nan, 338.
Chamier, Anthony, 256, 257.
Chapter coffee-house, 187, 189, 190, 191, 192.
Charnock, Robert, 149.
Charing Cross, coffee-houses of, 222.
Charing Cross, inns of, 110.
Charles I, 16, 44, 57, 70, 72, 73, 147, 341.
Charles II, 20, 21, 125, 142, 165.
Charles V, 58.
Chatelaine's, 124, 125, 126.
Chatterton, Thomas, 180, 190.
Chaucer, Geoffrey, 4, 5, 6, 7, 8, 9, 11, 13, 189, 353.
Chaworth, William, 145, 146, 147.
Cheapside Cross, 57.
Cheshire Cheese, 79, 80, 81, 82, 83.
Chesterfield, Lord, 318.
Child's coffee-house, 186, 187, 192.
Chinaman, Goldsmith's, at Vauxhall, 304, 305.
Christ's Hospital, 66, 67.
Churchill, Lady Mary, 247.
Cibber, Colley, 128, 211, 219, 220.
Cicero, 133.

Cider Cellars, 120, 121, 122.
"Citizen of the World," 322.
Claypole, Elizabeth, 235.
Club, definition of, 267, 268.
Clubs of old London, 243.
Club, The, 255, 256, 257, 259, 260, 261, 262.
Clutterback, James, 62.
Cock tavern, Fleet Street, 83, 84, 85, 86, 87, 88.
Cock tavern, Leadenhall Street, 46.
Cock tavern, Suffolk Street, 147.
Cocoa-Tree Club, 228, 229, 230, 231, 232, 233.
Coffee, 164, 166.
"Coffee House, The Character of," 167, 168, 169.
Coffee-houses in London, 163; first to be opened, 163, 164; subject of a play, 166; pamphlets for and against, 167, 168, 169, 170; petition against, 171; proclamation suppressing, 172; influenced by locality, 173.
"Coffee, Women's Petition against," 171, 172.
"Coffee House Vindicated," 169, 170.
Coleridge, S. T., 65, 66, 67, 150.
Colin, Farmer, 297.
Collier's, Jeremy, "Short View," 52.
Congers, The, 187, 188, 189.
Connoisseur, The, 174, 175, 176, 187, 206, 301, 306, 331.
Cony, Nathaniel, 149.
"Country Mouse and the City Mouse," 212, 213.
Covent Garden, coffee-houses of, 205.
Covent Garden, taverns of, 124, 125.
Coverley, Sir Roger de, 295.
Cowley, Abraham, 93.
Cowper, William, 197, 198.

Craven Head inn, 103.
Crown and Anchor, 103, 104, 105, 106, 107.
Cromwell, Oliver, 70, 71, 72, 73, 235.
Cruikshank, George, 153.
Cumberland, Duke of, 286.
Cumberland, Richard, 254.
Cuper's Gardens, 136, 137.
Curran, John Philpot, 222.
Cuthbert, Captain, 151.

Dagger tavern, 68, 69.
"Dark Walks" of Vauxhall, 299, 300, 306.
Davidson, John, 82.
Davies, Thomas, 104.
"Decline and Fall of the Roman Empire," 109, 110.
Defoe, Daniel, 64.
De Moivre, Abraham, 225.
Devil tavern, 93, 94, 95, 96, 97, 98, 99, 100, 101.
Devonshire, Duke of, 286.
Dibdin, Charles, 330.
Dickens, Charles, 29, 152, 155, 156.
Dick's coffee-house, 197, 198.
Dolly's chop-house, 64, 65.
Don Saltero's coffee-house, 238, 239, 240.
Dorset, Duke of, 273.
Dorset, Earl of, 115.
Douglas, Bishop, 223.
Dover House Club, 286.
Drinkwater, Thomas, 15.
Drummond, William, 98.
Drury Lane, inns of, 115, 116.
Dryden, John, 64, 98, 210, 211, 212, 213, 214, 215.
Dudley, Lord, 287.
D'Urfey, Thomas, 248, 249.
Dutton, John, 124.

Edward VI, 92.
Edwards, Mrs., 164.
Egan, Pierce, 153, 304.
Elephant and Castle tavern, 158.

Elephant tavern, 43.
Elizabeth, Queen, 12, 42, 43, 92.
England, John, 139, 140.
E O tables, 274.
Essex, Lord, 140.
Essex Street Club, 262, 263.
Ethrage, Sir George, 112, 113.
Evans, Widow, 137.
Evelyn, John, 60, 100, 147, 164.

Falcon tavern, 159.
Falkner, Mary Ann, 337.
Falstaff, Sir John, 22, 23, 30, 32, 33, 34, 35, 38, 169.
Farr, James, 92.
Fastolfe, Sir John, 21, 22, 23.
Fantom, Captain, 116.
Feather's tavern, 136, 137, 138.
Fielding, Henry, 64, 69, 2u5, 207, 297, 298, 299, 309.
Finch's Grotto Gardens, 353, 354.
Finch, Thomas, 354.
Fireworks at Vauxhall, 3C0; at Ranelagh, 330; at Mary-lebone, 339; at Bermond-sey Spa Gardens, 351.
FitzGerald, Edward, 87.
" Fitzgerald, Fighting," 230, 231, 280, 281, 282.
Fleece tavern, 126, 127.
Fleet Street, taverns of, 62, 77, 78.
Ford, Parson, 130, 131.
Foote, Samuel, 90, 91, 132, 133, 205.
Fortune Theatre, 59.
Fountain tavern, 246.
Fountayne, Dr., 339.
Fox, Charles James, 105, 106, 256, 261, 272, 275, 276, 278, 279.
Franklin, Benjamin, 186, 193.
Froude, James Anthony, 75, 76.
Fuller, Isaac, 45, 46.
Fuller, Thomas, 22.

Garraway's coffee-house, 176, 177.
Garraway, Thomas, 177.
Garrick, David, 62, 63, 180, 205, 251, 256, 258, 259, 260, 313, 326.
Garth, Sir Samuel, 247, 248, 249.
Gaskell, Mrs., 191.
Gay, John, 117.
Gentleman's Magazine, 343.
George I, 245, 249.
George II, 269.
George III, 107, 196.
George's coffee-house, 203, 204, 206.
George inn, 23, 24.
Gibbon, Edward, 108, 109, 110, 228, 229, 256, 257, 276, 284, 285, 286.
Gibbons, Grinling, 76.
Gibraltar, Siege of, 351.
Gifford's, William, Life of Ben Jonson, 54.
Gillray, James, 275.
Golden Cross tavern, 110, 111.
Golden Eagle tavern, 147.
Goldsmith, Oliver, 31, 33, 34, 38, 76, 78, 79, 81, 89, 190, 203, 204, 225, 228, 234, 256, 257, 260, 304, 322, 324, 345.
Goose and Gridiron, 62, 63, 64.
Gordon, George, 224.
Gough, Daniel, 337.
Grant, Andrew, 224.
Gray, Thomas, 321, 322.
Grecian coffee-house, 200, 201, 202, 203.
Green, J. R., 8, 9.
Green Ribbon Club, 93.
Gregorie, Robert, 138.
Gresham, Sir Thomas, 92.
Grimes, Jack, 116.
Guardian, The, 216, 218, 219.
Guildhall Museum, 34, 38.
Gwynne, Nell, 346.

Hackman, James, 206, 207.
Hal, Prince, 31, 32.

Hales, John, 17.
Hales, Robert, 103.
Halifax, Earl of, 247, 248, 337.
Hall, Jacob, 19.
Halley, Professor, 203.
Hamilton, Lord Spencer, 329, 330.
Hand and Shears tavern, 156, 157.
Handel, George Frederick, 339.
Hanover Club, 245.
Harley, Edward, Earl of Oxford, 194.
Harper, Bishop, 101.
Harrington, James, 235, 236.
Harvard, John, 21.
Haslam, Dr., 224.
Hawkins, Sir John, 256.
Henry II, 5.
Henry III, 68.
Henry IV, 31, 36.
Henry V, 23.
Henry VI, 25, 26.
Henry VIII, 314, 315.
Herrick, Robert, 57, 58.
Hill, Aaron, 220, 221.
Hill, Dr. John, 218, 325, 326, 327.
Hobson, Thomas, 48, 49.
Hogarth, William, 43, 44, 60, 61, 93, 115, 154, 158, 296.
Holborn, inns of, 68, 69, 72.
Holland, Lord, 276.
Horden, Hildebrand, 128.
Horn tavern, 78.
Horseshoe tavern, 116.
Horseshoe tavern, Covent Garden, 124.
Howard, Lord, 76.
Howard, Major-General, 141.
Howard, Sir John, 15, 16.
Howell, James, " Familiar Letters " of, 49, 50.
Hughes, Mr., 346, 347.
Hummums tavern, 128, 129, 130.
Humphries, Miss, 195.
" Humphry Clinker," 65.

Hunt's, Leigh, " The Town," 111, 113, 129.
Hyde, Abbot of, 4, 12.
Hyde, Lady, 248.

Inspector, The, 218, 326.
Irving, Washington, 36, 37, 38.

Jacobites, 115, 116, 149, 179, 229, 313.
James I, 50, 111.
James III, 180.
Jay, Cyrus, 81.
Jerusalem coffee-house, 179.
Jessop's, 117.
Jonathan's coffee-house, 177, 178.
John's coffee-house, 179, 180.
Johnson, Dr. Samuel, 30, 62, 63, 79, 80, 81, 88, 89, 90, 91, 103, 104, 105, 117, 130, 137, 138, 174, 189, 207, 211, 252, 255, 256, 258, 259, 260, 261, 262, 263, 267, 309, 322, 323, 339, 340.
Jones, Sir William, 256, 260.
Jones, William, 314, 315, 316.
Jonson, Ben, 39, 40, 54, 55, 57, 58, 68, 69, 88, 93, 94, 95, 96, 98, 99, 100, 111, 140, 166.

Keate, Roger, 138.
Keats, John, 55, 56.
Kenrick, William, 190.
Kensington, South, Museum, 51.
Keyse, Thomas, 350, 351, 353, 354.
Killigrew, Harry, 293.
King's coffee-house, 205, 207.
King, Thomas, 207.
King's Head tavern, Fenchurch Street, 42.
King's Head tavern, Fleet Street, 92, 93.
King John's Palace, 153.
Kingston, Lord, 249.
King Street, Westminster, taverns of, 139.

Kit-Cat Club, 243, 244, 245, 246, 249, 282.
Kit-Cat portraits, 246.
Knapp, Mrs., 83, 84.

Lacy, James, 313.
Laguerre, Louis, 116, 117.
Lamb, Charles, 65, 66, 67.
Lambe, John, 59.
Lambert, George, 283.
Langton, Bennet, 137, 256.
Lee, Sidney, 23.
Leg tavern, 141, 142.
Leslie, Charles Robert, 193.
Lill, William, 236, 237.
Lincolnshire, Fens of, 178.
Lion's Head at Button's coffee-house, 217, 218, 219.
" Lives of the English Poets," 189, 190.
Lloyd, Charles, 190.
Lloyd's coffee-house, 173, 180, 181, 182, 183.
Lloyd, Edward, 180, 181.
Lloyd, Sir Philip, 199.
Locket's, 110, 111, 112, 113, 126.
Locket, Adam, 113.
Locket, Mrs., 112, 113.
Lockier, Francis, 211, 212.
London Bridge, 3, 15, 21, 23, 26, 38, 75.
London coffee-house, 193.
London, Fire of, 34, 45, 51, 63, 79, 83, 292.
London, Plague of, 44, 45, 49, 158.
London tavern, 42.
Long's tavern, 148.
Lonsdale, Earl of, 151, 204.
Loughborough, Lady, 273.
Loughborough, Lord, 273.
Louis XVI, 261.
Lowe, Thomas, 338, 354.
Lowell, J. R., 7.
Lowther, Sir James, 204.
Lunsford, Colonel, 139.
Lupton, Donald, 335.
Lyttelton, Lord, 271.

Macaulay, Lord, 115, 209.
" Mac Flecknoe," 211, 212.
Macklin, Charles, 131, 132, 133, 134, 135, 202.
Mackreth, Robert, 269.
Maiden Lane taverns, 119, 120.
Malone, Edmund, 257, 258.
Man, Alexander, 222, 223.
Man's coffee-house, 222, 223.
Manchester, Lady, 246.
Marlborough, Duchess of, 228.
Marvell, Andrew, 119.
Marylebone Gardens, 336–341.
Maxwell, Dr., 91.
Medici, Mary de, 57.
Melford, Lydia, 306, 307, 325.
Mermaid tavern, Cheapside, 53, 54, 55, 56, 57, 94.
Mermaid tavern, Cornhill, 53.
" Mermaid Tavern, Lines on," 56.
Miles's coffee-house, 235.
Mitre tavern, Cheapside, 57.
Mitre tavern, Fenchurch Street, 44, 45.
Mitre tavern, Fleet Street, 88, 89, 90, 91.
Monmouth, Duke of, 125.
Montagu, Captain, 179, 180.
Montagu, Lady Mary Wortley, 249, 250.
Montagu, Mrs., 250, 251, 252, 253, 254.
More, Hannah, 251.
Morris, Captain, 106.
Mounsey, Dr., 104.
Mozart, W. A., 330.

Nag's Head tavern, Cheapside, 57.
Nag's Head tavern, Drury Lane, 116.
Nando's coffee-house, 195, 196, 197, 198.
Nash, Beau, 228.
Newport, Young, 293, 294.
New Spring Gardens, 291.
Newton, Sir Isaac, 203, 225.

# Index 363

Norfolk, Duke of, 105, 106, 107.
North, Dudley, 107.
North, Lord, 278.
Northumberland, Duke of, 104.
Nottinghamshire Club, 144.

Oates, Titus, 93, 198, 199.
Observer, The, 254.
" Oceana," 235.
October Club, 143.
Oldisworth, William, 193, 194.
Orford, Lord, 204.
Ormonde, Marquis of, 312.
Oxford, Earl of, 193, 194, 268.

Pall Mall taverns, 143.
Pantheon, The, 285, 323.
" Paradise Lost," 209.
Paris Garden, 335.
Paterson, James, 62.
Pellett, Dr., 131.
Pembroke, Earl of, 148, 149.
Pepys, Mrs., 83, 84.
Pepys, Samuel, 19, 20, 40, 41, 44, 45, 51, 52, 83, 84, 88, 100, 125, 126, 127, 141, 142, 143, 166, 167, 210, 291, 292, 293, 294, 336.
Percy, Dr., 104, 105, 256.
Petres, Lord, 272.
Philips, Ambrose, 220.
Phillips, Sir Richard, 265.
" Pickwick Papers," 28, 29.
Pierce, Mrs., 83.
Pie-Powder Court, 156, 157.
Pindar, Sir Paul, 49, 50, 51.
Pindar, Sir Paul, tavern, 50, 51.
Pindar, Peter, 129, 130.
Pitt, Colonel, 231.
Pitt's Head tavern, 151.
Pitt, William, 231, 288.
Poins, 32.
Pontack's, 59, 60, 61, 111, 126.
Pope, Alexander, 64, 117, 205, 219, 220, 271.
Pope's Head tavern, 51, 52, 53.
Porson, Richard, 120, 121.

Portland, Duke of, 193.
Preston, Robert, 37.
Price, Dr. Richard, 186.
Priestly, Dr., 193.
" Prince Alfred," 173, 174.
Prior, Matthew, 114, 115, 212, 227.
Prior, Samuel, 114.

Queen's Arms tavern, 62, 63.
Queensbury, Duchess of, 196.
Quickly, Dame, 33, 35, 36, 37, 38.
Quin, James, 52, 53, 205.

Rainbow tavern, 91, 92, 172, 198, 199.
Raleigh, Sir Walter, 54.
Ranelagh, 312–334; Rotunda at, 314–317; fête at, 318; amusements of, 324; riot at, 327, 328; poem on, 332, 333; closing of, 333.
Ranelagh, Earl of, 312, 313.
Rann, John, 349.
Rawlinson, Dan, 44.
Rawlinson, Mrs., 45.
Rawthmell's coffee-house, 205, 207.
Ray, Martha, 206, 207.
Red Lion inn, 72, 73.
" Retaliation," 234.
Reynolds, Sir Joshua, 80, 103, 252, 255, 256, 257, 258, 259, 262, 276, 322, 353.
Rich, John, 282.
Richard II, 6.
Richardson, Samuel, 65.
Richmond, Duke of, 20, 21.
Ridley, Bishop, 57.
Robinson, Sir Thomas, 313, 314.
Rochester, Lord, 214.
Rock, Richard, 76, 77.
Rogers, Samuel, 253.
Rosee, Pasqua, 164, 165, 172, 177.
Rose tavern, 127, 128, 337.
Rossetti, Dante Gabriel, 91.

Rota Club, 235, 236.
Rousseau, J. J., 90.
Rowlandson, Thomas, 59, 179, 274.
Rummer tavern, 113, 114, 115.

St. Albans, Duchess of, 247.
St. Alban's tavern, 143, 144.
St. James's coffee-house, 200, 233, 234.
St. James's Palace, 196.
St. Paul's churchyard, 62, 63, 64.
St. Paul's coffee-house, 185, 186, 192.
Salter, James, 238, 239, 240.
Salutation tavern, 65, 66, 67.
Sam's coffee-house, 177, 178.
Sanchy, Mr., 127.
Sandwich, Earl of, 206.
Saqui, Mme., 300.
Saracen's Head tavern, Snow Hill, 155, 156.
"Sarrazin's Head," Westminster, 138, 155.
Savage, Richard, 221.
Scott, Peter, 139.
Scott, Sir Walter, 41.
Sedley, Sir Charles, 127.
Sedley, Jos., 309, 310.
Selden, John, 156.
Selwyn, George, 233, 269, 271, 272, 273, 277, 278, 279, 286, 288.
Shadwell, Thomas, 126.
Shakespeare, William, 21, 22, 23, 26, 30, 31, 33, 34, 36, 38, 88, 159.
Sharp, Rebecca, 309, 310.
Sheffield, Lord, 110.
Shepherd, George, 12.
Sheridan, R. B., 106, 205, 256, 279, 280.
Ship and Turtle tavern, 46, 47.
Slaughter's coffee-house, 225.
Slaughter, Thomas, 225.
Sloane, Sir Hans, 203.
Smith, Adam, 256.
Smith, Captain John, 156.

Smith, J. T., 351.
Smollett, Tobias, 64, 65, 306, 322, 324, 325.
Smyrna coffee-house, 226, 227, 228.
Snow, Sophia, 354.
Somerset coffee-house, 205.
Southey, Robert, 65, 66.
South Sea Bubble, 178.
Southwark, map of, 1; meaning of name, 2; inns of, 3; Tabard inn, 3; Bear inn, 14; fair of, 19; Boar's Head inn, 21; George inn, 23; White Hart inn, 24.
Spectator, The, 74, 178, 182, 183, 186, 187, 233, 295.
Spenser, Edmund, 140, 141.
Spotted Dog inn, 103.
Staple inn, 68.
Star and Garter tavern, 143, 144.
Steele, Sir Richard, 100, 101, 181, 200, 215, 216, 217, 219, 226, 227, 238, 239, 240, 249.
Steevens, George, 339.
Stella, Journal to, 144, 227.
Stevens, George Alexander, 121, 122.
Stewart, Admiral Keith, 280, 281.
Stewart, General William, 231.
Stillingfleet, Benjamin, 251.
Stony, Captain, 108, 109.
Stow, John, 4, 11, 24, 39, 47, 51, 103, 141.
Strand, Inns and taverns of, 102.
Strype, John, 103.
Stuart, Frances, 20, 21.
Suckling, Sir John, 17, 18.
Suffolk Street taverns, 147.
Swan inn, 110, 111.
Swift, Jonathan, 61, 64, 100, 144, 227, 268.

Tabard inn, 3, 4, 6, 7, 8, 9, 10, 11, 12, 13, 14, 33, 353.
Tarleton, Richard, 64.

Tassoni's *Secchia Rapita*, 212.
Tatler, The, 101, 200, 215, 226, 233.
Tearsheet, Doll, 33.
Temple Bar, 75, 84, 196.
Tennyson, Alfred, Lord, 84, 85, 87, 88, 255, 256.
Thackeray, W. M., 309.
Thatched House tavern, 149, 150.
Thomson, James, 228.
Three as sign of London taverns, 41, 42.
Three Cranes' Lane, 39.
Three Cranes in the Vintry, 39, 40, 41.
Three Nuns tavern, 42.
Three Tuns tavern, 57.
Thurlow, Lord Chancellor, 150, 195, 197, 198.
Tibbs, Mr. and Mrs., 304, 305.
Tickell, Thomas, 277.
Till, William, 208.
Tom's coffee-house, Birchin Lane, 180.
Tom's coffee-house, Covent Garden, 208, 209.
"Tom Jones," 69, 70.
Tonson, Jacob, 244, 245, 246, 248.
Tooke, Horne, 106.
Torre, 339, 341.
Totenhall Court, 154.
Turk's Head coffee-house, 235.
Turner, J. M. W., 119.
Tyers, Jonathan, 296, 297, 299, 309, 335, 337.
Tyers, Tom, 309.

"Vanity Fair," 309.
Vauxhall, 83, 230, 291-311; plan of, 299; Rotunda at, 300; attractions of, 300, 301, 307; supper party at, 301–304; closing of, 309.
Vernon, Admiral, 118, 119.
Vittoria, victory of, 308.
Voltaire, 119.

Wales, Prince of (George IV), 228, 232, 279, 280, 286.
Walker's "The Original," 267.
Walpole, Horace, 76, 119, 143, 204, 205, 206, 223, 230, 252, 275, 317, 318, 319, 321.
Walton's, Isaac, "Complete Angler," 93.
Ward, Ned, 244, 282.
Warren, Sir William, 142.
Warwick, Countess of, 215.
Washington, George, 106.
Washington, Purser, 142, 143.
Waterman's Arms tavern, 350.
"Webb, Young," 232.
Weller, Sam, 28, 29.
Wellington, Duke of, 308.
Weltzie's Club, 286, 287.
West, Captain Thomas, 209.
Westminster taverns and coffee-houses, 234, 235.
"Wet Paper Club," 264.
Wheatley, Henry B., 74, 283.
White's Chocolate-house, 200, 268, 269, 271, 272, 273, 274, 275, 278.
White Conduit House, 341-345.
White Hart inn, 24, 25, 26, 27, 28, 29.
White Hart inn, Bishopsgate Street Within, 47, 48.
White Horse Cellar, 152, 153.
"White, Mary, or the Murder at the Old Tabard," 14.
Wildman's coffee-house, 205.
"Wilkes and Liberty," 196.
Wilkes, John, 119.
William III, 115, 120, 173.
William, King, statue of, 38.
Wilson, "Long-Bow," 265, 266.
Will's coffee-house, Belle Sauvage yard, 193, 194.
Will's coffee-house, Covent Garden, 200, 209, 210, 211, 213, 215, 216, 217.
"Will Waterproof's Lyrical Monologue," 85, 86, 87.

Windmill tavern, 58, 59.
Wittengamot Club, 264, 265, 266.
Wolcot, John, " Peter Pindar," 129, 130.
Wren, Sir Christopher, 66.

Wright, Thomas, 31.
Wyatt, Sir Thomas, 75, 76.

Yarmouth, Lady, 319.
York, Duke of, 20, 142, 308.
Young, Edward, 250, 271.

www.ingramcontent.com/pod-product-compliance
Lightning Source LLC
Chambersburg PA
CBHW031228090426
42742CB00007B/119